# CHARLUTZ

# CHARLUTZ

Charles Valenti

Copyright © 2024 by Charles Valenti.

ISBN: 979-8-89465-082-1 (sc)
ISBN: 979-8-89465-083-8 (e)

All rights reserved. No part of this publication may be reproduced, distributed, or transmitted in any form or by any means, including photocopying, recording, or other electronic or mechanical methods, without the prior written permission of the author, except in the case of brief quotations embodied in critical reviews and certain other noncommercial uses permitted by copyright law.

Printed in the United States of America.

**Integrity Publishing**
39343 Harbor Hills Blvd Lady Lake,
FL 32159

www.integrity-publishing.com

# Preface

This book has been written with the intention that it will serve to encourage a sense of confidence on the part of the American soccer coach. It is hoped that newfound confidence in traditional American concepts will encourage the coach to share his rich sports background with our younger generation of athletes.

The American soccer coach may not even be aware of just how much he has to offer his athletes, and by reading this book, he will experience a renaissance that may serve to enlighten far more people than just the reader. Within these pages are revelations that are so simple to the point that they have been overlooked in our search for more complex solutions. For years, we have been struggling to obtain an understanding of soccer and an ability to teach the concepts to our players in a way that we can all relate to and in terms that the American coach and athlete can identify. Had we been aware that solutions reside in our own athletic background, so much could already have been accomplished.

This book will benefit readers searching for a way of delivering knowledge so long held within themselves.

*All American: An American Approach to Soccer* has been written in the hope that it will serve to enlighten the American coach and his athletes, both foreign and American. Hopefully, it may awaken the American coach so that he may discover a forgotten natural resource.

The background possessed by most American coaches is one stocked heavily with ideologies inherent in football, basketball, and baseball. He has surmised that this background does not qualify him with experience enough to expect proficiency on the soccer field in his role as leader and teacher of foreign and American athletes. In attempting to bring the point home, let the record show that I never played organized soccer and yet I have been successful enough to develop a style based upon my American sports background, the principles of which warrant the writing of this book. You will soon realize that much of your valuable and extremely diverse knowledge has been withdrawn from application to the sport of soccer up to this point. It is to reverse this trend that the writing of the *American Approach to Soccer* has been undertaken.

This book differs from all others on the subject in that it implies we need learn very little more than we already know. This book will serve to awaken the reader to his own untapped potential. The writer does not pretend to offer magical solutions to complex problems. Instead, it is shown that by adaptation of his vast source of athletic knowledge, the American coach may already have the natural ability to offer his athletes more than anyone.

Finally, it is hoped that we might identify culturally by infusing our American sports techniques into the sport of soccer. We may be able to offer enlightenment to the extent that soccer may one day be accepted as an American sport.

If we pursue an American approach, as indicated in this book, we may witness as our ultimate reward the American sports fan embracing soccer with open arms.

In closing, I would like to address my attention to my peers who coach football, basketball, or baseball. Because of the proficiency you enjoy at your sport, you are already more than qualified to become a coach of soccer. Therefore, on behalf of all our young athletes, both girls and boys, I invite you to come and join me. Let this book serve as your invitation.

Welcome aboard!

—— Charles L. Valenti
Coach, Soccer and Baseball
Cleveland High School, NYC

# FAIRYTALES CAN COME TRUE, THEY CAN HAPPEN TO YOU

I had drifted off to sleep with the ample time afforded by the long flight from Milano to New York. My dreams were quite vivid in replaying all of my experiences as a young man living in Italy. There were many dreams, interrupted by waking up for a bite to eat, or a trip to the bathroom, or conversation with my family. There had to he many dreams in order to replay all I had been so fortunate to find in the treasure trove that I can only refer to as "Saturdays Paradise".

The hum of the engines combined with the boring expanse of the clouds and ocean below, soon brought me to another place. I found myself once again on my bicycle, this time circling around a patio near the statue of "Juliet", as I looked above at her famous balcony. This paradise was known throughout the world as Verona, Italy. And here on this patio stood Romeo, as I imagined him looking up to her and saying. "When are you going to realize that it was just the timing that was wrong, Juliet?"

In my dream, Romeo continues as he reasons with her. "We came up on different streets, so they were not at all the same, but our dream was just the same. And I dreamed your dream for you and now your dream is real. When are you going to realize that it was just the timing that was wrong, Juliet"?

I am on the plane bound for New York City, on a flight from Milano, as my dream continues. Looking down from the balcony where I visited frequently, Juliet began to explain. "The dice were loaded from the start. When we met, you exploded in my heart. When are you going to realize that it was just the timing that was wrong, Romeo"? And Romeo replies, "I can't think of everything, but I'll do anything for you". And then it is Juliet, who from that balconey I visited answers, "I can't do anything right now, but be in love with you, Romeo"!

And now, I am pedaling out of that courtyard under the archway that enters onto a nearby street. The very same archway under which Romeo had left dejectedly as he said to Juliet, "All I do is miss you and the way it used to be, all I do is keep the beat with my friends as company". And I can just hear her now as I am pedaling for home as she calls out to him. "All I do is kiss you, although only in my dreams".

The flight from Milano to New York City provided me with ample time to wonder about the paradise I had to leave. We had received orders to return to stateside, since our three year tour of duty had run its course. We are a military family, and when you receive orders to relocate, well, an order is an order, and the only acceptable answer is, "Yes Sir" my Uncle Vincent picked us up at Idlewild Airport and now I'm looking at tons of traffic as he drives through the crowded streets of Manhattan. We will be staying at his place in Yorkville for the time being. I don't know about this whole thing. All I can think about is my paradise lost. Somehow, I found it, and now I have lost it. Somehow, it found me, and now it has lost me, in this new world called New York City.

On the way to Yorkville, I am wondering not so much where I am going, instead I find myself holding on tightly to the memories of where I have come from. I'm a New Yorker, so this should be a moment of joy and great expectation, however I have reservations in that regard. Too much in the area of great expectations has already occurred in a distant land and I am confused. Have I arrived home or have I left home? That is the quandary I am now beginning to ponder. As you may begin to realize my feelings of misgiving and melancholy, by putting yourself in my situation, understand that I am a young man of thirteen years of age. How could a kid of that age have such complex and confusing interpretations about life? You might wonder.

Of course you are now thinking about how life was for you when you entered your own teenage years, in order to identify and bring into perspective a time in life that I am relating. I will wager that you believed with all your heart that the whole world was before you, and soon you would begin to learn about life and all its wonders. But what if I tell you that by the age of thirteen I have already learned much of what I will need to carry me through a lifetime. Could you make that claim? Of course, I didn't know that at the time, for only the passing of time has brought forth that realization. However, those uneasy feelings of misgiving that I have alluded to were early signs. Signs that my roots had taken to soil in another place, like it or not. A place where learning doesn't end with dismissal from school on Friday of every week.

And so, forgive me as I am prone to drift off into memories of a time gone forever. However, these memories appear and reappear in vivid colors with a pace of perpetual motion. One moment, I am skirting through the crowded marketplace, trying to avoid the pedestrians who shout, "Americani, Americani!", to the reckless youngster on his bicycle. And then, I am crossing the beautiful Adige river that flows lazily through the heart of Verona. Now, I am on the Castle Vecchio bridge, making my way downhill to my home overlooking the river passing below.

All this, I remember vividly, yet it still causes my heart to race all over again. The sights and the sounds of the city were a gorgeous mosaic that resonated with a cacofony found nowhere but here, in my own corner of the world. And always, the Italians would call out to me, "Americani, Americani", as they laughed when I shot by at great speed. "Dove va"? Where are you going?, they would ask, as I responded simply by a shrug of the shoulders while raising both hands high in the air, until I was out of sight. It was the universal gesture of expressing, "Who knows". How did they know that this Italian boy was an American? I was the only kid in the entire city that owned a Schwinn!

Often, I wondered why none of my American friends were to be seen on my many numerous routes through the city and even to parts unknown outside the city, in pursuit of a new fishing hole upriver, on the other side of the dam, where the water became calm. Where I could cast a fly rod to the "trutta", the trout. Or use my Mitchell 300 spinning reel with a #3 Mepps spinning lure, for lesser gamefish found in this paradise, this fairytale place of mine.

Frank Sinatra explained it best in the movie we went to see last night at the U.S. Army post theater, called "Young at Heart", (1954) starring, Sinatra and Doris Day. It just came out recently, and here is the advice that only the voice of Frank Sinatra can sing.

> "Fairy tales can come true, they can happen to you
> If you're young at heart
> For it's hard, you will find

> To be narrow of mind, if you're young at heart
> You can go to extremes with impossible schemes
> You can laugh, when your dreams, fall apart at the seams
> And life gets more exciting with each passing day
> And love is either in your heart, or on the way
> Don't you know that it's worth every treasure on earth
> To be young at heart
> For as rich as you are
> It's much better, by far, to be young at heart
> And, if you should survive to a hundred and five
> Look at all you'll derive out of being alive
> And here is the best part, you have a head start
> If you are among the very young at heart".

No, I did not dream this, for my memory vividly recalls having experienced everything that you will share with me in the ensuing pages. Each adventure is a piece to a puzzle and I learned as I went from one learning experience to another, in the open air classroom of life.

However, you indeed, will have a head start in fulfilling an education in many regards. The intricasies of the beautiful game of soccer were learned by me in this fairytale world and taught by teachers one could never have imagined. The joys found in all the sights and sounds would flavor my love for a game that I had not yet met.

Busy, busy, busy on my bike, pumping my legs tirelessly on my travels to the river upstream, or to the Castle Vecchio bridge crossing, downstream. And then, a sprint across that bridge and downhill to the other side of town where my eyes would grow wide with wonder as the wind of my speed brought tears to them.

And therefore, there is more to this story of soccer, than meets the eye. Each new experience or adventure would eventually find it's way out onto the field of battle, and yet none of the knowledge gained would come from a book. I was too busy learning and absorbing everything, there was no time to sit still for a moment to read anything.

So, I have done the legwork for you, and you may take with you what you wish knowing that everything learned in this fairytale was a lesson put out onto a field. And the fruits of each and every lesson produced a beautiful way to play the beautiful game.

Now, return with me, to the beginning. To the beginning of my fairytale. To Verona and the marketplace over the river Adige that is being crossed by a kid pedaling a bike on the Castle Vecchio bridge.

There is at all pedestal rising high from the center of a bustleing marketplace called Piazza delle Erbe, in the town of Verona, Italy. I find myself returning to this spot so that I may look up and gaze at the statue resting atop that pedestal, where it has resided for hundreds of years. It must be there for a reason to have remained in place for so long. As I look around, no one seems to pay any attention to the regal statue that appears to be guarding their marketplace. Everyone is busy scurrying about in a hectic pace to buy groceries. What does this statue mean to them? Nothing. What does it mean to me? Everything!

It is 1956. I am eleven years old, and therefore, very impressionable and so you may begin to surmise that this statue has made a lasting impression upon me, as I begin to write this story for you, some fifty-eight years later. It is a story of a journey we all must embark on, whether we wish to or not. Each of our stories of our life journeys had to begin somewhere. Think back to your own as you travel with me through mine, so that we may become kindred spirits and walk the road together.

I am acutely aware that every soldier in the detachment wears a patch on his shoulder and it appears to picture exactly, the statue watching over the people of Piazza delle Erbe. We have been ordered and deployed to Verona, Italy for a reason. The reason is to watch over and guard the marketplace known on the map of the world as, Italy. The detachment is known as the Southern European Task Force known by the abbreviation S.E.T.A.F. This abbreviation rests beneath the symbol on the patch worn by every soldier from private to the General himself. What does that mean to me? Everything!

High atop the piazza is a statue of a Lion. What is so special about that? You may wonder. This Lion has wings! What does that mean to the people of Verona, I am not yet certain. In time, I may discover the answer. What does this mean to me that the Lion has wings. It means that he can fly! That means that I too, as a young Lion, can fly. The implication is enormous. It means to me that anything is possible if you spread your wings and are resolute, as that Lion appears in stature and demeanor.

Well, I certainly hope you didn't think I was an eleven year old soldier sent halfway around the world to assist the security of post-war Italy. I couldn't fly that good! My status is that of military dependent, as is the case shared by all of my friends, classmates, and teamates. Some irreverent types refer to us as Army brats. We come from Georgia, Texas, California, Alabama with a banjo on our knee. The only instrument I can play is the radio, and I'm from New York City. I don't know if that is good or bad, for when I first arrived, all of the southerners gathered in groups to marvel at me when they heard from whence I came, since I was a rarified type of dubious distinction. I was a New Yorker!

I came from a place notorious for hustle and bustle necessitating a fast pace. You could say, I was wired, and I began to appreciate the slower pace and more gracious style offered by my southern countrymen. Italy was about to offer all of us an even slower and far more gracious pace than any of us had ever anticipated. An education for all was in the offing. As Olivia Dehavilland said, in her screen role on the set of "A Light in the Piazza".

> "Nobody with a dream,
> Should come to Italy,
> No matter how dead,
> And buried, you think it is.
> For, in Italy, it will rise,
> And walk, again".

It is to that end that this story will begin to take on a life. I had often dreamed of sailing a boat and of skiing rapidly behind one. What would it be like to travel to the mountain top by bicycle? Or, how about skiing down the slope of the mountain with my hair flying in the wind? I had dreams of shooting a real rifle and of dancing with a girl to the lindy-hop. I had dreams of hitting a baseball like Mickey Mantle or catching one like Phil Rizzuto. Another dream saw me catching a fish. Wouldn't it be wonderful to master a jackknife dive from the high board? Or how about diving deep into the depths in order to chase all the fish? I told you I was wired. Do you believe me now?

Would any of these dreams be possible? In Italy, it would be more prudent to query if any of these dreams could be impossible.

What kind of learning can take place on Saturday? School is closed and there is no access to the classroom or to the teachers. Normally, one would subscribe to that assertion, but not where. I have just come from. To me, it was a veritable Paradise of learning and it always began on Saturday. To me, it will always be home, and a place akin to a springboard into enjoying life through learning about subject matters that cannot be taught in school. These subjects were reserved for the weekend in paradise. These were to be experienced in a unique educational experience one could only find in my "Verona, Italy Paradise". Or so I thought, for, as you will see as this story unfold. I invite you to come along and join me in my discoveries. But first, let me begin at my first discovery. The first of many, that appeared to be a dominoe for all that would follow.

And I would, on many a day, pedal for home, on Saturday, after visiting the courtyard, for I am in love with this place called Verona, Italy. As I pedal my bicycle along these old Italian cobblestone streets, I have become acutely aware of all the sights, sounds, and personal interactions that are taking place all around me. It is as if I have gone back in time, as a trolley car passes by, taking its power from overhead electrical cables that emit sparks falling harmlessly to the street onto the cobblestone as if by magic. Could this be Paradise, I wondered?

There was much to see and even more to do in this magical place being witnessed by a young boy. Perhaps, I was viewing things that way since I was at an impressionable young age. However, I'll let you be the judge of that if you will join me in my adventures that still seem to me to have been somewhat of a dream.

Dream along with me, as I dream my dream for you. However, be advised as you close your eyes, that each and every dream is true. These dreams tell many stories that you will soon not forget, for this story is a dream told to you by an army brat you have just met! Now, where do I begin? Well, I'm a New Yorker and my father is a career Army officer and as a family, we are called upon for active duty overseas. Let's begin there.

Ooh ah, ooh, cool cool kitty. Let's talk about the boy from New York City. He's kind of cute, in his mohair suit, and he keeps his pockets full of spending loot. He's kind of tall, and he's on the ball. He's the kind you know will never trip and fall. Oh yes siree, just wait and see, there's something about that boy from New York City. We're kind of glad, we're glad he came, even though we don't even know his name. You can see, it's very plain, this place may never ever be the same. Ooh ooh ah eee, oh yes siree, let's talk about that boy from New York City.

They were from places like Georgia, Alabama, Tennessee, Kentucky, and Virginia. They were southerners. My name is Charley, and I'm from New York City. These would soon be the best friends this cool, cool, kitty would ever make. First impressions mean alot. They were impressed with me, and I with them. Perhaps the reason was that we were so different, and welcomed a change.

Well, one thing we all had in common was certainly that, we were all in for a change. We are all Americans, however, we are meeting each other for the first time in this foreign land called, Italy. Another thing we all had in common was our fathers. We were all extremely proud of these men of the armed service. We are their dependents, we are their army brats.

So, what impressions have I made here in the U.S. Army dependent school courtyard on my first day? What have I brought with me that has caught their eye already? Well, like it or not, there is a certain life we live, back in New York. It is fast paced, and the streets are tough, so you learn early, how to take care of yourself. That confidence projects itself in a natural way. Without even trying. It's just the way it is, and it is therefore, just the way I am.

Conversely, what impressions have the local populace made upon yours truly, in the courtyard of the school on that first day? They were very kind young people who made the stranger feel welcome right from the start. Southern hospitality is the stuff of legends, I had heard. And now, I know what it feels like. They have come from a slower pace, a calmer life style than the one I am used to living.

The difference appeared to be magnetic, as one needed the other, and we were drawn together. They began to take my city edge off immediately, with their relaxed demeanor and sincere welcome. And, the twinkle of mischief, in my eyes, seemed to be well received as it appeared to be right up their alley. They were a little bit country, and I was a little bit rock and roll. It was a perfect fit.

My new friends had names like Tom Lloyd, John Dotson, Patrick Conran, and Michael Whelan. And the girls had names like Deanna Nolan, Caroline Cole, and Jacquelyn Smith. And so something slowly began to dawn upon me with regard to my warm welcome. You see, they had been here for awhile in this strange land where Italian strangers were everywhere. Strangers that they may never get to know. And now, from out of nowhere, they have a real live Italian to call their own, so that they may make a connection with another culture.

In my wildest dreams, I couldn't have wished for more than what this development could portend. I would soon see myself as two dimensional, whereas, back in the states, the aspect would never occur. I was eager to make friends with these Americans, however, my eyes were receiving sights and sounds from this brief interlude. The signals were beginning to become obvious. This strange land my friends were visiting is the land of my fore fathers. This strange land was my country, it's in my blood.

And so, it seems that I have returned to where I come from, while being greeted by a warm welcome from many strangers I would soon call friends. It was like the story of a cast away who somehow survived an ordeal at sea, only to wash up on a shore where there would prove to be plenty of sustainence. As would the fortunate castaway I began to open my eyes wide, so that I could picture everything that this new land has to offer. It was a beautiful place and so, so pretty. A sight to behold in the eyes of the boy from New York City.

My family checked into the Grand Hotel for the time being. It was located in the heart of town, and would be temporary lodging until permanent quarters could be located. My friends assured me that this would take about a week or two in order to find a place of our choosing. Well, the wait would certainly prove to be well worth the time spent for the search. What we found was certainly befitting the family of an officer and a gentleman.

*???  two baseball players from New York could figure anything out*, I thought.

So I returned to the piazza later that week to get some answers and found Alfredo had set up shop in his usual corner of the piazza bra. He recognized me as I approached to buy an ice cream pop. "Quanta costa questa?" was the classic question one would ask if you wanted to know how much the price of something would cost.

"Sesanta lire," he said. In American language, it meant ten cents value.

"Mile gracie," I said as I gave him one hundred lire coin Dad had given me.

"Prego," he responded with a smile and a question, "Como se chiama?"

"Me chiama Charlie," I replied.

"Ah! Charlutz," he replied.

*Okay*, I thought, *just so long that this doesn't get back to any of my American friends. They would never let me live this one down.* This was strictly classified or top secret as they say at G2.

Dad was right; Alfredo did speak half-Italian and half-English. At least, this gave me half a chance to get some answers. "Alfredo, como se chiama," and I pointed to some of the boys passing the ball around down in the fountain.

"Calcio," he replied. "The game is called calcio."

"Calcio is soccer, Alfredo?"

"Yes––si!"

### ???

*I must return and talk to Alfredo in partial English and partial Italian. I must ask him to explain to me what my dad and I had just heard and seem from our aerial recon park bench at Piazza Bra.*

Dad and I had just been introduced to a sport we had never seen before. He had played quarterback for Franklyn High School in New York City. He even competed successfully in the passing accuracy contest held his senior year at Yankee Stadium. Weekends, he would quarterback the Uhlans from the upper west side of Manhattan, in the neighborhood known as Yorkville. In the classic movie *Casablanca*, Humphrey Bogart, when interrogated by the German police in Morocco, gave some advice. He thought it would be wise that when Germany invades the area of Manhattan, there are certain areas they had best stay clear of, and Yorkville is one of them.

Dad was hardnosed, and he displayed that attribute as captain of the US Army Baseball team of Trieste, Italy, on his prior tour of duty from 1950 through 1953. He was assigned to the Aleutian Islands during World War II as sergeant in charge of a squad whose mission was to help defend the island from attack by the Japanese. He witnessed the final days of the war in the area referenced by the description, the Battle of the Bulge. So you might say, he had seen it all. And then he was assigned to the G2 intelligence sector because he had a good head on his shoulders. He might have seen it all, but this was the first time either one of us had ever seen this new game, and we saw it together. *We are both baseball players from New York City.*

# Chapter 1

# The Ghost And The Darkness

Dad and me, Garmisch, 1952

My soccer teams met with success experienced by many in the first five years. We had our moments in the sun along with our share of rainy days. We became more and more powerful with the passing of the years because of the doctrine that became invincible. This doctrine was woven tightly together from the fine fabric of two distinctly different cloths. This is the doctrine that resulted in the famous streak of an unheard of run spanning ten consecutive years of never losing a regulation game of soccer by more than one goal! How could that be possible? Has the Azzurri ever put together a streak equal to that? Has Juventus, Real Madrid, Manchester United? Has Brazil, Germany, England, or

Argentina? Does anyone know of any team of any sport of any tie that has done this?

Well, my boys out of Ridgewood, New York City, did just that. And they did it against division-A Public Schools Athletic League talent. These opponents played club soccer for Inter-Giuliana, Gottschee-Bauweise, and other numerous sports clubs. Our opponents were trained and accomplished by fine soccer coaches from all over the world. Indeed, the athletes themselves were from all over the world, trained by former coaches, fathers, brothers, uncles in all the best ideas and strategies available worldwide. And we, from Ridgewood, New York City, put them all on a streak that will never be matched. We were Italian, German, Yugoslavian playing alongside the two components of Serbian and Croatian for our own common cause. We were Rumanian, Polish, Spanish, and we came from Haiti, Jamaica, and the Orient. Where in the world except here, in New York City, could such an army be assembled?

We loved to win, and for this common cause, we learned American sports, but we learned wisdom from another fabric of a clandestine nature.

This second fabric comes from the world of G-2 Intelligence sector, US Army Department of Counterintelligence. Major Charles N. Valenti has crossed the river to the other side. The name of that river is the Adige, and it flows beautifully through the town of Verona, Italy. When he arrived on the other side, there was a dried-up old fountain in a place named Piazza Bra.

In the Piazza are my friends Sergio, Claudio, Paolo, and they are playing soccer. Watching them intently is Alberto, the ice cream vendor, and another good-looking Italian man. They are sitting above the fountain on the park bench overlooking the boys. Next to Albert sits a coach with a book in his hands. The coach is my dad, and the book in his hands is *Nosce Hostem*.

DISTINCTIVE UNIT INSIGNIA    COAT OF ARMS

## Distinctive Unit Insignia

Description: A gold color metal and enamel device 1-1/8 inches (2.86 cm) in height overall consisting of the shield adapted from the coat of arms and blazoned as follows: Checky azure (teal blue) and Or a horse rampant Sable fimbriated of the second. Attached below, an arcing Teal Blue motto scroll doubled to the sides inscribed with the words "NOSCE HOSTEM" in Gold letters.

Symbolism: Teal blue and yellow are the colors formerly used for Military Intelligence Battalions. The black horse alludes to Stuttgart, Germany, the place of organization of the unit. The horse and checky field combined, symbolic of a chess board, refer to the strategic and tactical functions of an intelligence unit.

Background: The distinctive unit insignia was approved on 22 December 1959. It was amended to update the description and symbolism on 2 January 1987.

## Coat of Arms

Blazon:
Shield: Checky Azure (teal blue) and Or a horse rampant Sable fimbriated of the second.
Crest: None

Motto: Nosce Hstem

Symbolism:

Shield: Teal blue and yellow are the colors used for Military Intelligence Battalions. The black horse alludes to Stuttgart, Germany, the place of organization of the unit. The horse and checky field combined, symbolic of a chess board, refer to the strategic and tactical functions of an intelligence unit.

Crest: None

Background: The coat of arms was approved on 22 December 1959.

What an ominous-sounding pair of words are these two. When taken separately, they appear to have a meaning or a definition of an ambiguous nature. For instance, *nosce* in Latin simply means "to know." *Hostem* in Latin simply means "your enemy." Taken separately, they appear just as neutral and nonoffensive as any other word. However, when combined as equal parts of a team, these words become an extremely powerful proposition.

For example, a few years ago, a movie appeared at many local theaters here in the United States. The movie portrayed Michael Douglas and Val Kilmer as the two big game hunters hired by a railroad company in India. Progress in laying the track had come to a standstill due to a lion that found the workers to be easy prey. The fatalities began to accumulate to totally unacceptable proportions. Truth be known, one fatality is indeed totally unacceptable. So these two men were hired to put an end to the attacks by the lion, which would always occur under the cover of darkness. There were many witnesses to this nocturnal event, and people who had been working to lay the track were now four deep on the train leaving the workplace. Panic has shown itself in the justified fear exhibited by the mass exodus.

The name of the movie is *The Ghost and the Darkness*. Naturally, when one finds that these two superb actors are playing alongside each other, one wonders which one is the ghost and which of the two is named "the darkness." For when there are two characters, confusion becomes part of the equation. So who is who and which is which? Already things have become much more complicated, to say the least.

With all the workers almost evacuated, the hunt begins. The two men have a cavalier attitude, since they are both accomplished big-game hunters with plenty of kills to support their résumés. It is agreed they will make short work of this lion, and a wager is made as to who will be the better of the two. For when there is two, there is confusion, and the wager becomes the issue as focus is lost upon the lion.

The actor portrayed by Michael Douglas is sure the next day of only one certainty. He will not win this wager, for the lion now has only one hunter left to deal with, and now there is less confusion. The hunter portrayed by Val Kilmer must now avenge his partner. The odds, however, have dropped to even money. The odds are even. The odds are one to one, but the advantage must be with this clever lion since he has proven superior already. The hunter has become the hunted.

They finally come face to face with a villager is attacked and the lion is seen standing on the victim's rooftop. He takes aim; however, the lion has placed the sun behind himself as the shot is taken. Then there is a blur of a shadow as the hunter is knocked to the ground. Another shot is fired, and finally, the confusion comes to an end.

There were two lions! Both are in a museum today, and the inscription under the glass case reads "The Ghost and the Darkness." They are now part of India's history because of the terrible toll they took upon human life. However, they are wild beasts, and hunting prey is how they survive. The reason for enshrinement at the museum is to respect what they had done. Individually, each was quite formidable in his own right. Each was a male with the same appearance, and either one could wreak havoc as an individual. They were put in the museum because of the havoc they were responsible for as hunting partners. They were a team, and they were unstoppable.

While attention was being drawn to the Ghost by the rail workers, the Darkness would strike. When attention was drawn by the Darkness, the Ghost would strike. Under the cover of confusion and disinformation, it was assumed that there was only one lion. No one had ever heard of two male lions behaving in this manner. They stumbled upon something, and so have we!

*Nosce Hostem* is the partner to *All-American*. Each, when taken separately, is a handful. However, when all-American concepts are combined with nosce hostem doctrine, the result is, for lack of a better word, invincible!

Just as the Ghost was partner to the Darkness, each was a separate entity. *All-American* and *Nosce Hostem* are partners; however, each is a separate entity. As such, it is not possible or even appropriate to combine both in the same book. *All-American* must be digested first on its own merits. Time must elapse for this assimilation to run its course, or confusion would be introduced by introducing two remarkable concepts, and I do not wish to confuse the reader. I only wish to help the reader confuse his or her opponent––as I have.

Besides, who among us really wishes to dive into a four-hundred-page book? If you read *All-American*, then you are halfway there. If you haven't and you are only reading *Nosce Hostem*, then at the conclusion of this doctrine, you also will be halfway there. I never liked the feeling of being halfway there. It felt unsettling to feel that way before a game. It meant the issue would have a little bit too much of what I call intangibles.

When all-American concepts accepted help from the nosce hostem doctrine, the intangibles were all but eliminated. Now my boys and I could enjoy the game. Now we were well armed and well versed. We had prepared for each opponent separately and had trained specifically for that opponent. The weaponry we took from our all-American arsenal and the preparation was made available from our nosce hostem classified information.

This was how we did what we did here in Ridgewood, New York City, while the Cosmos nearby were crumbling. These pages are not being compiled to infer that this is the way one should coach soccer; it is merely the story of how I coached soccer. *Nosce Hostem* is the second part to that story.

We know what to do as a team from ideas discussed in *All-American*. Now it is our intent to know what you wish to do as a team when we meet. We wish to know you very well––all your strengths, weaknesses, and habits. We will analyze these particulars and then devise a plan for you. And then we will train specifically for you and execute that plan. Does that sound military? Well, it is, and this was how I was taught to think by a G-2 counterintelligence major named Charles N. Valenti. Nosce Hostem is the seal logo of his intelligence detachment US Army!

Once again, an innuendo arises with respect to an effort attempted by two entities; a unified effort by two working as one to achieve the interest shared by both. One entity called. All-American comes from the experience of an-American athlete. The other entity called Nosce Hostem comes from the experience of a career US Army major. The first would liken itself to the Ghost, since my opponents never did have a clue what my boys were doing as we subjected them to one American sport tactic after another, and it all remained a mystery. The second would liken itself to the darkness since these tactics operated in the clandestine world of the cloak and dagger. This is the world of obtaining information secretly and using that information you obtained to destroy your opponent without him even knowing you were in his camp!

So now I am beginning to tip my hand by divulging information, by revealing to you who was the Ghost and who was the Darkness. Each was an expert, both were a team. As did the two lions, we ran wild for over fifteen years as we consumed the prey called the Public Schools Athletic League. However, unlike the two lions, we were never mastered or even understood. Everything we did was classified, and like old soldiers, we didn't die, we just faded away, if I may use that famous line from General Douglas MacArthur.

The Ghost has already shared much of his approach with you in the book called *All-American*. Now the Darkness invites you to share much of his approach in this book called *Nosce Hostem*. The time has come to reveal what we did and how we did it since I believe that my coaching days ended a long time ago. Now that the Darkness has passed away recently, I fear the Ghost just doesn't have it in him anymore. Perhaps that is why the second lion took that final jump at the hunter when he could have run off into the wild. It just wouldn't be the same. However, keeping this knowledge to ourselves wouldn't be right, as all we were ever about was helping people by teaching.

Thanks to the *pescadors* of Verona, my two sons have grown up to love fishing and water sports. My older son, Ted, has been instrumental in developing the preliminary manuscript. My younger son, Chris, was relentless in finding the publisher. My wife, an Italian *ragazza* who is quite beautiful, has been a faithful supporter of mine. And by the way, it is only fitting that a shortstop must have a beautiful *ragazza*, don't you agree? Ted has two children who have taken an interest in this project. Christina, my granddaughter *e una ragazza moulta* bella, and thanks to her as my secretary sorting out bits and pieces of an old manuscript, an idea has become a reality. Her brother, Ted Jr., asked if he could have a copy of the book to take to school as he finds much humor between these pages and wants to make his friends laugh. I took that as a positive reinforcement. And of course, there is my dad, Major Charles N. Valenti, whom I was so fortunate to have for a father and a best friend. He was my professor, he was my consigliere, and he never let me down whenever I needed him, which was quite often.

Now it should be noted that if you have taken an interest in all that has preceded this page, my dad has a whole lot of classified information available for publication once I declassify everything. My dear friend has passed away recently, but his spirit lives on. I know this to be true, for when I was asked by the publishing house to proceed with this venture, I was at a loss and clueless. After all, I am only a mere shortstop, and shortstops do not write books. So I thought it prudent to visit Dad at the cemetery site and, for lack of knowing what to do or say, I brushed my hand over his name on the stone and asked him to help the shortstop write a book. When I returned home, I took this old Omega typewriter out from mothballs, and the whole thing came pouring out like water over the falls.

So he is still with us, and we together await your call so that we may tell you about the other half of the story. My teams did not go ten years with no opponent beating us by more than one goal just because we used American sports on the soccer field. That is only half the story, and the other half warrants the writing of another book called *Nosce Hostem*.

As we went into Germany, thoughts of Yorkville and life before the war entered my mind.

# Chapter 2

# Yorkville, 1935

It was spring of 1935, and I was sitting by the East River near my neighborhood of Yorkville, in the city of New York, where I was born seventeen years ago. I would be graduating from Benjamin Franklin High School that June, and I was wondering what the future has in store for a kid from New York City. I couldn't help but wonder what my future might be if I just could have completed one more pass that day at Yankee Stadium.

I was the quarterback at Franklin High School, and all I had to show for that is a varsity letter *F* in the school colors of orange with brown trim. I had another for playing baseball for the school. I guessed I'll hold onto them just in case I someday might have a son to show and tell football and baseball stories.

That day at Yankee Stadium came to a close after many football players from all over the area came to test their accuracy throwing the football. After a long day, it narrowed down to just the two of us as we entered what was thought to be the final round. Wow! What was this I see out there in the river?

It was a huge cargo ship passing through, and it was full to the brim with all sorts of rusty metal junk. Who would even want that scrap metal that appeared so unsightly? I looked closer to find the flag on that junk collector and saw a white flag with a huge red ball at its center. Odd, I thought.

So we entered the final round. We each had five attempts at passing the football through a tire suspended thirty yards away.

Many were watching from the sidelines to see the result. I went five for five—and so did he! This guy was good! An extra round was now necessary, and we went at it again, each competing for the college scholarship awarded to the winner. Somehow I hit the side of the tire on my last attempt, and he finished without a miss. I guess that's the way it goes. Now college is out of the question. Mom and Pop are having a hard time raising the five of us and putting food on the table. We were five brothers and lived in a railroad flat in Yorkville. Pop was a tailor who brought his skill here from Italy, and I would help him with deliveries.

Pop could play the mandolin and loved to play "Fratelli Di Italia." However, his favorite song next to that was "God Bless America." He would make the five of us sit on the couch and sing every word as he played that mandolin. When Luigi was satisfied, we could all get up and look forward to Mom's pasta and the delicious sauce we all loved.

Pop had a dog that took to him at the peril of the rest of the family. I would never want to upset Pop, but the other day, he wasn't around, and "Kutchie" went for me and removed part of my sleeve and a button. What would you do? No one was home except me and the dog, so I rushed him, threw a football move on him in the hallway. He fell for it just like all the guys I played against. So I quickly picked him up and ran through the halls and dumped him in the toilet; even flushed the toilet for good measure. I wondered where that dog was; I hadn't seen him around lately. It's a good thing dogs can't talk.

It's a good thing my four brothers aren't like me. I think they all have a more low-keyed way about them for a reason. You see, they are all musicians and took after Pop in that way. Vincent, my older brother, could play the bass fiddle. Johnny, my younger brother, could play the guitar. Tony, the youngest of us, could play the trumpet. And Alphonso could play the guitar and mandolin as good as anyone I ever heard in my young life; he has a gift. And then there is Charlie, that's me, and the only thing I can play is the radio—unless you can count quarterback or first base.

I feel as comfortable on the ball field as my brothers do playing before an audience. It seems that I have a sense of knowing what to expect before it happens. I'm good at spotting defenses and analyzing them before I shout out my audibles to the team. I'm team captain and their leader. That and a penny can get you two pretzels at the corner candy store.

So I was sitting there by the river as the Japanese cargo ship steamed out of New York City with everybody's junk, and I was wondering about my future. Each of my brothers had a skill that enabled them to earn some money for the family. It looked like I'll have to find a job so that I can help Vincent and Al support the family.

Vincent and Al were the breadwinners. Al has the musical talent one can only be born with and was pulling his weight and then some. Vincent played his bass as a job and eventually would play on the cruise ships going to Havana, Cuba. However, Vincent had another side to him.

Vince is the oldest of the five, and we all look up to him for two reasons. He is a good role model for the rest of us and shows great respect for Mom and Pop. If one of us got out of line, Vincent may make his presence felt rather dramatically. Vince could hit. He has a right hand that will put you on the seat of your pants before you could blink an eye, and now maybe you couldn't even open your eye. The four of us were safe in the neighborhood when it was known that he was our big brother.

The people in the neighborhood who weren't safe, however, were the opponents chosen to step into the ring against him on Friday night. He made money for the family and became welterweight Golden Glove champion of Yorkville. He would also become a US Marine during the years ahead.

Johnny had his circle of friends, and I never really saw him all that much, although I know he had a good heart like the rest of us. I feel that Mom and Pop had something major to do with that blessing.

And then there was Tony, who would eventually be the soldier who was selected to wake the barracks up at the post he would be assigned to as an army bugler in the future trial that awaited all of the brothers. The best way I can describe Tony is an episode that occurred one afternoon as I was taking a walk with the girl I would eventually marry. As we approached the corner of our high school, we were both startled as the doors flew open and out came Tony running at full speed up the block with the truant officer in hot pursuit.

Tony and I kind of took to each other since we were closer in age and interests. We also may both have had a screw loose here or there. Tony and I eventually found a job working together as the dynamic duo in Glauber Plumbing Supply Company a few blocks from the house. Tony noticed that there was a problem getting bread for the table; maybe the money situation had something to do with the shortage. At any rate, he came to me because he was certain he had the solution and placed his trust in me as I was the other half of the dynamic duo.

"Charlie, listen. I know where we can get fresh bread for Mom and Pop."

I was all ears and went along wholeheartedly with the plan. It seemed that Tony had spotted a bakery one day as he was outrunning the truant officer somewhere over by the Fifty-Ninth Street bridge next to a coal factory. He claimed to have smelled a wonderful aroma as he shot past in full stride but couldn't put on the brakes, so he made a quick mental note of the area as he flew by and noticed something interesting.

He explained that the bread was put out on the windowsill high above. There was a high pile of coal waiting shipment, and he skirted through that coal pile in order to lose the truant officer, so all we had to do was climb that coal pile, grab the bread, and run home. "I'm with you," I said, and the dynamic duo left bright and early the next morning. He was right; the bread was placed out on the windowsill, and the coal was piled high enough to reach the bread. So up we went. We reached the top and each of us grabbed as much bread as we could possibly hold when a dog from inside the bakery suddenly appeared at the window, snarling at us as though it was his bread or something. Well, down we went, both of us clutching onto the bread for dear life as we rolled all the way to the bottom. We reached the bottom and couldn't even recognize each other. We were as black as the Ace of Spaces. So was the bread, but we ran like hell through the streets of Yorkville with the soiled bread tucked under our arms as though it were a football. We got home and knocked on the door. Mom answered, took one look at us, and said, "*Povero mia!*" It was her way of feeling sorry that she had raised two nutjobs.

Tony had an idea, and then I had one for him. I asked him to tag along with me one afternoon so that we can go to a great place for stickball batting practice. Tony and I were good enough at stickball to hustle anyone whom we played in Yorkville. It was okay because like the bread, we would always bring everything home to Mom and Pop. That made everything all right.

So the dynamic duo arrived at the local horse stable for batting practice, each with stickball bat in hand.

"What are we doing here, Charlie?" he asked.

"Watch this," I answered as I began swatting one fly after another into smithereens. Tony joined in and in his exuberance slipped and fell in the manure that drew the flies to the stable. I told Tony I had to stop off and see my girlfriend and I would see him later. I wound up getting home earlier than Tony and was there when he knocked on the door and Pop answered and just stood there looking at him in silence.

Tony and I spent the next two years working for Glauber Plumbing, and it began to appear to offer no future. Tony remained there, but I felt compelled to search for something more rewarding. My future brother-in-law, Jules Stollack, played on the UGLANS football team that I quarterbacked on Sundays in Upper Manhattan. We became good friends for several reasons. Jules was a good athlete and was going out with my girlfriend's sister. However, our relationship grew because of another feature. It began to dawn on me that this kid who spent much time down at the East River watching Japanese ships pass or watching his older brother Vincent swim across to Randalls Island needed to become something.

Jules and I would devise football plays and tactics to be used on Sundays and spent time during the week rehearsing his movements downfield, in coherence with the delivery of the football. The Uhlans were a good football team; however, we were having a hard time scoring because our linemen were forty pounds lighter than teams we would face each Sunday, so Jules and I put our brains to work. In order to help this Yorkville football team, we took to the air, and it brought dramatic results. What we both became aware of is that each had met the intellectual equal.

We were both very curious and inquisitive about everything. Then one day, after the season ended, we were walking through Manhattan together when we saw this poster to enlist in the armed forces of your choice. He was attracted to becoming a paratrooper, and I was to choose the infantry, so we enlisted.

Trouble was brewing over in China, and it evidenced itself in some horrible accounts regarding the Japanese attack (1937) and occupation of the Chinese main city of Nanking. The local draft board was becoming more active, and some of our friends were learning that they would have no say in the matter.

Jules was to become a member of the 82nd Airborne, and we would meet again in Germany. My choice was to continue quarterbacking a team where there would be no football. I always felt comfortable being a leader and taking responsibility for making decisions for the group. So I entered the area responsible for training the men and preparing them for the big game on Sunday. There was a big game coming all right, and no one could have ever imagined just how big that game would be and how the world would suffer. Vincent chose the Marines, and we would meet again at a train stop in California. Tony and Johnny were drafted into the army. Al was left behind to take care of Mom and Pop, and that was life in Yorkville.

There were more accounts coming from another part of the world. It seemed that the British prime minister, Neville Chamberlain, had offered Germany a free hand in the takeover of an area of Czechoslovakia known as the Sudeten (1938). And that time, October 1939, Germany had taken over the entire country of Czechoslovakia without even firing a shot. No wonder the draft board was becoming more active.

I was to report to Fort Jay, on Governors Island, right here in New York City.

# Chapter 3

# You're In The Army, Now!

Things were moving fast now as we said good-bye to family and friends. Fort Jay, on Governors Island, in the heart of New York City, was where the First Army was located. The overall mission of the First Army was commanding and training regular army, army reserve, and national guard units in the northeast area of the United States. That was where I would begin my assignment in training a cadre of men. It wasn't quarterbacking, and then again, maybe it was in a way.

These training responsibilities grew in size as the First Army relocated to Louisiana and North Carolina. Large-scale maneuvers were conducted here during 1940 and 1941. As an old quarterback used to leading a team, I felt right at home training my teams of new soldiers. Before I knew it, Uncle Sam felt he needed a sergeant and pushed me up the ladder. I was assigned to train men as first sergeant the 159th Infantry. It set me on a path away from First Army, although I would see them again down the road in Germany. The First Army under General Omar Bradley was to participate in Operation Overlord in the invasion of Normandy on D-Day, the Sixth of June, 1944. Jules Stollacks, 82nd Airborne, would be in on that, and he survived to tell his story.

So the 159th Infantry was detached from the First Army because the training it provided was needed elsewhere. Events unfolded at an alarming rate as Germany overran Poland and France. Suddenly the United States found itself honor bound to defend Great Britain after news came in that Churchill gave the order to sink the French fleet at anchor to prevent Germany from obtaining the French warships.

It was hot down in North Carolina, and I had the men take a timeout for water and salt pills to replace what they had lost on the long overland hike with full pack and camping equipment. It reminded me of a time out with my old Uhlans from Yorkville, water and salt pills and a brief respite, before the second half resumes. And before we rose up to resume training, we heard the news that took our breath away. This was December 7, 1941, and the word spread rapidly around the detachment that Pearl Harbor had been struck by Japan. What does this awful news mean to men who had been training by way of overland hikes and maneuvers? We did not know! I thought that the Japanese have cleverly turned all that East River junk against us by changing the steel into ships and planes, to be used as weapons.

During the next few months, I often wondered how it could be possible that we were so unprepared. I would never had allowed my football team or my men here to be so unprepared, if I had a say in the matter! What the hell happened? Maybe I needed to switch gears and get out of the training business and into the area of military intelligence. My thoughts were leaning in that direction for the future because of this event. However, right then my job was to train the men.

We found out bits and pieces about the attack on Pearl Harbor. All my men were happy to learn that none of our aircraft carriers were in port on that day, but I couldn't help but wonder about that.

How could a massive fleet engage in a mission of such enormity, which had to be meticulously planned, and travel undetected across the Pacific Ocean? How is that possible? How could the planners have been so intelligent? How could we have been so stupid? And how could they have picked December 7th as the arrival date and not know that none of our aircraft carriers would be in port? How could they have been that stupid? Something doesn't add up here.

At the time, I had no other information. However, eventually more facts emerged from the swamp. Our intelligence units knew that the Japanese fleet set sail from their port on the northern Kuriles Islands on November 26, 1941. Our intelligence units knew that the normal intercepts of radio traffic between the ships of that fleet had ceased. Was no one astute enough to put these two bits of intelligence together?

Something just doesn't add up here. And then the scuttlebutt came down that we had our boys up at Opana Point call in a large flight of aircraft coming in from the north. This intelligence was dismissed as a flight of our own incoming B-17s? and then our B-17s came in from another quadrant altogether. I never went fishing much down at the East River in New York City, but there were times when dead fish floated up onto the rocks below, and I know something fishy when I smell it! As a baseball player, I know what it takes to strike a batter out or to be struck out by the opposing pitcher. It takes three strikes right down the middle of the plate unless the batter is fooled by a bad pitch. Three strikes to a batter just doesn't happen. The batter gets a warning. He may foul one off, or a pitch or two may go by for a ball so that there are more warnings as the count builds. Eventually, the batter may indeed strikeout, and he may even go down swinging, but at least he had processed information and tried to do something with it. We don't stand up at the plate with a blindfold on, do we?

We had three pitches and ignored each of them while standing at the plate with a bat. How could it be? That did it. I was a baseball player out of New York City, and where I came from, you just don't take three strikes! Someday, if I get the chance, I must become an army intelligence officer––someday.

In the meantime, I just informed the boys that our new deployment orders just came in, and I don't know what to make of them. It appeared that the 159th had been redesigned as something called the Seventh Motorized Division. We are to be transported to the Mojave Desert in preparation for deployment to the Africa theatre of operations. This is an example of a word being invented here in the US Army. The word is abbreviated as SNAFU––that is short around here for situation normal, all fouled up! What the hell were we going to do next? Learn to ride camels? We were not a motorized division. I'll bet most of my men haven't even tried for their driver's license yet!

Well, at least the brass realized something and came to their senses. We have instead been deployed to California. It was January 1943. Ever since we received the order back in April to become a motorized outfit, it became obvious to the men that all our vehicles were being reassigned little by little, where they may have been in short supply. Until finally we realized that we weren't a motorized division anymore. Now what? Another abbreviated word started to make the rounds around the camp, FUBAR, translated what described our situation aptly––fouled up beyond all recognition.

We were now deployed in sunny California as a light infantry division. Now the training program had switched gears to amphibious assault operations. We were expecting this training in preparation to fight in the Pacific theatre instead of Africa. Rommel, the Desert Fox, was a formidable German opponent I North Africa as head of his motorized Africa corps. At least we no longer had to worry about running into that bunch, I thought. And then I had another worry that I don't even want to tell the men, as some regarded me as their fearless leader. The East River was not the cleanest body of eater around back home, so I would just s on the bank and watch Vincent swim. He would call and holler "Charlie, you chicken, come on in!" and I would always decline. So I never learned how to swim, and now I'm involved in the training of men for amphibious landings on beaches in the Pacific as an element of the Seventh Infantry Division. Much had happened in the Pacific.

The Japanese had advanced throughout the entire Pacific and were approaching the Alaskan coastline. They had actually occupied the Aleutian Islands of Adak, Kiska, and Attu. They were getting too close for comfort. Training accelerated as one contingent of men after another were being prepared for their mission.

Elements of the Seventh Infantry Division first saw combat in the amphibious assault on Attu Island, the westernmost Japanese entrenchment in the Aleutian chain.

It was May 11, 1943, when elements landed, spearheaded by the Seventeenth Infantry Division. Ever since June 3 and 4, 1942, when the Battle of Midway proved decisive for the United States Navy, we felt that maybe the tide of war in the Pacific may be turning in our favor. The Japanese Navy lost all four of their carriers those two days in that epic battle. They were the Akagi, the Kaga, the Soryu, and the Hiryu.

The Japanese plan was to capture the island in the middle of the Pacific called Midway Island. Once that was achieved, Midway would be used as an airfield for the Japanese to dominate the area and threaten the coast of California. These were trying times, and everything was very uncertain.

My research about this event years later revealed that the US Navy was aware of the Japanese plan through communications intercepts and had devised its own plan to destroy his forces despite the odds being stacked against us. Once again, my interest gravitated toward becoming a military intelligence officer. Those intercepts and their analysis proved crucial to the outcome of the battle. We knew their plan, but they did not know ours. Part of the Japanese's plan was sending a diversionary force to occupy the Aleutian Islands. The American Task Force 16, commanded by Admiral Chester Nimitz, had taken the battle with the carriers Hornet, Enterprise, and I'm very proud when I learned that the Yorktown was the third.

The very outcome of the war in the Pacific hinged upon that battle. We had the advantage, even though they had the superior force and a meticulous plan of execution. They were to lure our carriers out into the open when we would attempt to defend midway, and that would be a moe at our own peril. The diversion at the Aleutians would serve to divert some of our attention and thereby weaken our overall defense. Everything was planned to perfection, just as it had been at Pearl Harbor, except for our lesson we had learned the hard way.

This time we listened to our intelligence reports. Our intelligence had long before put out a message that Midway was low on water. After close monitoring of communication signals, we were able to identify the Japanese version of the word "Midway." It was enough to tip us off that they were planning something, and that plan had something to do with Midway. And we even knew when this would occur. So into the parlor, said the spider to the fly, and the hunter became the hunted.

Years would pass before I would belong to a military unit of intelligence and counterintelligence that identified themselves by their logo, "Nosce Hostem," a Latin reference to "know your enemy." We certainly were beginning to know him very well, for we received some news the other day about a significant event.

On April 18, 1943, a flight of our P-38 Lightings, referred by the Japanese as the "fork-tailed devil" intercepted a top secret flight transporting Admiral Isoroku Yamamoto to the Solomon Islands. He was their commander-in-chief of their combined fleet and the architect of the raid on Pearl Harbor. "We got him!" shouted the boys.

Years later, I became aware that our navy had developed a technology named "ULTRA." This enabled us to "nosce hostem" as we were able to break their code, and we knew the itinerary of the flight on that fateful day. We also threw a curveball at the enemy during the months ahead, thanks to Navajo Indians in our armed service who would just send signals back and forth in Navajo during our "island hopping" campaign. Only a Navajo could possibly interpret this natural coded language. The reference to island hopping reveals itself as a tactical tool used to avoid the enemy where he is strong so that you may attack him where he is weak, or at the very least, beat him by winning the war of attrition. By cutting off his supply lines, you may render him irrelevant. These are all tactical and strategic tools that are essential to emerge victorious in battle.

Now we had to deal with the Japanese diversionary force that has become a problem in that they were well dug in on Attu. Our assignment was to land there on May 11, 1943. An intense battle was fought over the tundra against strong Japanese resistance. The fight for the island cumulated in a battle at Chicago of Harbor, when the division destroyed all Japanese resistance. This occurred only after a suicidal Japanese bayonet charge.

During its first fight of the war, six hundred soldiers of the division were killed while the Japanese suffered 2,351 dead, and only twenty-eight were taken prisoners.

My 159th Infantry Division was relieved from the Seventh Infantry Division in August 1943 and assigned to the Alaskan department of defense. A polar bear patch would identify the outfit during our stay there. It wasn't easy, and the men had a tough time. I remember one of the guys because of my baseball background; I sure respect a strong arm. This soldier went up into the hills for two days and wouldn't come down. He kept pelting all his buddies with rocks. We left him alone until he came to his senses. There was absolutely nothing up there but a few fox and some goats that could climb like a spider. One night, a few of us grabbed some tins of peanut butter and ran up there to fetch our friend, whom we thought must be real hungry by this time. We all sat up there for hours eating gobs of peanut butter and finally got him to come down. I don't know if he thought we were helping him or trying to kill him with the peanut butter, but I haven't had the interest to eat peanut butter ever since.

The Japanese Navy would pass close by, and the order came down to dig 8 caliber antitank guns into the beach in order to disguise them as coastal artillery, of which we were sorely lacking. They decided to leave us alone as they were more interested in rescuing their own men on one of the neighboring islands called Kiska. We were planning to hit them with airpower based at yet another Aleutian Island called Adak. Several bomb runs and we went into Kiska only to find that all 5,200 men had been evacuated, under the cover of fog, several days earlier. We had been bombing a deserted island all the while. We finally departed Attu on August 9, 1944, arriving at the stateside Seattle port of embarkation eleven days later. Our army had been in Europe since D-Day, the Invasion of Normandy on June 6, 1944.

The 159th Infantry Division was transferred to Camp Swift, Texas, on August 28, 1944. We moved to Camp Callan, California, on December 20, 1944, before returning to Camp Swift on January 28, 1945. Something was up, and we all could feel it by these latest moves. Something big had happened in a forest called the Ardennes, in Europe, near the Belgium border on December 16, 1944, and it very well may be the reason for our return to Camp Swift where the Fourth Army was based. That base was responsible for what I do best––train men. My guys and I took to each other a lot like you may expect on a close-knit ball team, only even closer due to all of our harrowing experiences back on Attu. After we hit the beach, we were ordered to dig large pits over which we could pitch a tent sufficient to withstand the elements for a squad of men. We followed our orders and were about to take up quarters when a group of officers threw us out and laid claim to the place.

My men looked at me with that same look I used to get quarterbacking the outclassed Uhlans football team back in Yorkville. It was the look of "Now what, Charlie?" So I took a huge gamble and marched into the commanding officer's tent and objected vociferously about the intrusion and the exclusion.

"Sir, I respectfully submit to you that this is just not right."

He agreed and demanded that the officers relocate so that my men could rest in the tent they erected and would indeed call home. These were my guys. This was my family now on that long isolated stay away from my wife back home in Yorkville. It was all for one and one for all, and that's the way it would be until we shipped out. Mary and I had been married in June 1941, and like all the girls and guys, it hasn't been a normal life, to say the least. This past Christmas was a brief return to a normal life as I was reunited with my wife at Camp Callan, California.

All hell had broken loose in Europe in what was being called "the Battle of the Bulge." Indeed, our training here at Camp Swift, Texas, was to prepare us for our assignment ahead.

The regiment staged at Camp Kilmer, New Jersey, on February 27, 1945, before departing from the New York Port of Embarkation on March 7, 1945. Mary was three months pregnant, and this was a rough departure for all of us. Would I ever see my newborn son? This I did not know, but if I ever do, I had much to tell him and much to teach him. I had already learned firsthand much about our opponent. This information I will pass on to him in the event that he will need to know about the events that have transpired. Perhaps they may be of use to him something in the future.

I intended to keep an account on all I will learn in the days ahead of all the battles fought––battles won and battles lost––so that one day he may analyze that information and put it to use. I would not keep this knowledge to myself. I must share all of this someday with my son. I must learn all I can about this Battle of the Bulge because from what I was being told, it appeared once again to have resulted due partly because of the failure of our intelligence community. I must, in the trial ahead, allow my new warrant officer status to promote me into the intelligence community of our armed forces––the sober, the better.

My intent was the gathering of information. What happened in the Ardennes forest, and how was it even possible? Where will I find the answer to that question? The 106th Infantry Division unit called "the Golden Lions" by the patch they wear was taken by surprise after being placed in what intelligence believed to be the quietest sector on the front. Those guys didn't have a chance. Two of the three regiments were overrun and surrounded in the initial days of the battle, and they were forced to surrender to German forces on December 19, 1944. I had to get answers to what happened. I had to know, but who can tell me all I need to learn? And will I ever be able to pass that knowledge on to my son? My 159th Infantry Division arrived in France eleven days later.

The 106th (Golden Lions) relieved the Second Infantry Division at a section of terrain designated by name as the quietest sector on the front. The 106th consisted of three infantry regiments, the 422nd, 423rd, and 424th. The 424th joined the Second Infantry Division and were sent to an area called Winterspelt. The Ardennes-Alsace German campaign was thrown in force at the 106th on December 16, 1944.

The 422nd and 423rd Infantry Regiments were encircled and cut off from the remainder of the division by a junction of enemy forces in the vicinity of Schoberg. They regrouped for a counterattack but were blocked by the enemy and were lost to the rest of the division on December 18, 1944. The two regiments surrendered to the Germans on December 19, 1944.

The rest of the division, reinforced by the 112th Infantry Regiment of the Twenty-Eighth Infantry Division, withdrew over the Our River and joined other units at St. Vith. Along with the city of Bastogne, to the south, St. Vith was a road and rail juncture considered vital to the German goal of breaking through Allied lines to split American and British forces and reach the Belgium port city of Antwerp.

A scratch force of 106th division personnel, in particular the divisions Eighty-First Engineer Combat Battalion, began a five-day holding pattern (December 17-21) on a thin ridge line a mile outside St. Vith against German forces vastly superior in numbers and armament (only a few hundred combat green Americans against many thousands of veteran Germans). For this action, the 81st Combat Battalion was later awarded the Distinguished Unit Citation for gallantry.

The defense of St. Vith by the 106th (Golden Lions) had been credited with ruining the German timetable for reaching Antwerp and hampering the bulge offensive for the German Army. The 81st and its allied units, including the 168th Engineer Combat Battalion, all pulled back from St. Vith on December 21, 1944, under constant enemy fire, and withdrew over the Saint River at Vielsalm on December 23. The following day, the 424th Regiment (Golden Lions) attached to the Seventh Armored Division fought a delaying action a Manhay. From December 25, 1944, to January 9, 1945, the division received reinforcements and supplies at Anthisnes, Belgium, and returned to the struggle. The Golden Lions secured objectives along the Ennal-Logbirme line on January 15th after heavy fighting. After being pinched out by advancing divisions, the 106th assembled at Stavelot on January 18th for rehabilitation and raining. It moved to the vicinity of Hunningen on February 7, 1945, for defensive patrols and training.

In March, the 424th (Golden Lions) advanced along the high grounds between Berk and the Simmer River and was again pinched out at Olds on March 7, 1945. A period of training and security patrolling along the Rhine River followed until March 15, 1945, when the division moved to St. Quentin for rehabilitation and the reconstruction of lost units. Here is when my 159th became "Golden Lions."

The 159th Infantry Regiment moved from Camp Swift to Camp Callan, California, on December 20, 1944. It looked like we were headed back to the fight in the Pacific, when word came of a change because of an event that was stunning to all the men. The German Army has broken out in Europe. We were ordered back to Camp Swift for a month of training. The Germans had come though the Ardennes on December 16th and decimated many allied elements in that area. We were told to mobilize and join the fight. (So that is where I first heard the word.)

We were moved quickly and arrived in France in March 1945. Our orders were to mobilize and move rapidly across France to the city of St. Quentin where the remnants of the mauled 106th Infantry Division was waiting for us. They had lost two-thirds of their unit in the breakout.

# Chapter 4

# The Race Across France

"How was France, Dad?" I had taken a seat, now in the living room of our home in Whitestone, Queens, New York years later. "How were the people at that time?"

"Well, Charlie, it was like this," and he began.

We knew that we were about to play a personal part in the final stages of the way in Europe and the wining of the peace. Whatever part you have been mobilized to perform––infantry, artillery, gunner, truck driver—you will be an essential factor. This would be a mobilization that has one objective. The destruction of a system and ideology opposite to all freedom-loving men.

"My 159th Infantry Division reconstituted the lost 422nd and 423rd, arrived in France at St. Quentin. By April 1945, the Allied Armies swept across the Rhine deep into Germany. About two hundred thousand German prisoners were already taken, and the number increased day by day."

"The Ruhr pocket brought in an additional three hundred thousand men, which had to be processed through allied hands. As the German Army surrendered unconditionally on May 7th, thousands of German soldiers were heading west to avoid capture by the Russian Army."

"Meanwhile, my 159th Infantry Division made its way through France to the city of St. Quentin and then eventually to the French city of Rennes. It was here in these two French towns where the decimated 106th Division received two new combat teams, the Third and the 159th Infantry Regiments, and two new field artillery battalions, the 401st and the 627th. We wore a new patch on our sleeve; it was a patch of the Golden Lions!"

"We were one of them now! Where better than from these survivors could I possibly learn what happened at that battle? As a member of the Golden Lions, I would have much to tell my son in the years ahead. It would be a story told by the Lion to his cub."

"In time, let us all see what he can do with that knowledge, of the Battle of the Bulge, as told to me by the men who were there. Immediately after joining the remnants of the 106th, I began to gather information and started putting the pieces together about the epic battle that they were a big factor in for our side."

It should be noted for clarity purpose that my 159th Infantry regiment and the 106th Infantry Division were both elements of the US First Army. As an element of the First Army, my 159th, while reconstituting the lost units of the Golden Lions, received its new task.

It would be responsible for guarding and protecting Germans in the area around the Rhine River. The battle and capture of many of these POWs took place on March 7 and 8, 1945. The First Army had to take a bridge called the Ludendorff at the town of Remagen. We took that bridge intact and quickly advanced on to the other side of the Rhine. This was a stroke of luck as the Germans failed to destroy the bridge.

We crossed the river in force quickly. By April 4th, an enormous pocket had been created by First Army and our Ninth Army. This pocket contained the German Army Group B, the last significant combat force in the north west of Germany.

We then headed east, creating another pocket containing the German Eleventh Army. First Army reached the Elbe by April 19th, where the advance met Soviet forces on April 25th.

In May 1945, we were awaiting the possibility of a deployment to the Pacific as I received word that advance elements had already returned to New York City. There they were preparing for the dreaded invasion of Honshu, the main island of Japan, in the spring of 1946. Thankfully, the Japanese in August 1945, terminated that effort.

The 106th Infantry Division returned to New York Port, October 1, 1945.

The Wehrmacht had failed in France. "They had failed to contain the beachhead, Charlie. They had failed to stop our armored spearheads. The race was on once we broke out of Normandy and developed a salient at the French town of St. Lo. Our air force pounded and strafed their troop movements. The German supply lines were log and tenuous, with no air force to defend them, and they still believed the allied main landing may be yet to come at the Pas de Calais. Coupled with this was a brilliant, bold strategy, which turned the American armor loose."

"The Pas de Calais is an area of France in closest proximity to the coast of England. Because of the short distance across the water barrier, the German 15$^{th}$ Army totaling 250,000 men were awaiting the invasion where none would be forthcoming." This always intrigued me, from a soccer coach point of view. Overextending your capabilities is daring but foolish and should be thought through thoroughly. Furthermore, it appears that the Pas de Calais was a masterful ploy. This will be a useful tool for my effort as a coach in order to keep the pressure off our point of attack. By the way, across this narrow channel, the Germans witnessed tanks, trucks, and other equipment through their binoculars and from the air. However, what they didn't know was that the equipment were inflatable dummies! This ploy froze in place 250,000 German soldiers who could have been used to push the allies back into the sea and off the Normandy beaches. This was a lesson in both intelligence and counterintelligence. These were the fulcrum from which my teams drew their identity and reputation for unpredictability. The Germans were outfoxed, and that feature became part and parcel to our nature. These studies influenced the nature of my team dramatically. Simply stated, freeze the enemy where he is strong so that you may attack him where he is weak. This was done during the allied invasion of Normandy and gave us our foothold in France. This was also done in Ridgewood and gave us our foothold in New York City!

"Once we had broken into the open, Charlie, many possibilities became apparent. Hodges and Patton quickly formed two gigantic hooks into the rear of the German formations, still fighting the British and Canadians around Caen and, I conjunction with a Montgomery drive to the south, created the Falaise Gap. Over one hundred thousand Germans escaped through this gap near the French town of Falaise."

"It was here that many of the Germans found the way to flee back into Germany, as the German army maintained strong flanks in order to hold off the allies until their men could pass through, after which the gap was closed. This gives merit to the value of an organized and methodical retreat under great pressure. There are times when the other side is just too powerful and cannot be challenged, and therefore, discretion is the better part of valor."

They would live to fight another day, and so can you, if you have a plan that does not include panic, but is well organized. We had to retreat many times during our battles on the fields of the Big Apple, and we always lived to fight another day, or at least refused to be headstrong and foolhardy at that moment. Back up fast and defend. We'll be back later at a time and place of our own choosing, but right now, you're just too strong, and we'll take our hat off to you. Just don't get too comfortable with our hat because we are coming back to get it sooner than you think! We must now retreat, regroup, and reconstitute so that later we may hear you say, "Oh no, here they come again!"

He continued. "The German army in France was licked. From mid-August until mid-September, all hell broke loose in France. My battle-weary buddies told me that they had wished that all war was like those early days." It was a tactic the Germans chose out of necessity and a well-remembered one, from my point of view. The connection I identified with was when we would run helter-skelter back to set up our perimeter at or near the sixteen-meter line. We didn't really want to, but we had to, or we would be overrun and scored upon. Stiff resistance here is better than a weak resistance upfield––the lesser of two evils.

At this point in his review, his description of events took on a type of behavior that we at Cleveland would never experience, a rout! We could not be routed because our fail-safe protocol was just too sound and had several layers, contingencies, and a stubborn state of mind reinforced by a huge measure of pride. However, there were numerous occasions where the opponent was so exposed and downtrodden that a rout appeared eminent. When this began to occur, everyone on the sideline began to stretch their legs, and all entered the contest. They had their orders to maintain control of the contest but not to pull the trigger if we were ahead by three goals. Enough is enough; there will be no ore scoring against a team less fortunate than ours. Let them depart with a measure of respect, and let us not do something we may regret by piling it on. It's just not us.

"Charlie, the Germans were in full retreat and heading due East for the safety of their homeland. There were times when we would be chasing them, and we could actually see each other on parallel roads. However, our main mission was to reach a point certain and so was theirs, so it was off to the races and either side took the time to stop and engage. We had our orders, and they had theirs."

"Here in France they found their situation to be untenable. They had overextended their logistical capabilities and were unable to match the sheer tonnage of supplies, including men and machine, pouring onto the beaches of Normandy. Two hundred and fifty thousand men representing the German 15th Army were still not convinced that the main landing had yet to come across from the Pas de Calais and were decimated by allied air attacks as they too began the nasty retreat to the east."

Wow! If I ever thought the adrenaline rush was high at any of my baseball games, this story put those to rest, hands down. It was difficult to sit still and listen as he described the rest. "Never overextend" was my lesson learned. "Never think you are so good that no opponent can even come near you" was my lesson. An intelligence officer must be an eternal pessimist, my dad would always remind, and never fall for the euphoria of the optimist.

"Why the all-out retreat, Dad? Why didn't they turn and fight?"

"Well, Charlie, this wasn't like the time you came home from playing basketball at the night center earlier than usual. You took a big risk that night when you turned to fight, remember?"

Indeed I did. It was a hotly contested game of three-on-three basketball. The winner remains on the court, loser waits on the sidelines. Punches were thrown. I could hear fists rapping off my head like someone was playing the drums. The problem was my head was the drum. Where were my college buddies whom I teamed up with? *Aren't they going to break this up before I get killed?* I thought. The three opponents were not kids, they were men, and I kept ducking and moving with my fists covering my face like the peekaboo style of Floyd Patterson until I turned and risked it all with a right hand uppercut to end the fight with one punch. Then again, I'm not German, I'm Italian, and this worked for me. For the Germans, discretion indeed was the better part of valor, and they had their reasons just as I had mine.

"They had to make it back over the natural barriers, Charlie. There were rivers between France and Germany that for generations had provided sanctuary from invaders. The Germans fled to cross the river Our, the Meuse, and the river Rhine. When they arrived on the other side, many bridges were destroyed. Finally, they could breathe a sigh of relief and regroup for the terrible fight ahead."

"After we broke through at the French town of St. Lo, we created a salient through which the entire combined allied armies poured through. The logistics had changed. This was not a fistfight, Charlie! The Germans were wise to retreat with as much men and equipment as was possible and get back in over the safety of the West Wall of Germany where allied penetration was nearly impossible due to rivers and terrain."

"But why such a hurry?" came the question from a baseball player turned prize fighter. "Because of a couple of guys named Patton and Montgomery," he answered.

"Montgomery and his powerful British force were coming down from Holland to the north. Patton and his powerful Third Army were racing along France to the south and were preparing to meet Montgomery in a tactic of encirclement near the French town of Falaise. They had to escape the trap, and there wasn't much time. So they moved quickly and guarded their flanks against Montgomery on the north and Patton on the south. Then they moved quickly through the twenty-mile corridor known as the Falaise Gap."

Good stuff. A retreat that is measured and methodical may succeed while providing an essential protection of the main force on both flanks until the main force has safely returned to their sanctuary—sound doctrine that we would put to use many times on the battlefields of the Big Apple.

"What happened after the retreat into Germany?"

"Well, Montgomery and some other high-ranking authorities wanted to push for a salient deep into Germany in the direction of the German capitol of Berlin. However, it was a plan by Montgomery earlier in the war that reminded General Eisenhower to call for a time-out and assess the situation."

"What happened?"

"Did you ever hear of the story about *A Bridge Too Far*?"

"I saw the movie, Dad. Michael Caine, Sean Connery almost pulled it off."

"Almost, and the bridge at Arnhem was called a bridge too far because the allies attempted too many variables depending upon chance and luck. Therefore, the mission to end the war resulted in failure, and the lesson was learned. It's kind of like that story I told you about the turtle and the hare. Slow and steady wins the race. Remember?"

"What did you think about the whole picture, Dad?"

"At that time, General Marshall, upon his inspection of these events in France, decided more troops were needed immediately to support any offensive actions in pursuit of the German army. So we of the 159$^{th}$ were ordered to deploy along with countless thousands of troops who had assembled and were training back at stateside. We were off to England and then joined in on the rapid deployment across France. I didn't know what to think then, but I do now."

"What does that mean, Dad?"

"Anyone can be a Monday morning quarterback, Charlie."

How often I would hear those very words as the years flew by, and we would sit and watch football on Sunday afternoons. And then on Monday morning, after all the games were finished, we would criticize everything we had seen and decided what we would have done in that particular situation. That is "Monday Morning quarterbacking."

"Tell me what you think now of those events as a 'Monday Morning quarterback,'" I asked.

"The facts, when carefully evaluated, indicate a planned German withdrawal."

*Uh, oh, here we go. Back to a military intelligence officer*, I thought. He had many suits of clothing, and they all looked real good on him. I imagined him as the quarterback of old, in his helmet and colorful Uhlans uniform, and then I could see him as an astute and pessimistic army intelligence officer who would question even the spelling of his own last name.

"Facts don't lie, and this is what the facts revealed. The Germans avoided any major pitched battles as they streaked across France. Although thousands of German prisoners were captured, among them many combat troops, the majority of those captured were service and rear echelon troops left behind in the precipitous retreat. In many cases, the fighting cores of divisions and armies were maintained. A series of covering actions in a progressive leapfrogging withdrawal took the German armies back into the West Wall."

*Leapfrogging actions*, I thought. What a great idea to use when the other side is just too strong in a particular area of the field. This was a wise tactic used in time of need by the boys under my command back in Ridgewood, New York City.

"Hey, Dad. Do you remember the time when we had to get that lizard off my shoulder without letting Mom know?"

"Yeah, Charlie. We sure had a good laugh over that one, didn't we?"

That just came to my mind when he mentioned the tactic of leapfrogging in order to defend each other's positions. I wondered if I could use a tactic also based on that lizard adventure of years ago. Don't be surprised if that episode rears its comical head somewhere in these ensuing pages.

"Our attention went back to the German retreat to the safety of the West Wall: the Fifteenth Army on the north, the Seventh Army covering the Aachen Gap, Fifth Panzer Army further to the south, linking with the First and Nineteenth Armies, hastily pulling within the shelter of the West Wall from the south. We moved too fast for the Germans to establish a line along the Scheldt-Albert canal, but failure of the Arnhem drop gave the Germans the lion's share (pardon the expression) of Holland. This gave them hope, ideas, and intentions of a full-fledged counterattack."

My interest was keen, and I listened carefully, even more than I was aware. For in the future, this is exactly what the Cleveland team was known for and feared by many who would chase us too far into our own turf. "We could counter," said referee Richard Kilm, "better than any college team in the area of New York City." I wonder where we learned that strategy?

And from this historical account eventually would develop one of the most famous counterattacks by any army in the history of armed warfare. The Sixth Panzer Division was put in plain sight, and their mission remained unknown. Other Panzer divisions were relocated under the cover of darkness, and their mission remained unknown. Tanks were heard rumbling through the Ardennes sector every night before December 16, 1944, and their purpose in that area went as a routing exercise. Then came the morning of December 16, 1944, when the massive counter attack came to fruition through the "ghost sector" put aside by both armies as an area for rest and rehabilitation. The Golden Lions were put there for that express purpose after their arduous trip across France. Intelligence officers were too optimistic, and the clues went unheeded. Many paid the price for this negligence. However, they may have had somewhat of a chance. The only certainty would be repeated over and over throughout the years by my dad, and that is the following: "The Golden Lions didn't have a chance!"

And so we in Ridgewood learned from our own "Golden Lions," and it was déjà vu all over again, only this time it was the other side that wouldn't have a chance! "Come into our parlor," said the spider to the fly!

"That great allied effort my men took part in was based on evidences we were sad to witness with our own eyes as we moved through France. We saw what the enemy did to a democracy when they could get it down by itself. That was why we received our orders to mobilize, Charlie! The plan was to destroy France first, then get England, after which the United States would be compromised. We have mobilized with our allies in order to open up conquered France and reestablish the liberties of the past."

"Were you and your men welcomed there, Dad?"

"Well, we all heard about the welcome the allies received in the liberation of Paris. Americans have been popular in France ever since we fought for their liberties against the Germans in the first war. Charlie, guess who gave us the Statue of Liberty?"

"The French people were hurting ever since 1940 when in June, the German Army came through the very same Ardennes sector that they came through this time. Maybe on another day, we can sit down, and I'll tell you more about the Ardennes breakthrough that forced us to mobilize and join an infantry regiment called 'the Golden Lions.' We began to meet the French people. The French men, women, and even children learned what happens to a great democracy when a hostile occupying force takes over. Every town we passed through, we would notice the same words on public building."

"What words, Dad?"

One word was spelled *Liberte*, the second was *Egalite*, and the third was *Fraternite*. These stood for "Liberty, Equality, and Fraternity." She lost all three when the German Army marched in.

"How could they have just marched in?" I asked.

"The French built defensive structures after the first war. This structure of cement, bunkers with armaments I pillboxes was called the Maginot Line. The French felt safe behind that line and felt it could never happen here. When France felt, the biggest democracy in Europe went down. As Europe's leading republic, France was the nation representing freedom on the continent of Europe. Winston Churchill had pleaded with France to sail her Navy into British ports across the channel before the German Navy could take them. France refused."

"What happened then?"

"Well, what choice did he have? England would be next. The French fleet was sunk and destroyed at anchor by the British. That is another sore spot, and I could never understand why the French Navy made that decision. They should have sailed when they had the chance."

"Anyway, we finally reached the tow of St. Quentin and were welcomed by the remnants of the 106$^{th}$ Infantry Division. They had lost their 422$^{nd}$ and 423$^{rd}$ regiments, and here we met up with the surviving 424$^{th}$. The 106$^{th}$ was reconstituted when the Third Infantry Regiment and my 159$^{th}$ Infantry Regiment were attached to replace the two lost regiments. Two new field artillery units, the 401$^{st}$ and the 627$^{th}$, rounded out the new Golden Lions."

"We had the patch sewed on and told them, 'We're with you. Let's go back in together.' And off we went into Germany! We had a score to settle!"

"My men of the 159$^{th}$ were sent halfway around the world and across two separate oceans and fought two distinctly different enemies in those five years. We started as First Army out of Fort Jay, New York City. Our orders took us to the Aleutian Islands, where we engaged in hand-to-hand combat with hardened Japanese. On our arm, we wore the big A in its camouflaged version for battle."

"Then we wore the 'Polar Bear' as we were assigned the Defense of Alaska from the Japanese. After that, it was off to England and then France, where we became members of a mauled 'Golden Lion' regiment as part of the 106$^{th}$ Infantry Division. Here I became acquainted with the men of the 106$^{th}$ Counterintelligence Corps Detachment. They encouraged me to pursue my interests in that regard, and one member wrote these words to me in the back of my Army Field Manual: "The Army is just what you intend to make out of it. At times you may cuss yourself out for joining it, and then there are times when you can proudly say, I am an American soldier. And you stop to think. Just as all men do. Was it worth the trouble or should I enlist again. Think it over." (I'll turn this over to my son for now.)

# Chapter 5

# An Intelligent Man

AUTHOR:

I recently found these words written on the back of Field Manual 21-25 issued by the war department. This manual had become yellow and brittle with the passing of time. This particular manual has the title printed in boldface: **ELEMENTARY MA AND AERIAL PHOTOGRAPHY READING**. It had been issued by the War Department—15 August 1944.

This archival evidence indicates two interesting clues from the past. It appears that Dad had a close friend who may have come from the southern part of the United States, as we from the New York area would use the expression "curse."

More important, he had been carrying that manual around with him for quite some time as there was no thought of reenlisting until war's end. So he had been studying for advancement into the intelligence community even as guns were blazing all around him, and the war had no end in sight! He was determined to become a US Army intelligence officer, and that message written to him was the first step.

Many left the army after the war. Dad did not. He would be part of the "big team" forever. He had many manuals that he would ceaselessly study in the years ahead. I know of all the manuals and all of the corresponding maps associated with those manuals. I even know of all the onion skin overlays connected to the manuals and maps. Dad would need a study partner in his career years ahead.

That study partner was me! Together we were the Third Army of Patton, racing across France, in pursuit of the retreating German Army elements. Together we were with Montgomery's British Thirtieth Corps, in the sixty-four-mile dash to take the bridge at Arnhem. Together we studied the June 6th D-Day Invasion of Normandy resulting in an allied breakthrough in France at St. Lo.

Together we watched on the map before us the retreat of the German Army through the Falaise Gap to the River Seine. For him, this was required military intelligence study, required for advancement. However, what good was it for me to be looking over his shoulder or taking up a chair right next to him? I had no idea. I knew only of a game called chess, and the similarity of that game to his studies was remarkable. I could relate to his interests, and we became birds of a feather.

The intricacies of the Battle of the Bulge took much time. There seemed to be many errors, and he would point to these as intelligence failures with the sharp end of his pencil. The German Army took us both to school here, since these lessons learned by studying he actually lived through. These particular lessons learned by studying alongside him, I would put to use and live through also. This lesson of the Golden Lions in this particular event would count exponentially. I took it personal. These were his guys, and this hurt him badly.

From this intelligence, I would eventually train an army out of Ridgewood, New York City. All right, it was only a soccer team. But it was the best damn soccer team you ever saw! Operating with the best damn intelligence that the Golden Lions could provide!

But hold on a second! I'm getting a bit ahead of myself. All of that will unfold in the pages ahead. Let's return to the story.

After the war ended, Dad returned to Yorkville and was there in time to meet his son who was born on September 26, 1945. We lived in a nice apartment near Second Avenue off Seventy-Ninth Street. Nearby lived his mom and dad. With them were Vincent and Al. Johnny and Tony were newly married, and everything was returning to normal here in Yorkville. Dad decided he would make a career in the army and remained on active duty stateside. He finally began to realize his dream of becoming an intelligence officer while taking the prescribed military courses for advancement in that field. His rank then rose to captain, and he began to specialize in the area of military counterintelligence.

That particular focus suited him especially well since he possessed a bilingual skill, thanks to his mom and Pop. He was fluent in the Italian language, and that, coupled with his newly acquired credentials, led to his next assignment.

Five of my early years in Yorkville, and now I would begin to taste army life firsthand. Dad received orders to ship out to a place called Trieste, Italy. It was a peacetime assignment, so military dependents would accompany the officer to his post overseas. And so it was goodbye Yorkville and *buon giorno* Trieste. We were to be a member of the 17th Counterintelligence Corps Detachment.

The detachment was part of the command designated as TRUST, which stood for "Trieste United States Troops." As part of the 351st Infantry Regiment, the 17th Counterintelligence Corps was assigned to deploy to the Free Territory of Trieste as agreed upon by the Italian postwar accord.

Dad, US Army Baseball Team, Trieste, Italy, 1952

As part of that accord, TRUST was established on May 1, 1947. TRUST gained a reputation as a spit-and-polish command. Uniforms were altered for better appearance. Troops wore blue scarves and lacquered helmet liners with decals of the TRUST patch. Web pistol belts were dyed black and brass fittings shined. Bayonets and mess kits were chrome-plated. During this tour of duty, I was ages five, six, and seven years of age. To me, it appeared that the army always looked this good. I had never seen them any other way. Even to a little kid, they sure looked sharp and made an everlasting impression upon me.

However, Dad was never to wear such uniform for he was working for the counterintelligence corps, and they operated in a more clandestine nature. Plain clothes and an undercover approach better suited the nature of their job. There was a general uneasiness in postwar Europe at that time. The US had to keep an eye and ear on the dictator residing across the border. Tito and his forces next door in Yugoslavia were a matter for our concern, so Dad and his Seventeenth Intel. men had to mix in with the local Italian population in order to gain as much information as possible about the intentions of our next-door neighbor. I was busy peddling my tricycle and going to military dependent school and learning how to swim at a place called Miramare Castle, which bordered nearby on the Mediterranean Sea. I remember it as being quite beautiful. The beach had high cliffs behind it where lived scorpions that we were advised to watch for. We were told by Pete the lifeguard to check our beach blanket prior to sitting for scorpions as their sting was somewhat dangerous to people. We called the lifeguard "Pete"; however, he was a muscular Italian man who was employed by the army to keep us under his wing. His real name was Pietro, but we called him Pete. He spent many hours teaching me how to do something that Dad never learned to do—swim. So I learned to swim in Italy, near the Miramare Castle. The headquarters bulletin described Miramare Castle as "that gleaming pearl in an emerald setting," on the outskirts of Trieste. What an appropriate description indeed.

I remember walking through the castle with Mom and Dad. The castle served as headquarters for TRUST, and since Dad was a counterintelligence officer, rank had its privileges. I remember that castle was filled with beautiful oil paintings, hand-carved woodwork of intricate design, embossed wood carvings, and other signs of the lavishness of the old Austrian Court. It was built by Maximilian, the younger brother of the emperor of Austria. Dad would always remind me of that in the years ahead.

We weren't the only ones impressed, Dad often told me when I grew older. He mentioned that even the hard-bitten "old soldiers" who had entered Miramar were found staring open-mouthed at the splendor of the castle, as if it was their first visit to a candy store. He also told me that the very word "Miramare" means look at the sea."

On weekends, Dad would take us out for a drive in the country. This was where I was told he taught Mom how to drive a beautiful dark-green Studebaker that I loved because it had a pointed noise and looked like a jet, and my dad looked like a jet pilot as he avoided all the stones spewing about on the open fields of Opicina. We would bring lunch and picnic in the open green fields decorated by many various rocks of assorted sizes. There was a dark side to these fields, however. There were huge natural cavernous holes that went down so far that one could not see the bottom. It was in some of these holes that prisoners of various nationalities were thrown into by partisans of one side or the other in that terrible war that ended several years ago.

The headquarters of the 351$^{st}$ Infantry Regiment was in Opicina. Two of its infantry battalions were stationed in the Opicina area on the plateau above Trieste. One infantry battalion was stationed in Trieste. Nonregimental units, like my dad's Seventeenth Counterintelligence Corps, were stationed at a number of locations in the free territory, including the city of Trieste, the Opicina area, and nearby Duino. We lived in the city of Trieste itself.

My dad showed me an article years ago taken from *The Saturday Evening Post* dated March 1948. In that article, TRUST was described as follows:

> It's hardcore consists of the crack 351$^{st}$ infantry regiment, most of those officers and men belong to the de-activated 88$^{th}$ division and carry on in the tradition of that famous fighting unit. During the war, not too long ago, these men were referred to as "The Blue

Devils." There lineage comes from the infantry and field artillery units of W.W.2 responsible for the taking of Anzio, Rome, Arno River, Mt. Battaglia, Verona, Vicenza and all the way up to Innsbruck, Austria in their relentless pursuit of the German Army up the "boot" of Italy.

No wonder Dad would often march around to the cadence of this tune with me happily in tow: "Well, it's high-high-hee, in the field artillery. Shout out your numbers loud and strong. For wherever we go, you will always know, that the caissons go rolling along. Keep them rolling. That the caissons go rolling along. Forward march, step about and then you begin to shout, that the caissons go rolling along." And we would wear out the living room rug with that march through our house. Pots and pans were used to keep the beat!

The TRUST shoulder patch was made up of the Coat of Arms of Trieste superimposed on the blue Eighty-Eighth Infantry Division patch under a scroll with the letters TRUST.

It went by in three years, and the tour was over—back to the states for us. But my impression of Italy would remain forever. *Che bella*— how beautiful! I guess I grew up in Trieste learning how to swim, how to march, and even how to drive a beautiful dark-green Studebaker in Opicina while steering around the rocks of the field sitting upright on the lap of a military counterintelligence officer named Dad!

We returned to America, and Dad bought a new house in a place called Whitestone, New York. It is out in the suburbs in a county called Queens. The yard is very big, and here I began to have daily catches with an intelligence officer who taught me how to throw a curveball, a slider, and something called a screwball. He studied all the time and rose to the rank of major.

The call came from G-2 Intelligence sector US Army SETAF (Southern European Task Force) located in Verona, Italy. The rest of that part of the story is available in the prior book called *All-American*. And off we go to La Bella Italia to lie in a magical hamlet of Verona, near the river Adige, which passes under the Castelvecchio Bridge near a soccer field in the center of Piazza Bra—a time long ago in a place far away!

Read on now with regard to strategic and tactical deployment put together by the two Golden Lions. Read on with regard to intelligence and counterintelligence that originated here in Piazza Bra, right in that very fountain!

There are three coins in the fountain. What wish will the fountain bear? And through the ripples, how they shine. What wish will the fountain bear? Make it mine, make it mine, make it mine!

I remember huge cheers emanating from outside our hotel room at the Grand Hotel in Verona, Italy. It was Sunday. We checked in at the Grand Hotel, and we could hear the crowd cheering from the open window overlooking the field. My dad had met us at the train station the night before looking a lot thinner that he was when we had last seen him at stateside before he went on ahead of the rest of the family. Perhaps it may have been from missing my mom's cooking, or it may have been from the stress associated with the clandestine work associated with G-2 section to which he was assigned in which he specialized in counterintelligence for the US Army SETAF (Southern European Task Force). My dad was fluent in Italian and had a good head on his shoulders.

Either way, and for whatever the reason, we were so happy to see him, and he was thrilled to have his family back and reunited once again in this faraway land called Italy. United once again in the city of Verona, known worldwide for Shakespeare's *Romeo and Juliet*. It was 1956. I was almost eleven years old, and loud crowd cheers were certainly a cause to arouse my curiosity. I loved the New York Yankees and had seen many of their games including the no-hit perfect game turned in by Don Larsen. I watched as Yogi Berra elatedly jumped onto the hero after the last pitch, for as the famous catcher, he had been the huge partner in that effort. The ensuing cheers were of an extremely joyous nature with much celebration by players and fans alike. But this cheering coming from outside the window of the Grand Hotel in Verona, Italy, was different.

I went to the window and saw a huge crowd, and their attention was focused upon a green field occupied by many moving players in two brightly distinct colors. A large white ball gathered the interest of everyone, and the cheers were associated with every movement of that ball. I turned to ask my dad, "What is this?"

He replied, "It's what they do here in Italy."

I wondered as I looked upon the game. *Who is their Mickey Mantle? Who is their Joe DiMaggio? Why is that ball so big?*

Spring was in full swing, and spring in Italy was already a sight to behold. The SETAF detachment had just constructed a beautiful baseball field for us military dependents fondly known as army brats. Tryouts and team selections were underway, and there was much excitement and enthusiasm generated by the parents, the kids, and the soldiers who were to be their coaches and teachers. My dad had played for the Trieste Yankees US Army team on our prior tour of duty when I was five years old. He knew how to throw a curveball and a screwball. He knew a lot more than that. We practiced daily when opportunity permitted. He taught me how to pitch, for I was blessed with a strong arm. He explained how ball rotation resulted in movement used to fool the batter by causing the ball to move toward, away, or even down. The team was selected, and the call was put out for a coach.

(L to R) Charlie Valenti, General Fischer and Delmar Meadows.
US Army Photo

The general cutting a cake

General Fisher, the commander of the detachment, had me chosen to assist him in cutting the first slice out of the cake symbolizing the opening of the baseball season. He told me he had heard of my curveball and screwball from the soldiers conducting the tryouts. The officer who had so far assembled the team had just been reassigned to stateside duty, and the general was so notified.

Now my dad, who is fluent in Italian, was assigned undercover duty in the clandestine and perilous area of counterintelligence. It was an assignment that by its nature kept him out in the field at night with his partner, Bruno Francase. Both were armed. *Bruno Francase?* I thought. What a name for the job! My dad was playing ball on the wrong field, and the call from General Fisher finally came through in the form of a reassignment to G2 intelligence sector, desk duty. After his military duties were addressed, he was encouraged posthaste to get down to the field for practice and games, and that's an order! His schedule at G2 was amended to provide for the kids on the Verona Red Sox Little team. He was out of harm's way.

With the passing of the season, Dad taught everybody who would listen everything about baseball. The parents, the soldiers, the kids—everybody—and listen they did! He taught us things everyone had heard of and other things no one even ever imagined. Who better to teach us how to hit a baseball than a man who as a kid grew up in the streets of Yorkville, in Manhattan, swatting flies out of the air with a stickball bat! Who better to teach all who would learn how to catch and throw a baseball than a man who could right in front of the whole team catch a fly out of midair flight, then another one, and then open his hand as we watched as both flies flew free!

We all began to love the game because of him. He had great patience and kindness. He would never criticize a player or hurt their feelings. Privately, and on the side, he would tend to the business of winning in a tactful manner. You could see why he was a US Army officer. We were proud of him and proud to win for him—and win we did. Break up the Red Sox was soon heard to our dismay. It was baseball by day for us, and it was studying by night.

He was taking courses all the time for military advancement prospects from current rank of captain to major. I studied with hi. Although no rank would be forthcoming for me, it was more stimulating than watching Italian TV after my schoolwork was completed. Now I entered the world of logistics, reconnaissance, enfilading fire, troop displacement, numerical superiority, azimuth, and reverse azimuth. I learned of gathering information, known as intelligence, and giving disinformation in the form of counterintelligence.

Maps were spread out on the table after dinner, or if necessary, we used the entire living room floor. On top of each map would be a corresponding overlay that when superimposed would make some sense of it all. This was getting very interesting—almost as interesting as baseball. A similarity prevailed. In baseball, as a pitcher, I had to know the other team using information gained through intelligence while guarding not to allow the opponent to gain knowledge of my ability or intentions.

Soon we found a nice place of our own for the three-year tour of duty. The apartment had marble floors throughout, three bedrooms, a huge living room, and a spacious balcony overlooking the beautiful Adige River that ran elegantly through the heart of Verona, Italy—very benefitting the family of an officer and a gentleman. My mom, sister, and I were very happy to reside in this luxury. Years later, I designed my beach home in Amagansett, Long Island, with similar balconies that afford ocean views to all. The living room is huge here as well. There is a fireplace with a large striped bass hanging over it and a weakfish on the opposite wall. The ocean is my Adige River now, and this book is being written from this location so as to improve memory skills for all that I have to tell. For in this place, I feel as though I am still in that wonderful place where I learned so much. For here, I am still in Italy.

There were other military families in the building, and I soon made friends with several other army brats. There were five boys my age, all sons of military officers. They had little interest in baseball at first but a great interest in another game, chess! We formed a club and had a structure in place for a tournament in no time. My dad was happy to hear about the chess club and gave me a medal that I have to this day. The medal is the logo for his CIC division. The medal displays itself as a chessboard with the squares colored yellow and teal blue. The words "Nosce Hostem" appear at the top of the medal. Teal blue and yellow, dad told me, is the chosen colors to represent counterintelligence. What has chess got to do with counterintelligence? Everything!

Chess is the intellect of counterintelligence. Intelligence and counterintelligence are the heart and soul of chess. Gathering information and disseminating disinformation is what chess is all about. So is intelligence and counterintelligence. Nosce hostem, in Latin, means "know your enemy." You learn to know him by testing him and committing to memory his response to your constant prodding. Films of Rocky Marciano reveal Rocky memorizing the onslaught being dished out to him by Jersey Joe Walcott in a famous heavyweight title fight. Suddenly Rocky saw a pattern coming in and absorbed it, memorized the moment he had seen before, and ended the fight with one punch. Walcott could not get up.

Chess dictates the need to memorize and to feed disinformation. Planning three moves ahead is not an option—it is a necessity––unless you want to wind up like Jersey Joe. We were a bunch of kids playing a game, but chess is a serious endeavor with lasting education and implications. Our tournament went well into the winter months and were hotly contested affairs. Chess, when paired with counterintelligence dogma, prevailed. Guess who won? To the winner goes the spoils, and so the bargain was settled. If I, the baseball player, could possibly win the tournament, then they would have to join Little League in the spring. And so I recruited four more ball players to the cause.

I joined Dad regularly at the cleared off kitchen table after dinner. A huge map was spread out on the table. Out of a cardboard cylinder, he removed what he called an onion skin. He carefully placed the onion skin over the map, and the onion skin was made to fit precisely. The onion skin derived the name because you could actually see through it much like you might see through the original article. When I asked him what was on the map, he replied that this was a topographical map of the terrain. He explained by pointing out areas of elevation, mountains, hills, rivers, trees, and it all looked to me like a very interesting game board. But there was more to it than that.

On the map, he showed me what he called enemy positions and supply dumps, including ordinance and weaponry, and even troop strength and displacement. Here, he pointed out, is where they are strong. Tanks appeared, as did barbed wire and minefields. I began to see that this indeed was the real deal, and it was unsettling. No one gets hurt too badly laying baseball. This was totally different. I was surprised he even showed this to me, and when he saw my expression, he asked, "Well, you do want to learn about this, don't you?"

The map, he went on, was obviously the enemy, and this onion skin represents the US Army. He laid it over the map and said, "This is an overlay. Now one could see the strengths, deployment, capabilities, and even the strategy of the US Army compared to that of the enemy." It was amazing. He just made his own board game!

"How does the army gather all of this information?" I asked.

He replied, "Through aerial reconnaissance or reconnaissance gathered from high ground. Now look at this and look at it good. What do you see?" And the big picture would begin to unfold before my eyes.

"Don't be in a hurry in making your assessment," he would order as if I were a soldier under his command. "If you hurry, you may overlook something and make a costly mistake that could influence the very outcome of the battle."

He told me of the story of the turtle and the hare.

"What is a hare?" I asked.

"It's a rabbit," he answered. "They had a race, and the rabbit should have won easily, but he was too overconfident and took a nap on the route to the finish line. The turtle took his time, applied himself diligently, and won the race."

There was a lot going on between the map and the onion skin overlay. A lot of information was appearing on the kitchen table, and one needed time to decipher and interpret all the information in order to arrive at a solution that would be met with success. If one onion skin did not show much promise, then another must be selected and reviewed and studied in detail. Perhaps a combination of two or even more than two overlays would be necessary to arrive at the solution. There were many overlays available that were applicable to the battlefield displayed by the map on the table. The carrying case looked like a quiver full of arrows as indeed it had the solution if only one could think it through and select the right combination. This technique would prove to be very valuable in the soccer years ahead.

These kitchen table overlay events occurred frequently during the evenings. One afternoon, however, I biked down to the Piazza Bra park in search of something more tangible. The Italian boys were there every day after school playing that game they play over here, inside a dried-up fountain the size of a modern-day hockey rink. Well, international hand signals made me realize that I was invited to play along with the words *"Americani, vien qua e giocomo."* Hey, American. Come down here and get in the game.

There was one large white ball and two goals with a goal tender in each. It appeared to be eleven against ten and my addition would provide for an even match. The ensuing match proved to be bewildering and exhilarating—twenty-one Italians and I running all over the dried up fountain with that ball at the center of our attention. This became a daily after-school event at the park, and I became a regular. They taught me skills relevant to ball control, passing, teamwork, and strategy. I began to learn their language, for I had the initiative to interact with another culture and had been rewarded by making so many new friends with names like Cesare, Guiusseppe, Claudio, Antonio, and last but not least, Sergio.

To show my appreciation, I offered to bring down to the park the next afternoon some of the Little League equipment my dad kept in the closet so that I may teach them how to play baseball. Everything went so well as I showed them how to catch that piccolo ball as they described the small size of the baseball. I pitched to them one after another as if it were on assembly line as they began to learn the hand-eye coordination necessary to strike a baseball properly. I hit soft grounders to each and had them throw over to first base and found that throwing was difficult for them and foreign to that game of theirs. They were used to throwing with two hands over their head, and accuracy was a serious problem. I began to wish I had brought the batting helmets for protection, but how much equipment could one bring down on the back of a bicycle?

We had a big league game the next day, so I asked some of the boys to help me prepare with some extra batting practice. Sergio, the biggest one of them all, offered to pitch. Now down at the other end of the park were some older men flying gasoline-propelled plywood, homemade airplanes in a circular pattern guided by a handheld device attached to thin line controlling the plane. Soon into the batting practice, I hit one that the famous Yankee broadcaster would have said is "Going, going, gone!" It flew up, up, and away. It could be seen by all that this didn't look good. It was a direct hit, and the plane was blown out of the sky. A one in a million shot, but they didn't buy it, and I was on my bike peddling for my life with the whole park on my tail.

I made the peace eventually; however, baseball was out of the question for the time being, and we played soccer exclusively. I began to learn the foreign way of thinking while interacting with them on the soccer field. Their reaction to things was a bit more spontaneous and more intense than that of the American athlete. More patience was needed, it seemed to me, in order to advance the ball downfield in numbers that would dictate a better outcome in the back of the goal. However, there is a way to get your thoughts across, and there are American ways that you would be best served to not even attempt. Diplomacy was essential to making friends in this faraway land. We rewarded ourselves after each game with some gelati down at the corner of the park where the vendor set up shop daily to await the outcome of the game. Alfredo, the ice cream man, became our number one fan as he took an interest in the outcome of the game and congratulated the victors on their performance. He was also our liaison with the big Soccer Club Verona as he would provide us with the standings of the league and the place the Verona club found itself residing in on Monday morning, after the big game on Sunday. Alfredo reminded me of our stateside Good Humor man in more ways than one. His presence added to the daily event and made it feel bigger than it would have been without his input and his gelati. My American friends were invited to join these daily events as I spread the word at the military dependent school, but they would always decline in favor of baseball. I crossed the line and was rewarded in the present and did not realize just how big a reward was coming my way in the future years as teacher and coach of that game they play over here.

Little League playoffs were arriving, and it is hard to imagine the excitement this generated. You have to understand that we are Americans living in Italy. We are from Alabama, Georgia, Texas, New York, California, and we need baseball just as much as the Italians need soccer. The Little League was a source of pride for the whole detachment because the sense was that we brought a piece of home with us. The teams were even named after the big league teams in the states. We were the Red Sox, and if you were a soldier in Verona, you knew what that was synonymous with winning.

Livorno was coming in by train for a three-game series. Yes, we traveled in style and even wore a sports jacket and tie, complete with white buckskin shoes and a crew cut. You're in the army now!

My dad offered our services of hospitality and offered to billet the Livorno star hitter at our place for the series. That is how the army would make sure to house the players who were the visiting team. Tony was the big stick's name. After settling him in for the night, we had breakfast and headed to the park where my Italian friends offered to field batting practice for Tony.

My American rival took his turn at the bat and yelled, "Let me see your curveball. I heard it is a real good one!"

"Sure," I conceded and proceeded to pitch him one slow hanger after another. He hit that curveball all over the place and was very full of himself. My Italians friends felt bad for me as I heard them utter things like "povero Charlie" and "mama mia!" What my friends didn't know was that my dad set the table with intelligence, and I was providing disinformation, and as a team, we were about to apply the counterintelligence the next few days. We took two out of three and my American rival couldn't even smell my real curveball throw as a slider or fast breaking ball. It's a pitch Dad taught me using the combination of speed and rotation that amounted to a fast breaking curveball and not that hunk of junk that I showed to my rival at practice. That screwball was also a factor. Many a night, my dad would have me grab the doorknob in the kitchen and open the door. That, he said, is the same way to release a ball so that the spin develops the opposite way of the natural curveball. So I was thus named with a pitch that could curve in and another one that could curve out. This was to come in very handy with another white ball somewhere down the road on a field with no diamond! Thus, armed with a good team and a clandestine coach, the Red Sox won the US Army Little League Championship in 1957. But it wasn't that simple.

Somewhere along the way, that clandestine coach stumbled upon something no one had ever seen. It may have come from his days as quarterback for the ULANS in Yorkville, Manhattan, NYC. Dad learned that he could move players around on the field like chess players on the checkerboard by using code signals. For example, if I was a shortstop and he wanted me to relieve the pitcher, he would signal the first baseman if we were using the dugout near him or the third baseman if we drew that dugout. They, in turn would call time out and make the pitching change by switching positions. Other switches were done as well, and my dad never even moved from his sitting position.

Managers and parents complained, but the umpire would just point to Dad and say he never did a thing and hasn't even moved. That was the big reason why we won. The whole team was changed around numerous times to suit the coach, and all he did was to touch his nose or pull the string on his sweatshirt. He outfoxed the game of baseball. Years later, using this lesson, I began to outfox the game of soccer in New York City, for there are no timeouts in soccer. American football had arrived on the baseball field. What other field would it find its way to in time?

Something happened between the second and third games of the playoffs. Sunday was reserved for church and tie off from work. Tony paired up with one of his teammates to figure out how to handle my curveball, so I strung my mitt around the handlebars of my bike and went to the park to seek out my Italian friends and found them laying that beautiful game of theirs and happily joined the melee. By game's end, my mitt had disappeared and could not be found as Sergio began interviewing the spectators who gathered to watch on Sunday. I went home to tell my dad the bad news, and Sergio came with me. It was the only time I ever saw Sergio angry.

This news did not sit well with Dad since he knew my intentions were good and I was teaching the baseball. He also appreciated that they took a liking to me and were teaching me all about soccer.

"What do you know?" he asked Sergio.

They spoke in Italian for a while, and then my dad turned and told me Sergio knows who took the mitt. He said that the only way it will be returned was if I go with him to San Zeno! "He will trust you on this mission and only you."

Sergio was the biggest and strongest of all the Italian boys. He was tall and had curly brown hair and very strong legs. At the game, no one could clear the ball like Sergio. They nicknamed him catenacio, which refers to an Italian form of defense known throughout the soccer world as the "locked gate." And this too will be a word I remember for the trial ahead. *"Andiamo,"* Sergio said to me, and off we went to San Zeno!

We took some water and a couple of oranges with us since Sergio knew that it would be a long ride to the old church neighborhood known as San Zeno. It was described to me as a poor neighborhood on the other side of the river. I took my seat on the handlebars, and off he pedaled over the nearby beautiful Castelvecchio Bridge in order to cross the river. *Castelvecchio* means "old castle," and indeed that is how the bridge looks to this day, awesomely beautiful! We arrived on the other side, thanks to those big Italian legs pumping away below the handlebars as San Zeno began to appear in the distances.

Already it became obvious we were entering another world. The war took a big toll on Italy, and there were no stores or parks, and the only thing to sustain us was the items Sergio knew we must bring along for the ride. The war ended only eleven years before this journey on his bike, and everything appeared lacking in color as white and shades of gray were predominant. This aroused apprehension in me since I really didn't know Sergio that well at this time in the tour of duty. Now I began to understand what my dad must have felt like when he would team up with Bruno Francase for counterintel operations. *So, I thought, I am my dad, Sergio is Bruno Francase, and I hope I come back alive with my mitt!*

A cheerful note occurred to take the edge off things back at the Castelvecchio crossing. It was Sunday, and that roar erupted, and this time it lasted longer than ever before.

"What does that mean?" I asked Sergio.

"It means we won! Verona has won, Charlie, and this is a lucky day," and he began to sing a song that made him pedal a lot faster than before. I know that song; I heard it before from my grandfather a long time ago.

"What is that song called?" I asked.

"Fratelli Di Italia, he said. "It is a happy song that we like to sing when we win a soccer game. It is the song of my country!"

Wow. Here I was in a war-torn section of Italy on the handlebars of a bike being pedaled by an Italian singing his country song with gusto!

We were passing all the car now; it was downhill full speed ahead. Sergio was on a roll, singing all the way down that hill! From this I learned that a song can mean a lot to a person. "Without a song, the day would never end. Without a song, the day road would never bend. When things go wrong, a man ain't got no friend without a song. That field of corn, would never see a plow, that field would be deserted now.

I've got my troubles and woes, but sure as I know the garden will grow. I'll get along as long as I know a song is strong in my soul. I'll never know what makes the rain to fall. I'll never know what makes the grass to grow. I only know there ain't no love a tall – without a song!" (Willie Nelson).

There is no doubt that I was feeling Sergio express love in that song. He was singing of his country and pride too. Finally, we arrived in the San Zeno area where we were encouraged not to venture as it was far from home; but we had split the series, and tomorrow was set for the rubber match. I was scheduled to pitch the final game, and a pitcher needs his mitt. Without my mitt, I would need a lot more than a song. As it was, they were onto my curveball after our close win in the first game. I had to have that mitt, and Sergio knew it and thought it was a lucky mitt. When we arrived at the address he had secured from the spectators, he asked me to wait down below in a spot he pointed to so that I could be seen from the window. He came down with the mitt and handed it to me saying, "*Eco es por loi.*" This is for you!

He pedaled us all the way back to Castelvecchio, over the river, and back to home where Dad was waiting. I did not know, but Sergio was put on a time schedule by the CIC.

Dad said, "*Mile gracia*" to Sergio and invited him to a drive the next day to the big game. He asked Sergio how he knew where the mitt was and who took it—just like Dad to seek some classified information.

Sergio replied with some counterintelligence of his own. "Your son, *tu fijo*, is a friend of all the Italian boys at the park, but on this Sunday, there was a newcomer who made a serious mistake. He has lost respect of the group, and they demanded the mitt be returned. "Sergio let them know of the urgency of that mitt being needed in the game tomorrow, just the same as the soccer ball would be needed in their game. It was a long day, and I thanked him for being my friend.

Get a good night's sleep, *bono nota*," he said. "*Veremo domain.* See you tomorrow."

It was a bright and sunny day, and on the way to the field and somewhere on the way, the line "buy me some peanuts and crackerjack" entered out of nowhere. I was nervous and remembered seeing a sign in the hallway at school. It said, *"En quest classe siamo tutti nervosi."* In this class, everyone is nervous. I hoped my teammates were calmer than me; I was going to need them.

They were a lot calmer than I was and kept us in the game. I really was tapped out from the San Zeno handlebar adventure of the day before, and it showed, but we found ourselves ahead by one run as the opponent stood in the batter's box for their last licks. Tony memorized my curveball and led off with a double. His buddy whom he had compared notes with singled sharply off the third baseman's mitt. It was first and third, nobody out, and my curve had been compromised, as they say in CIC jargon. Dad knew it and pulled on his sweatshirt string. "Time!" yelled Stanly Parker, our first baseman. "He wants to switch, Charlie."

"Break the rule, Stanly," I said. "Ask the coach to call time and come out here for a second."

Dad called timeout and came to get the ball. He took the ball and then asked, "Why did you change our rule?" This was a question I had to answer and couldn't.

"Do you want this ball back?" he asked.

I remember it all as clear as day because for some reason, I said it twice. "Give me the ball back, Dad. Give me the ball." He put it in my mitt, and we all went back to our positions.

By the time Dad returned to his seat in the dugout, Sergio did something crazy. He saw the situation and acted in that beautiful and puzzling foreign way. He stood up in the stands and bellowed out the song he so joyously sang the day before. He was not embarrassed. This one was for me! I summoned the catcher out before time was resumed. Sergio had finished, and the fans liked it from what I could see.

"Play ball!" shouted the umpire. Nine hard screwballs later and it was over. The place turned into a zoo.

My dad took congratulations and came out to see me. He asked, "What the hell just happened here? Did you hear Sergio?"

"Yea, I did, and that was pops' favorite song."

"But, where the hell did you get that screwball?"

"From the kitchen doorknob, Dad, but I was afraid to ever use it in a real game."

Bobby Poole, the catcher, came over and told the coach we had planned all screwballs the rest of the way. He told Dad I had told him, "If Sergio can stand up there like that and sing his song, then I can throw nine screwballs for strikes."

"Coach," he said, "Sergio is the one who pulled us through. As the famous Yankee broadcaster would often say, 'How about that!'" (Mel Allen, NY Yankees).

Dad had been telling the team all season long that you never can tell what you can achieve unless you apply yourself. He kept us up-to-date about a Little League team from Monterrey, Mexico; a team that didn't have a chance but began to win one game at a time. In August 1957, our season was not yet over, and we met in the dugout before the first playoff game. Dad told us the Little League team from Monterrey, Mexico, just won the championship against the best from all over the United States! They did that, and we could do this! It was a brilliant intelligence maneuver!

Sergio made many American friends at the baseball field that day. He was invited to come along with us as we had a basketball game for our team called the Verone Victors. We even used the tune from the Notre Dame fight song at the halftime cheerleader rally. It was a road game, and the army bus was transporting us to the city of Vicenza. An Italian bus driver was hired since he knew the roads. Shortly after we left Verona, something happened on the bus that I will never forget. The team of fourteen players and fourteen cheerleaders with a few coaches filled the bus. Sergeant Beck was our coach, and he worked us hard and taught us well.

A song broke out from the rear of the bus. A group began to sing, "O, I wish I were in the land of cotton, old times there are not forgotten, look away, look away, look away, Dixieland. I wish I was in Dixie, hooray, hooray, in Dixieland I'll take my stand, to live and die in Dixie. Hooray, hooray, away down south in Dixie."

That song was challenged well before it was finished by the other half of the bus. Some seats began to be switched around the bus for the challenge. And it went like this. "Mine eyes have seen the coming of the glory of the Lord, he has trampled down the vineyard where the grapes of wrath are stored, he's unleashed the lightning of his terrible swift sword, his truth is marching on. Glory, glory hallelujah, glory, glory hallelujah, his truth is marching on."

"O, I wish I was in the land of cotton" boomed again, and then mine eyes have seen the coming interrupted once more. On and on it went this way.

Sergio turned to me as we were sitting together and asked, "Charlie, *que su chesa*? What is going on here?"

I told him that we were still divided along the lines caused by the American civil war, and he became visibly saddened to witness this division.

"Stand again like you did for me that day," I told him, "and sing your song of unity. Do it now, Sergio!"

"No, not unless you stand with me."

"*Okay*," and up we went, many eyes wondering, *What is this now?*

Residual civil war songs were still being sung, and no end was in sight, and he booed with me at his side.

> *Fratelli Di Italia*
> *Fratelli di Italia, Italia se desta,*
> *Del elmo di scipio, se cinta la testa,*
> *Dove la vittoria, le porga la chioma,*
> *Che schiava di roma, iddeo la creo*
> *Stringiamici a corte, L, Italia Chiamo, Si!*

The Italian bus driver lost it and leaned on that horn, cheering, and he wouldn't stop. The civil songs ceased and was replaced by cheers for Sergio and his song. He had united them with that beautiful song, for it was the song of Italy, and whatever differences we had at the time, one thing was for sure—we all loved Italy. And we all loved that song!

I remember huge cheers emanating from outside our hotel room at the Grand Hotel in Verona, Italy. It was Sunday. We checked in at the Grand Hotel, and we could hear the crowd cheering from the open window overlooking the field. My dad had met us at the train station the night before, looking a lot thinner than he was when we had last seen him at Stateside before he went on ahead of the rest of the family. Perhaps it may have been from missing my mom's cooking, or it may have been from the stress associated with the clandestine work associated with G2 section to which he was assigned. In which he specialized in counterintelligence for the US Army SETAF (Southern European Task Force). My dad was fluent in Italian and had a good head on his shoulders.

Either way, and for whatever the reason, we were so happy to see him, and he was thrilled to have his family back and reunited once again in this far away land called Italy, united once again in the city of Verona, known worldwide for Shakespeare's *Romeo and Julie*. It was 1956, I was almost eleven years old, and loud crowd cheers where certainly a cause to arouse my curiosity. I loved the New York Yankees and have seen many of their games, including the no-hit perfect game turned in by Don Larsen. I watched as Yogi Berra elatedly jumped onto the hero after the last pitch, for as the famous catcher, he had been the huge partner in that effort. The ensuing cheers were of an extremely joyous nature, with much celebration by players and fans alike. But this cheering coming from outside the window of the Grand Hotel is Verona, Italy, was different.

I went to the window and saw a huge crowd, and their attention was focused upon a green field occupied by many moving players in two distinctly bright colors. A large white ball gathered the interest of everyone, and the cheers were associated with every movement of that ball. I turned to ask my dad, "What is this?" He replied, "It's what they do here in Italy." I wondered as I looked upon the game, *Who is their Mickey Mantle? Who is their Joe DiMaggio? Why is that ball so big?*

Spring was in full swing, and spring in Italy was already a sight to behold. The SETAF detachment had just constructed a beautiful baseball field for us military dependents, fondly known as army brats.

Tryouts and team selections were underway, and there was much excitement and enthusiasm generated by the parents, the kids, and the soldiers who were to be their coaches and teachers. My dad had played for the Trieste Yankees US Army team on our prior tour of duty when I was five years old. He knew how to throw a curve ball and a screwball. He knew a lot more than that. We practiced daily when opportunity permitted. He taught me how to pitch, for I was blessed with a strong arm. He explained how ball rotation resulted in movement used to fool the batter by causing the ball to move toward, away, or even down. The team was selected and the call was put out for a coach.

General Fisher, the commander of the detachment, chose me to assist him in cutting the first slice out of the cake symbolizing the opening of the baseball season. He told me he had heard of my curveball and screwball from the soldiers conducting the tryouts. The officer who had so far assembled the team had just been reassigned to Stateside duty, and the general was so notified.

Now my dad, who was fluent in Italian, was assigned under cover duty in the clandestine and perilous area of counterintelligence. It was an assignment that by its nature kept him out in the field at night with his partner, Bruno Francase. Both were armed. *Bruno Francase? I thought. What a name for the job!* My dad was playing ball on the wrong field, and the call from General Fisher finally came through in the form of a reassignment to G2 intelligence sector desk duty. After his military duties were addressed, he was encouraged posthaste to get down to the field for practice and games. And that's an order! His schedule at G2 was amended to provide for the kids on the Verona Red Sox Little League team. He was out of harm's way.

With the passing of the season, Dad taught everybody who would listen—the parents, the soldiers, the kids, everybody—everything about baseball. And listen they did! He taught us things everyone had heard of and other things no one even ever imagined. Who better to teach us how to hit a baseball than a man who as a kid grew up in the streets of Yorkville, in Manhattan, swatting flies out of the air with a stickball bat! Who better to teach all who would learn how to catch and throw a baseball than a man who could, right in front of the whole team, catch a fly out of midair flight, then another one, and then open his hand as we watched as both flies flew free!

We all began to love the game because of him. He had great patience and kindness. He would never criticize a player or hurt their feelings. Privately, and on the side, he would tend to the business of winning in a tactful manner. You could see why he was a US Army officer. We were proud of him and proud to win for him. And win we did. "Break up the Red Sox," was soon heard, to our dismay. It was baseball by day for us, and it was studying by night.

He was taking courses all the time for military-advancement prospects from current rank of captain to major. I studied with him, although no rank was forthcoming for me; it was more stimulating than watching Italian TV after my schoolwork was completed. Now I entered the world of logistics, reconnaissance, enfilading fire, troop displacement, numerical superiority, azimuth, and reverse azimuth. I learned of gathering information, known as intelligence, and giving disinformation in the form of counterintelligence.

Maps were spread out on the table after dinner, or if necessary, we used the entire living room floor. On top of each map would be a corresponding overlay that when super imposed, would make some sense of it all. This was getting very interesting—almost as interesting as baseball. A similarity prevailed. In baseball, as a pitcher, I had to know the other team using information gained through intelligence while guarding not to allow the opponent to gain knowledge of my abilities or intentions.

Soon we found a nice place of our own for the three-year tour of duty. The apartment had marble floors throughout, three bedrooms, a huge living room, and a spacious balcony overlooking the beautiful Adige River, which ran elegantly through the heart of Verona, Italy, very befitting the family of an officer and a gentleman. My mom, sister, and I, were very happy to reside in this luxury.

Years later, I designed my home in Amagansett, Long Island, with similar balconies that afford ocean views that remind me of my bella Adige. The living room is huge here as well. There is a fireplace with a large bluefish hanging over it, and an equally large weakfish adorns the wall adjacent to the fireplace. The ocean is my Adige River now, and much of this has been written from this location so as to improve memory skills for all that I have to tell. For in this place, I feel as though I am still in that wonderful place where I learned so much. For here, I am still in Italy!

There were other military families in the building, and I soon made friends with several other army brats. There were five boys my age, all sons of military officers. They had little interest in baseball at first but a great interest in another game—chess! We formed a club and had a structure in place for a tournament in no time. My dad was happy to hear about the chess club and gave me a medal that I have to this day. The medal is the logo for his CIC division. The medal displays itself as a chessboard with the squares colored yellow and teal blue. The words *nosce hostem* appear at the bottom of the medal. Teal blue and yellow, Dad told me, is the chosen colors to represent counterintelligence. What has chess got to do with counterintelligence? Everything!

Chess is the intellect of counterintelligence. Intelligence and counterintelligence are the heart and soul of chess. Gathering information and disseminating disinformation is what chess is all about. So is intelligence and counterintelligence; Nosce hostem, in Latin, means "Know your enemy." You learn to know him by testing him and committing to memory his response to your constant prodding. Films of Rocky Marciano reveal Rock memorizing the onslaught being dished out to him by Jersey Joe Walcott in a famous heavyweight title fight. Suddenly Rocky saw a pattern coming in and absorbed it, memorized the moment he had seen before and ended the fight with one punch. Walcott could not get up.

Chess dictates the need to memorize and to feed disinformation. Planning three moves ahead is not an option; it is a necessity, unless you want to wind up like Jersey Joe. We were a bunch of kids playing a game. But chess is a serious endeavor with lasting educational implications. Our tournaments went well into the winter months and were hotly contested affairs. Chess, when paired with counterintelligence dogma, prevailed—guess who won? To the winner went the spoils, and so the bargain was settled. If I, the baseball player, could possibly win the tournament, then they would have to join Little League in the spring. And so I recruited four more ballplayers to the cause.

I joined Dad regularly at the cleared-off kitchen table after dinner. A huge map was spread out on the table. Out of a cardboard cylinder, he removed what he called an onion skin. He carefully placed the onion skin over the map, and the onion skin was made to fit precisely. The onion skin derived the name because you could actually see through it, much like you might see through the original article. When I asked him what was on the map, he replied that this was a topographical map of the terrain. He explained by pointing out areas of elevation, mountains, hills, rivers, trees, and it all looked to me like a very interesting game board. But there was more to it than that.

On the map, he showed me what he called enemy positions and supply dumps, including ordinance and weaponry, and even troop strength and displacement. "Here," he pointed out, "is where they are strong." Tanks appeared, as did barbed wire and minefields. I began to see that this indeed was the real deal, and it was unsettling. No one gets hurt too badly playing baseball. This was totally different. I was surprised he even showed this to me, and when he saw my expression, he asked, "Well, you do want to learn about this, don't you?"

The map, he went on, was obviously, the enemy, and this onion skin represented the US Army. He laid it over the map and said, "This is an overlay. Now one could see the strengths, deployment, capabilities, and even the strategy of the US Army compared to that of the enemy."

It was amazing. He just made his own board game! "How does the army gather all of this information?" I asked.

He replied, "Through aerial reconnaissance or reconnaissance gathered from high ground. Now look at this and look at it good. What do you see?" And the big picture would begin to unfold before my eyes. "Don't be in a hurry in making your assessment," he would order, as if I were a soldier under his command. "If you hurry, you may overlook something and make a costly mistake that could influence the very outcome of the battle."

He told me of the story of the turtle and the hare.

"What is a hare?" I asked.

"It's a rabbit," he answered. "They had a race and the rabbit should have won easily, but he was too overconfident and took a nap on the route to the finish line. The turtle took his time, applied himself diligently, and won the race."

There was a lot going on between the map and the onion skin overlay. A lot of information was appearing on the kitchen table, and one needed time to decipher and interpret all the information in order to arrive at a solution that would be met with success. If one onion skin did not show much promise, then another must be selected and reviewed and studied in detail. Perhaps, a combination of two or even more than two overlays would be necessary to arrive at the solution. There were many overlays available that were applicable to the battlefield displayed by the map on the table. The carrying case looked like a quiver full of arrows, as indeed it had the solution if only one could think it through, and select the right combination. This technique would prove to be very valuable in the soccer years ahead.

These kitchen table overlay events occurred frequently during the evenings. One afternoon, however, I biked down to the Piazza Bra park in search of something more tangible. The Italian boys were there every day after school, playing that game they play over here inside a dried-up fountain the size of a modern-day hockey rink. Well, international hand signals made me realize that I was invited to play, along with the words, *Americani, viene qua e giocama* (Hey, American, come down here and get in the game).

There was one large white ball and two goals with a goal tender in each. It appeared to be eleven against ten, and my addition provided for an even match. The ensuing match proved to be bewildering and exhilarating—twenty-one Italians and me running all over the dried-up fountain, with that ball the center of our attention. This became a daily after-school event at the park, and I became a regular. They taught me skills relevant to ball control, passing, teamwork, and strategy. I began to learn their language, for I had the initiative to interact with another culture and had been rewarded by making so many new friends with names like *Cesare, Guisseppe, Claudio, Antonio,* and, last but not least, *Sergio.*

To show my appreciation, I offered to bring down to the park the next afternoon some of the Little League equipment my dad kept in the closet so that I may teach them how to play baseball. Everything went so well as I showed them how to catch that piccolo ball, which was how they described the small size of the baseball. I pitched to them one after another as if it were an assembly line as they began to learn the hand–eye coordination necessary to strike a baseball properly. I hit soft grounders to each and had them throw over to first base and found that throwing was difficult for them and foreign to that game of theirs. They were used to throwing with two hands over their head, and accuracy was a serious problem. I began to wish I had brought the batting helmets for protection, but how much equipment could one bring down at the back of a bicycle?

We had a big league game the next day, so I asked some of the boys to help me prepare with some extra batting practice. Sergio, the biggest one of them all, offered to pitch. Now down at the other end of the park were some older men flying homemade gasoline-propelled plywood airplanes in a circular pattern guided by a handheld device attached to a thin line controlling the plane. Soon into the batting practice, I hit one that the famous Yankee broadcaster would have said, "Going, going, gone!" It flew up, up, and away. It could be seen by all that this didn't look good. It was a direct hit, and the plane was blown out of the sky. A one in a million shot, but they didn't buy it, and I was on my bike pedaling for my life, with the whole park on my tail.

I made the peace eventually; however, baseball was out of the question for now, so we returned exclusively to soccer; it was safer.

"Dad," I said later that night, "some people who saw that shot called me Joe DiMaggio! Do they know who Joe DiMaggio is over here?"

"Of course they do, Charlie—this is Italy!"

# Chapter 6

# Crazy Like the Fox!

It was 1963, and the war in Vietnam was escalating. This was evidenced by nightly news reports and also by a more personal observation. One by one, all of my close friends were being drafted to serve in the armed forces. All four have been sent to fight in Vietnam. Tommy, Tony, Paul, Lonnie, and I formed the group of five. Our teenage years were spent incessantly playing baseball, football, and basketball. We even formed a rock band called The Blue Notes. One by one, they would be taken away by the army, navy, air force, or marines, with virtually no say in the matter. They vanished.

Finally, I was left alone, without a friend. I was now the Lone Ranger, and I don't even have Tonto for a companion. I knew this feeling very well from my upbringing as a US Army brat. How? I wondered, can I take charge of my own destiny and not leave it up to others?

Soon I was certain that the call will come for me, and this uncertainty was beginning to drive me crazy. This uncertainty had been interrupting my pipe dream of becoming a major league baseball player. Each and every member of the group shared this same pipe dream. Now I was the only one remaining, and there is a difference.

The difference between our pipe dream and reality was a telephone call received by my dad late last night from Al Harper of the Boston Red Sox! It was August 13, 1963, and the entire family had just returned home to Whitestone, Queens. Everyone had been to the game that night at Yankee Stadium. An offer had been made on my behalf to my dad to sign a major league baseball contract.

But soon I was certain they would come for me and pull me right off shortstop on some minor league field and force me into another type of uniform.

*What is to become of me?* I wondered. Something huge has just happened. It happened earlier that night at Yankee Stadium, in the five hole. It was the reason for the call from the Boston Red Sox.

I was one of only eighteen phenoms from New York City chosen to play against the United States All-Star team. I had a small window of opportunity, and I had used it well.

I had become crazy with the heartfelt loss of my friends, crazy with worry and fear for my future, but at 8:45 earlier that night in Yankee Stadium, everyone was standing and cheering for something crazy that a kid did down there in the five hole to the left of third base. They would not sit down as I looked up at the fans in awe. From our dugout came the order to tip my cap to the fans. With a tip of my cap, thirty thousand people returned to their seats. How crazy is that?

Seven weeks had passed since graduation day from Flushing High School where the tag of "Flushing Fence Buster" would appear that night on the scorecard handed out to the fans. In my locker at Yankee Stadium, my trousers were hung near the lockers of Mickey Mantle and Roger Maris. In the rear pocket of those trousers was a wallet. In that wallet was a draft card. The initials on that draft card were 1-A. Soon there would be a ping-pong ball lottery—a ball for each day of the year. If your ball popped up between 1 through 180, you were gone. What a way for a seventeen-year-old kid to grow into becoming anything but crazy—crazy like the fox!

A decision comes easy when one doesn't have a choice. What sense was there to accept a dream of a lifetime offer when you had such a cloud hanging over your head? I was not living in the land where Alice grew up, although at times like these I do begin to wonder. Alice knew that the Mad Hatter was indeed crazy, and that assumption was part of the story, but I'm an average easygoing guy who goes along with the flow. Maybe it was time to take a few lessons from the Mad Hatter. Would he just go along with the flow? Of course not. After all, he's crazy! Would he take the Red Sox offer? He probably would. After all, he's crazy! The difference between the Flushing Fence Buster and the Mad Hatter is that one is crazy, and the other is crazy like the fox! That is a huge difference indeed.

"Thanks, but no thanks!" was my reply to their offer. All my friends thought that I was crazy. What do you think? Instead, an offer to play baseball for Long Island University or St. John University was considered. Who cares which one just so long as my draft status would automatically change to 2-S, indicating a student deferment. That's all I cared about. Baseball and fishing took a close second and third—in that order.

I accepted the offer to play shortstop for Long Island University. The deciding factor rested with the curriculum liability at St. John where an education program did not exist. You see, the Mad Hatter informed me that college students were being whisked away from out under their desks. Only college students who were to become teachers would have a reprieve for the time being. I liked the sound of that word "reprieve." It was good enough for me. I couldn't care less about becoming a teacher. All I wanted to do was to play baseball and go fishing! I may be the only fox that ever took an interest in those two sports.

The college year began in September simultaneously with the ping-pong ball draft. My birthday ball popped up as number 18! You know what that means—except that I was wearing number 11 as the LIU shortstop studying to become a teacher. Jack the fox! Jack be nimble, Jack be quick. Jack jumped over the candlestick. Where did I learn to think like this? I wondered.

*So this is how life is going to be*, I thought as I enrolled in all the prescribed undergraduate courses on registration day earlier this month. I'm on my own, and I wound up right here on Flatbush Avenue in Brooklyn, New York City. Well, they say that Brooklyn baseball players are a rough-and-tumble bunch. This should be fun—let's see just how tough they are compared to a kid from Queens, New York City. But was that really where I was from? Remember, you are dealing with a Fox and therefore must hesitate to take anything at face value. It is toward that end where this story may have value to all who take the time to read these pages.

In a way, I was not expected by my guidance counselor back at Flushing High School to have qualified for this high honor. I never cared much for boredom. That was my assessment of geometry, however. One must pass the geometry regents in order to graduate with an academic diploma. I hadn't passed a single test all year; however, it was common knowledge that you would pass the course if you were capable of passing the regents. Interesting. Boring but interesting.

Summer school was in the offing, so said my pompous and somewhat aristocratic guidance counselor as he peered over his bifocals. When I told him that I would be attending LIU on an athletic baseball scholarship, he simply replied, "Oh, you're a jock!"

I thought to ask him, "And what in the world are you?"

Whenever I see reruns of the Arnold Schwarzenegger movie, *The Predator*, I am reminded of that insult to a seventeen-year-old baseball phenom. Of course, in my imagination, I am Arnold, and the counselor is the predator from outer space. That was all he had to say and all I had to hear. *This is going to be fun*, I thought as I began to memorize every single theorem, every angle or triangle known to mankind, and all the possible questions in just two nights.

The big day was at hand, and my friends, who were also my fans, were saddened to see me rise up out of my desk to hand in the regents exam prematurely. The geniuses weren't even halfway through when I left the room. Mr. Shapiro felt sorry for me and reminded me that there was always summer school.

I had to report for training down at the Long Island University campus baseball field that afternoon and was in a big hurry to get out of that room and into my world. "I was late, I was late, for a very important date. No time to say hello. Good-bye, I'm late, I'm late, I'm late!" It was a grade of 86 for Jack the fox. Jack be nimble, Jack be quick. Jack jumped over the candlestick. Where did I learn to think this way? I wondered.

So now I was standing on line here at the college bookstore with all of our country's future leaders and captains of industry. This was such an honor, and I can't believe I was in such company. *What*, I am thinking, *will I do with this book,* The History of Western Civilization, *when I am done with it? And this one regarding anatomy of physiology looks like a real winner. And then there is this one on group psychology and another on group games.* I left them all in the shopping basket and walked out the door. My four-year stint at the college was successfully accomplished without buying a single book! That's crazy—unless you have a photographic memory, borrow the book from your buddy and memorize it from cover to cover. It was a legal way for yours truly to refer to his handy "open book" resource on all the exams. I was not a scholar; I was a baseball player who must not lose his student deferment. But where did I learn to think like this? Who was my teacher, and what were his methods?

Where was he now? Off to Berlin. He had been summoned to report for duty. Something called "The Berlin Crisis" has occurred with our Russian adversaries, and the United States Army had need for his talents. You see, there are other people who need to be taught how to think, and that was what he did. Berlin, in Germany, had been isolated, and this event had become the tip of the spear in the military world of national security and the maintenance of freedom for all people—a noble cause for a noble man—and he was whisked away from me, but not before he made sure I would not be whisked away.

Down to the draft board in Main Street, flushing, he hurriedly took me in tow, a few weeks earlier. Into the waiting room and past the line, he pushed open the door leading to the office of the desk sergeant. Out flashed his credentials along with a stern order to the desk sergeant. "This is my son," he said. "Here are his registration documents to Long Island University as a full-time student. I am ordering you to reclassify him with 2-S at once!"

"Yes, sir. My apologies, sir," responded the desk sergeant.

And it was done, and now my photographic memory had to do the rest. And then he was whisked away! That is how it is in the army.

Three years is about all you could expect to remain in one place before being uprooted. He had been stateside for over five years and was urgently called out of retirement in order to report for duty in Berlin. There were security measures that needed to be addressed so that sabotage must not enter the equation. There were tanks and other weaponry in the motor pool that must remain operational and uncompromised. They must be lubricated with Cosmoline and made ready for action at a moment's notice. Someone with the wily ways of a fox had to see to it that all of the above orders would be present and accounted for in meticulous detail. There would be hell to pay if so much as a cigarette butt was found on the floor of the motor pool.

Now how far did this apple fall from the tree? It appeared that the apple not only fell from the tree but slid down the nearby hill and onto a passing truck to wind up in parts unknown—or so it appeared. However, the apple did come from that tree and would always be a part of that tree no matter where it wound up on the journey. The tree was structured and disciplined, but the apple certainly was not. The apple had become somewhat cocky and arrogant although extremely confident and sure of his capabilities—not a bad apple after all. What kind of tree produces such an apple? What kind of fox can produce such a fox? These pages will tell in time.

Much had happened in what we refer to as the formative years in our former tour of duty. It has become difficult to take anything or anyone serious when one learns about life and love in the manner that I have been called upon to experience. It was like this with the two of us as a team.

> I say I'll move the mountains,
> And I'll move the mountains
> If you want them out of the way.
> Crazy, you call me,
> Sure, I'm crazy,
> Crazy, like the Fox, I'd say.
> I say I'll go through fire.
> As you want it, so it will be.
> Crazy, you call me,
> Sure, I'm crazy,
> Crazy like the Fox, you'll see.
> Like the wind that snakes the bough,
> You move me with a smile.
> Thanks to you, the difficult

I can do right now.
And even the impossible may take only a little while.
I say I'll care forever.
And I mean forever.
If I have to hold up the sky.
Crazy, you call me,
Sure, I'm crazy,
Crazy, like the Fox am I!

The apple and the tree were constantly uprooted as the years passed. It was just fine with us, and it merely became a way of life. He just kept teaching, and I just kept learning. As long as the apple and the tree were uprooted together and never separated, who cares? We were happy to know each other, and did we ever get a kick out of our differences and also our similarities. We understood each other even when it would become apparent that not a single soul ever understood either one of us.

And the story begins—the story of two thinkers who thought only outside the box; two thinkers who were crazy like the fox!

It seemed that another kind of fox has entered the picture in the form of a third-generation crazy like a fox. Her appearance alone was well worth the description of a fox. However, it was her curiosity that encouraged her to sit down with my father one day in the recent past to find out something for herself.

I had spent many a day at the beach with her as we searched for shells. Little by little, I told her of my father as she listened intently. After all, the stories being told were of my father, and he was her grandfather. The apple doesn't fall far from the tree; but being the fox that she is, it was prudent for her to find out for herself, and so she did that warm, sunny summer afternoon in her grandfather's backyard—the same backyard where my dad and I spent countless hours practicing curveballs and groundballs and rarely spoke of history.

Christina, however, needed to find out what her grandfather was all about, and this indeed would result in a history lesson that she has apparently remembered quite well indeed, for recently my granddaughter asked me for some advice pertinent to a project that would entail the writing of a story. As she explained it to me, it appeared that her school district had been contacted by the local Veterans of Foreign Wars organization. The students were encouraged to participate in what was called "The Patriots Pen" and submit their essay.

The title of the essay would simply be "What Patriotism Means to Me." At a loss to begin, she came to me for advice.

"If you want to be crazy like the fox, Christina, then you have to think outside the box!"

"What do you mean, Papa?" she asked.

"Well, it is a topic that many will surely submit a fine version. However, there will be many similarities. In order to win, your entry has to be special. It has to be original."

"What do you mean?" came the question.

Once again, I replied, "You have to tell a story that only your feelings can possibly know from your own experience."

"I don't have a story of my own to tell, Papa, about patriotism."

"Oh, yes, you do, Christina. Remember that summer day when you sat for quite some time with my father? It was a sunny day, and he was sitting alone in his backyard. You noticed that as the family was having cake and coffee after the lasagna dinner that my mom had made for your birthday in July. We noticed that you went out back to keep him company because we have seen you do things like that before, since it is a beautiful part of your nature, and it made me feel happy for myself and proud for you."

"I remember, Papa, but how can I use that memory and apply it to what patriotism means to me?"

"That is for you to find out," I replied. "What did you talk about? What did you ask him? And what did he tell you? I know the answers to those questions as I went out to sit with him later that evening, and I asked him about the conversation. He doesn't talk too much about the war to anyone. My impression was that he felt quite comfortable to talk about his experiences with you, and that is to your credit. You have a nice way with people, and that is one of the reasons why people will engage in conversation with you. They call that being personable."

"I wish he was still here, Papa, so I could refresh my mind with that conversation," she said.

"He is still here, Christina. You will know that to be true."

"How, Papa?"

"If there is something in the memory of that conversation that may help you, then he is going to help you remember. You had better keep a pencil and paper handy when you return home and sit down in a quiet place in order to reminisce."

And so she did. Here is a copy of what she remembered sent to:

Patriots Pen Competition
Veterans of Foreign Wars
8th Grade

I had a name I called my great grandfather. I called him Ipa. Ipa was a Patriot. One day I sat with him in his backyard and I asked him to tell me about his experience as a young man serving as a Sergeant during World War Two. "Well dear, if you really want to know" "My men of the 159th Infantry Regiment were sent to Alaska in order to defend its freedom during 1943. The Japanese had invaded Alaska. "What happened Ipa?" "We fought and died for her. She had to remain free."

"Did you return home?" "Only for a brief training period." "We were sent to France in order to replace soldiers killed or captured there, by the Germans." "Ipa, what did you see when you were sent to France?" "Well, we saw with our own eyes what the enemy did to a freedom loving democracy." "We were sent to free France and re-established her liberties. "Christina, guess who gave us the Statue of Liberty?" "France!" "The French people were hurting ever since 1940, when in June, France was invaded by the German Army." "How were they hurting, Ipa?"

"They were lacking food and medical supplies, and something worse, freedom!" "Christina, every town the 159th passed through, we would notice the same words on public buildings." "What were the words, Ipa?" "Liberte, Egalite, and Fraternite." "These stood for Liberty, Equality, and Fraternity. She lost all three when the Gera Army marched in." "France was the nation representing freedom on the continent of Europe. When France lost her freedom, the biggest democracy in Europe went down." "So, your men were in France to give France what belonged to her." "That's right, Christina, and then we became part of the 106th Infantry Division and we became "The Golden Lions." "Here is the patch I give to you!"

"Did you finally return home after that Ipa?" "No, Christina, when we joined "The Golden Lions," we made them a promise." "What was it?" "They had lost many of their friends and we told them that we were now with them and let's go back in together!" "Go back in where together, Ipa?" "We had to go into Germany and settle a score for our fallen brothers of "The Golden Lions!" "And in the process, we must bring freedom to yet another country, Germany."

"My Ipa reminds me of a song about following a star. "No matter how hopeless, no matter how far. To fight for the right, without question or pause. He was willing to march into hell for a heavenly cause. And I know he was true to his glorious quest, and his heart did lie peaceful and calm when he was laid to his rest. And the world will be better for this that one man scorned and covered with scars. Still strove with his last ounce of courage. To reach the unreachable Stars." My Ipa was a patriot. And my Ipa is what patriotism means to me!

By Christina Valenti

Age 13

Symbolism:
The blue is for infantry.
The red represents artillery support.
The lion's face represents strength and power.

"Beware, all who wish to know. There are many who wish you not to know. Their name is Legion. Be brave, all who wish to learn, for as a soldier of The Brave Rifle, I have much to teach. Be brave, all who wish to know, for there are many who wish for you to remain ignorant. Their name is Legion!

I come before you now with knowledge gained from enduring the unendurable. My eyes have seen victory, and my ears have heard the sound of defeat. I have smelled the odor of battle and that of cordite. I have known sheer fright, and I have known jubilation. I have dealt with loneliness while separated from my family, thanks to the camaraderie I was blessed with from the men under my command.

I know what it is like not to know. It is frightening. I knew of this while serving on Attu Island in 1943 and 1944. Would the enemy come? We did not know. What would we do if they did come? That we did know!

Would they come through the Ardennes? We did not think so. Will I ever see my newborn son, of which I gave my name? I do not know; but if I do, I am holding this book at the ready for him should he need to learn the knowledge within these pages.

Surely, he will need to know what lies beneath these covers, for the knowledge within is what has kept me alive to tell this story.

Within lies the knowledge of my opponent. The knowledge of how he thinks. The knowledge of all his formidable assets. I know where he is strong and where lies his soft underbelly. This knowledge comes my way through the luck of the draw. The luck of the draw simply means that I have survived the war and am alive to tell my tale.

But beware, the faint of heart. My son is now in possession of this legacy called "the Golden Lions."

With it, he can help you understand the crucial knowledge gained from knowing your opponent. We are the last of the Lions. We are the Ghost and the Darkness. And we are here to teach you, it's what we do. Lions do not speak, but they know each other's thoughts, and these we will convey."

My son had the fortune of growing up in Italy as a military dependent. There he learned the sport of soccer through relationships made with his Italian friends. He would teach them how to play the American game of baseball, and they, in turn, taught him how to play soccer.

They may have in time forgotten all about baseball; however, my son fell in love with their sport of soccer. His book *All-American* reveals how he used his knowledge of American sports on the soccer field in order to lead a team that would put together a streak of ten consecutive years of not losing a single regulation game by more than one goal! That occurred in the highly competitive division-A league in "the melting pot" known as New York City.

And now, this book called *Nosce Hostem* contains the military intelligence and counterintelligence with regard to strategic and tactical deployment of members of his team. This is the second half of the story in explaining exactly how military philosophies based on actual events were used by his Grover Cleveland soccer team out of Ridgewood, New York City.

# Chapter 7

# Piazza Bra

The piazza of every town in Italy represents a place where people come from near and far to enjoy life's simple pleasures. Chances are high that the picture in the piazza will change from day to day, since by its very nature, the piazza is very cosmopolitan. All kinds of people at various stages of life will arrive here, and some will pass through daily. Some you see regularly, and others you may never see again. There is a walking path around the park and benches here and there for a rest and relaxation.

One can learn much in the piazza since it is a place akin to a library, a school, or even a museum. It is a place for social gathering and where people gather, thoughts are exchanged, people learn. As we proceed with this factual story, I would remind that I am not attempting to teach anything yet will recount all that I have learned and how I have learned so that it may help to explain an inordinate amount of success that these pages will eventually unfold. It all began at Piazza Bra.

Piazza Bra is situated in close proximity to the river Adige that flows lazily through the beautiful town of Verona, Italy. This piazza is extremely verdant with grass areas and tall Italian trees surrounding the park. Through the trees, one can see what appears to be a medieval bridge leading to the other side of town where much of the hectic businesses flourish in the form of small shops and food stores. Among the many attractions to be found on the other side is a marketplace called Piazza Erbe. Not too far from that piazza remains intact to this day the balcony of Juliet and the courtyard below the balcony where Romeo appears, as accounted for in Shakespeare's classic love story.

Returning over the medieval bridge to Piazza Bra, one may begin to understand how the bridge derived the grand name of Castelvecchio. This bridge is stunning in its beauty and appropriate in the name of old castle. It is constructed of red brick with white trim, tastefully done by the artesian of old. Other bridges upriver and downriver afford auto and truck traffic in and out of town. Castelvecchio, however, is for pedestrians and bicycle use only, and all who traverse this bridge arrive at the foot of Piazza Bra. Here they will certainly find something of interest to see or learn. It may be from someone they see or talk with—who knows? This is a magical place, and for me, the piazza was love at first sight. It soon would become apparent to me that anything I learned here, I would remember for a lifetime. That is why my memory of all the following accounts is so vividly and unerringly accurate.

All piazzas in Italy share a common denominator. They must have, at the center of the piazza, a fountain, for it is here where people gather and sit for a while in their slow pace in order to enjoy the beauty of the majestic fountain.

It was springtime, 1956, and I had been reunited with my dad, Major Charles N. Valenti, US Army. This began his three-year tour of duty as an American officer who is able to speak fluent Italian. He had been chosen for this assignment since counterintelligence work requires the bilingual skill. This was now tie for us to get back together, and he asked me to take a walk with him after mass on a sunny summer afternoon, or at least it felt like summer to me, as Italy can make you feel happy. So can my dad!

As we walked alongside the Adige River, we eventually arrived at a beautiful park. I asked him what is this place called, and he answered, "Piazza Bra."

"But doesn't a piazza have a fountain?" I asked him.

"It does," he answered, and there it is right in the center of the park.

I followed the direction of his pointed finger and became puzzled. There was no water in that fountain. It was dry and arid as a desert. In better times, the water would apparently approach depths of four to five feet, and it now appeared to be quite an effort to lower oneself down into what now passed for an arena. There were no stairs to step down, and the cement floor was brittle and old from decay. It must have been awesomely beautiful at one time. The lack of steps did not seem to hinder the Italian boys from taking advantage of a situation. They eagerly jumped down into the cement with no problem in their eagerness to play that game they loved to play over here.

There is plenty of room down there in that dried-up fountain for what appears to be a full-fledged soccer game. The fountain is the size of a modern-day hockey rink. The four-foot walls were being adeptly used by the boys to pass the ball off the wall a lot like the hockey puck is bounced off the boards in a similar passing maneuver. The goals at the end of the arena were drawn from with chalk. This was a no-holds-barred affair that was hotly contested, and my dad suggested we stay for a while, for this was right up our alley. We took a bench, although I noticed he stood up a lot in order to get a better view of the game being played down below.

People sitting on the benches are enjoying the match as were the passersby. Occasionally, the ball was kicked too hard and flew out of the arena to be returned swiftly by fans or people walking by—men, women, and children all eager to hit the ball back onto the field of action. There was plenty of communication going on down below as the boys moved the ball up, down, and all around the field. We heard words like "*fore giogo*," "*adestr*" and "*asinistra*." "*pase la pala*" and "*libero*." Then we hear shouts of "*medio campo*" and "*cruza la pale*" and "*pase al ale*" and "*tira la pale*." Dad is fluent in Italian but was shaking his head from side to side, indicating he does not understand.

"What are they saying, Dad?" I asked him.

"Well, *fore giogo* means 'outplay,' *adestra* and *asinistra* means 'left' and 'right.' *Medio campo*," he said, "means 'midfield,' and *libero* means 'free,' and *cruza la pala* means 'cross the ball.'" We looked at each other and burst out laughing!

As we walked home together alongside the bank of the Adige River, my dad began to hum a song and then began to match the tune with words I'll never forget. It went something like this, since I am certain he was making up his own version. He began:

> Like the wallpaper sticks to the wall,
> And like the seashore clings to the sea.
> Like you'll never get rid of your shadow,
> You'll never get rid of me.
> Let all the others fight and fuss.
> Whatever happens, we've got us.

I liked the sound of it so far, and I encouraged him to continue. Dad was on a roll, and picked up the pace of the walk, and I hurried to catch up so as to hear the next part because with him, there was always a next part. He continued.

> Me and my shadow,
> Strolling down the avenue.
> Me and my shadow,
> Not a soul can bust this team in two.
> We stick together like glue.

I looked up at him now, and he looked down at me and gave me a big wink of the eye. This song was for me! There was more.

> And when it's baseball time,
> We start to swing.
> Our bats don't chime,
> They ring a ding ding.
> Closer than pages that stick in a book,
> Closer than ripples that flow in a brook.
> Wherever you find him,
> You'll find me, just look!

He took my heart in the whole thing now because it became apparent that he had a very appreciative audience tagging alongside.

> Me and my shadow,
> "We're alone, but far from blue.

Before we get finished, we'll make the town roar!
We'll win a few games, and then a few more,
For my shadow and me!

And indeed, we would do just that in baseball, but what was this we had just witnessed?

My dad and I are baseball players and are clearly out of our element. Then we hear more calls to pass to the wing and finally just to throw the ball. Finally, something we identify with baseball. Then the game was nearing the end, and we heard a distinct shout of "*catenacio*," and Dad looked at me and declared the new word means "locked gate," and he shook his head in puzzlement.

"What a strange game," he admitted as he went over to the vendor to buy me an ice cream pop. I continued to watch as I waited for him to return, and I noticed that he and the vendor were having a conversation. Then we all heard cheers coming from deep within the tow of Verona. Dad returned with the ice cream and told me that the vendor explained the cheers indicated that the big Verona team had won their battle with rival Vicenza. He told me that the vendor's name is Alfredo, and he spoke some English as their conversation took turns from one language into another. A friendly man, my dad offered.

The sun was setting on this wonderful afternoon I shared with my dad, and the game below came to an end as the Italian boys got on their bikes for the ride home. They departed in many different directions, which meant to me that they had come to this place from all over the city. They waved to each other and shouted, "*Ciao!*"

"What does that mean, Dad? Are they that hungry?" He laughed so hard he couldn't finish his ice cream.

"No, Charlie," he said. It means "see ya!" In the army, anything that sounded like *chow* meant "food." What a strange game this would be to understand, I thought, as we walked home together along the path beside the river Adige to our beautiful home with that splendid view of the river passing below.

On that walk home, I thought of words my dad had translated for me that made no sense—words we heard in the piazza—words like "outplay," "freeman," and "locked gate." Words like "wing," "cross," and yet there was something else that Dad muttered under his breath as we sat and enjoyed the ice cream.

He said to himself, "I feel like I'm doing aerial recon."

When I asked him what he meant, he replied, "We were up high and could see everything down below on the field. We could see more from the bench than the players themselves could see of the game." He said, "We have a bird's-eye view."

"Because of the recessed fountain, we had witnessed much from our vantage point." He said it was like looking down into a microscope and seeing everything you had to see, but he admitted that even with that view, he still did not understand what he had just seen. "Someday I will need a vantage point, and from it, I will look down with my microscope, and I will understand—someday."

There was an ice cream vendor at the park. His name is Alfredo, and he spoke some English and, from what I saw, was an avid soccer enthusiast. Next Sunday, I must return and talk to Alfredo in partial English and partial Italian. I must ask him to explain to me what my dad and I had just heard and seen from our aerial recon park bench at Piazza Bra.

Dad and I had just been introduced to a sport we had never seen before. He had played quarterback for Franklyn High School in New York City. He even competed successfully in the passing accuracy contest held his senior year at Yankee Stadium. Weekends he would quarterback the Uhlans from the upper west side of Manhattan in the neighborhood known as Yorkville. In the classic movie called *Casablanca*, Humphrey Bogart, when interrogated by the German police in Morocco, gave some advice. He though it would be wise that when Germany invaded the area of Manhattan, there are certain areas they had best stay clear of, and Yorkville is one of them. Dad was hardnosed, and he displayed that attribute as captain of the US Army baseball team of Trieste, Italy, on his prior tour of duty from 1950 through 1953. He was assigned to the Aleutian Islands during World War II as sergeant in charge of a squad whose mission was to help defend the island from attack from the Japanese. He witnessed the final days of the war in the area referenced by the description, the Battle of the Bulge. So you might say he had seen it all. And now he was assigned to the G2 intelligence sector because he has a good head on his shoulders, as a matter of expression. He may have seen it all, but this was the first time either one of us had ever seen this new game, and we saw it together. We are both baseball players from New York City. Surely two baseball players from New York could figure anything out, I thought.

# Chapter 8

# Como Bella la Verona

So I returned to the piazza later that week to get some answers and found Alfredo had set up shop in his usual corner of the Piazza Bra. He recognized me as I approached to buy an ice cream pop.

"*Quanta costa questa?*," was the classic question one would ask if you wanted to know how much the price of something would cost.

"*Sesanta lire*," he said, or in American language, ten cents' value.

"*Mile gracie*," I said as I gave him a one-hundred-lire coin Dad had given me.

"*Prego*," he responded with a smile and a question. "*Como se chiama?*"

"*Me chiama Charlie*," I replied.

"Ah! Charlutz," he replied.

*Okay*, I thought, just so long that this doesn't get back to any of my American friends. They would never let me live this one down. This was strictly classified or top secret, as they say at G2.

Dad was right; Alfredo does speak half Italian and half English. At least, this gives me half a chance to get some answers.

"Alfredo, *como se chiama*," and I pointed to some of the boys passing the ball around down in the fountain.

"*Calcio*, he replied. "This game is called *calcio*. *Calcio* is soccer, Alfredo."

"Yes, *sì*! How many people? Show me," as I unfolded the small carton that housed the ice cream pop so that it now can be used to write or draw.

Alfredo put eleven numbers in very specific places on the backside of my ice cream pop box. Now it was time for my half Italian input.

"*Como se chiama questa?*" I pointed to one of the numbers.

"*La ale,*" he replied.

Wow. I heard the boys say that word. So that is what they meant. *E'questa*, I resume. *Medio campo*. Bingo, I thought. The best one is this one, *medio campo*, he revealed. That is their best player. *That is their shortstop*, I thought. On and on we go like this until my eleven players were all accounted for by both position and by number. Now I was beginning to get the big picture. Now I knew what aerial recon actually looks like when you can identify something from a vantage point just like Alfredo had drawn it on the back of my ice cream pop box. This wasn't as sophisticated as I thought. After all, how complicated could it be if an ice cream vendor can explain it all on the back of a carton? How complicated? It would take me many years later in life to learn all on that ice cream carton—all the combinations, all the variations, all the complications, all the consternation, all the aggravations. But most of all, all the jubilation! It was my first insight to what is rightfully described as "the beautiful game."

Later that night, back at the house, we had just finished dinner, and I lingered awhile at the kitchen table. I pulled the folded ice cream carton out of my back pocket and began to study and scrutinize it more closely.

"What is that you have there?" Dad noticed.

"This is what we saw down at the Piazza Bra fountain on Sunday," I answered.

<<<MISSING PAGES 102-105>>>

We rewarded ourselves after each game with some gelati down at the corner of the park where the vendor set up shop daily to await the outcome of the game. Alfredo, the ice cream man, became our number 1 fan as he took in the outcome of the game and congratulated the victors on their performance. He was also our liaison with the big Soccer Club Verona, as he would provide us with the standings of the league and the place the Verona club found itself residing in on Monday morning after the big game on Sunday.

Alfredo reminded me of our stateside Good Humor men in more ways than one. His presence added to the daily event and made it feel bigger than it would have been without his input and his gelati. My American friends were invited to join their daily events as I spread the word at the military dependents' school, but they would always decline in favor of baseball. I crossed the line and was rewarded in the present and did not realize just how big a reward was coming my way in the future years as teacher and coach of that game they played over here.

Little League playoffs were arriving, and it was hard to imagine the excitement this generated. You have to understand that we were Americans living in Italy. We were from Alabama, Georgia, Texas, New York, California, and we needed baseball just as much as the Italians need soccer. The Little League was a source of pride for the whole detachment because the sense was that we brought a piece of home with us. The teams were even named after the big league teams in the states. We were the Red Sox, and if you were a soldier in Verona, you knew what that was synonymous with *winning*.

Livorno was coming in by train for a three-game series. Yes, we traveled in style and even wore a sport jacket and tie, complete with white buckskin shoes and a crew cut. "You're in the army now!" My dad offered our services of hospitality and offered to billet the Livorno star hitter at our place for the series. That was how the army would make sure to house the players who were the visiting team. Tony was the big sticks' name. After settling him in for the night, we had breakfast and headed to the park, where my Italian friends offered to field-batting practice for Tony.

My American rival took his turn at the bat and yelled, "Let me see your curve ball. I heard it is a real good one!"

"Sure," I conceded and proceeded to pitch him one slow hanger after another.

He hit that curveball all over the place and was very full of himself. My Italian friends felt bad for me as I heard them utter things like "*Povero Charlie*" and "*Mama mia!*" What my friends didn't know was that my dad set the table with intelligence and I was providing disinformation, and as a team, we were about to apply the counterintelligence the next few days. We took two out of three, and my American rival couldn't even smell my real curveball thrown as a slider, or fast-breaking ball. It's a pitch Dad taught me using the combination of speed and rotation that amounted to a fast-breaking curveball and not that hunk of junk that I showed to my rival at practice.

That screwball was also a factor. Many a night, my dad would have me grab the doorknob in the kitchen and open the door. That, he said, was the same way to release a ball so that the spin would develop the opposite way of the natural curveball. So I was thus armed with a pitch that could curve in and another one that could curve out. This was to come in very handy with another white ball somewhere down the road on a field with no diamond! Thus armed with a good team and a clandestine coach, the Red Sox won the US Army Little League Championship in 1957, but it wasn't that simple.

Somewhere along the way, that clandestine coach stumbled upon something no one had ever seen. It may have come from his days as a quarterback for the Ulans in Yorkville, Manhattan, New York City. Dad learned that he could move players around on that field, like chess players on the checkerboard, by using code signals. For example, if I was at shortstop and he wanted me to relieve the pitcher, he would signal the first baseman if we were using the dugout near him or the third baseman if we drew that dugout. They in turn would call time-out and make the pitching change by switching positions.

Other switches were done as well, and my dad never even moved from his sitting position. Managers and parents complained, but the umpire would just point to Dad and say he never did a thing and hasn't even moved. That was the big reason we won. The whole team was changed around numerous times to suit the coach, and all he did was to touch his nose or pull the string on his sweatshirt. He outfoxed the game of baseball. Years later, using this lesson, I began to outfox the game of soccer in New York City, for there are no timeouts in soccer. American football had arrived on the baseball field. What other field would it find its way to in time?

Something happened between the second and third games of the playoffs. Sunday was reserved for church and time off from work. Tony paired up with one of his teammates to figure out how to handle my curveball, so I strung my mitt around the handlebars of my bike and went to the park to seek out my Italian friends and found them playing that beautiful game of theirs and happily joined the melee. By game's end, my mitt had disappeared and could not be found as Sergio began interviewing the spectators who gathered to watch on Sunday. I went home to tell my dad the bad news, and Sergio came with me. It was the only time I ever saw Sergio angry.

This news did not sit well with Dad since he knew my intentions were good and I was teaching baseball. He also appreciated that they took a liking to me and were teaching me all about soccer. "What do you know?" he asked Sergio. They spoke in Italian for awhile, and then my dad turned and told me Sergio knows who took the mitt. He said, "The only way it will be returned is if you go with him to San Zeno! He will trust you on this mission and only you."

Sergio was the biggest and strongest of all the Italian boys. He was tall and had curly brown hair and very strong legs. At the games, no one could clear the all like Sergio. They nicknamed him *Catenacio*, which refers to an Italian form of defense known throughout the soccer world as the "locked gate." And this too would be a word I remember for the trial ahead. *"Andiamo,"* Sergio said to me, and off we went to San Zeno!

We took some water and a couple of oranges with us since Sergio knew that it would be a long ride to the old church neighborhood known as San Zeno. It was described to me as a poor neighborhood on the other side of the river. I took my seat on the handlebars, and off he pedaled over the nearby beautiful Castel Vecchio Bridge in order to cross the river. Castel Vecchio means "old castle," and indeed that is how the bridge looks to this day, awesomely beautiful! We arrived on the other side, thanks to those big Italian legs pumping away below the handlebars as San Zero began to appear in the distance.

Already it became obvious we were entering another world. The war took a big toll on Italy, and there were no stores or parks, and the only thing to sustain us was the items Sergio knew we must bring along for the ride. The war ended only eleven years before this journey on his bike, and everything appeared lacking in color as white and shades of gray were predominant. This aroused apprehension in me since I really didn't know Sergio that well at this time in the tour of duty. Now I began to understand what my dad must have felt like when he would team up with Bruno Francase for counterintel operations. *So,* I thought, *I am my dad, Sergio is Bruno Francase, and I hope I come back alive with my mitt!*

A cheerful note occurred to take the edge off things back at the Castel Vecchio crossing. It was Sunday, and that roar erupted, and this time, it lasted longer than ever before.

"What does that mean?" I asked Sergio.

"It means we won! Verona has won, Charlie, and this is a lucky day," and he began to sing a song that made him pedal a lot faster than before.

"I know that song. I heard it before from my grandfather a long time ago. What is that song called?" I asked.

"'Fratelli d'Italia,'" he said. "It is a happy song that we like to sing when we win a soccer game. It is the song of my country!"

*Wow, here I am in a war-torn section of Italy, on the handlebars of a bike being pedaled by an Italian singing his country song with gusto!*

We were passing all the cars now; it was downhill full speed ahead—Sergio was on a roll, singing all the way down that hill! From this, I learned that a song can mean a lot to a person.

> Without a song, the day would never end,
> Without a song, the road would never bend,
> When things go wrong, a man ain't got no friend,
> Without a song.
> That field of corn, would never see a plow,
> That field, would be deserted now,
> A man is born, but he's no good no how,
> Without a song.
> I've got my troubles and woes, but sure as I know the garden will grow.
> I'll get along as long as I know a song is strong in my soul,
> I'll never know what makes the rain to fall,
> I'll never know there ain't no love at all,

Without a song!

I like the way Willie Nelson sings that one.

There is no doubt I was feeling Sergio express love in that song he was singing of his country and pride too. Finally, we arrived in the San Zeno area, where we were encouraged not to venture, as it was far from home. But we had split the series and tomorrow was set for the rubber match. I was scheduled to pitch the final game, and the pitcher needed his mitt. Without my mitt, I would need a lot more than a song. As it was, they were on to my curveball after our close win in the first game. I had to have that mitt, and Sergio knew it and thought it was a lucky mitt. When we arrived at the address he had secured from the spectators, he asked me to wait down below in a spot he pointed to so that I could be seen from the window. He came down with the mitt and handed it to me, saying, "Eco es por lui" (This is for you).

He pedaled us all the way back to Castel Vecchio, over the river, and back to home where Dad was waiting. I did not know, but Sergio was put on a time schedule by the CIC. Dad said "Mile gracia" to Sergio and invited him to a drive the next day to the big game. He asked Sergio how did he know where the mitt was and who took it—just like Dad to seek some classified information.

Sergio replied with some counterintelligence of his own. "Your son, tu fijo, is a friend of all the Italian boys at the park, but on this Sunday, there was a newcomer who made a serious mistake. He has lost respect of the group and they demanded the mitt be returned." Sergio let them know of the urgency of that mitt being needed in the game the next day, just the same as the soccer ball would be needed in their game. It was a long day, and I thanked him for being my friend. "Get a good night sleep, bono nota," he said. "Verremo domani. See you tomorrow."

It was a bright and sunny day, on the way to the field. Somewhere on the way, the line "Buy me some peanuts and crackerjack" entered out of nowhere. I was nervous and remembered seeing a sign in the hallway at school. It said, "En questa classe siamo tutti nervosa" (In this class, everyone is nervous). *I hope my teammates are calmer than me. I'm going to need them*, I thought.

They were a lot calmer than I was and kept us in the game. I really was tapped out from the San Zeno handlebar adventure of the day before, and it showed. But we found ourselves ahead by one run as the opponent stood in the batter's box for their last licks. Tony memorized my curveball and led off with a double. His buddy whom he had compared notes with singled sharply off the third baseman's mitt. It was first and third, nobody out, and my curve had been "compromised," as they say in CIC jargon. Dad knew it and pulled on his sweatshirt string.

"Time!" Stanley Parker, our first baseman, yelled. "He wants to switch, Charlie."

"Break the rule, Stanley," I said. "Ask the coach to call time and come out here for a second."

Dad called timeout and came to get the ball. He took the ball and then asked, "Why did you change our rule?"

This was a question I had to answer and couldn't.

"Do you want this ball back?" he asked.

I remember it all as clear as day because for some reason, I said it twice, "Give me the ball back, Dad. Give me the ball."

He put it in my mitt, and we all went back to our positions.

By the time Dad returned to his seat in the dugout, Sergio did something crazy. He saw the situation and acted in that beautiful and puzzling foreign way. He stood up in the stands and bellowed out the song he so joyously sang the day before. He was not embarrassed. This one was for me! I summoned the catcher out before time was resumed. Sergio had finished, and the fans liked it from what I could see.

"Play ball!" the umpire shouted.

Nine hard screwballs later, and it was over. The place turned into a zoo. My dad took congratulations and came out to see me. He asked, "What the hell just happened here?" Did you hear Sergio?"

"Yes, I did, and that was Pop's favorite song."

"But where the hell did you get that screwball?"

"From the kitchen doorknob, Dad, but I was afraid to ever use it in a real game."

Bobby Poole, the catcher, came over and told the coach we had planned all screwballs the rest of the way. He told Dad what I had told him, "If Sergio can stand up their like that and sing his song, then I can throw nine screwballs for strikes. "Coach," Bobby said, "Sergio is the one who pulled us through."

As the famous Yankee broadcaster would often say, "How about that!" (Mel Allen, New York Yankees)

Dad had been telling the team all season long that you never could tell what you can achieve unless you apply yourself. He kept us up to date about a Little League team from Monterrey, Mexico—a team that didn't have a chance, but began to win one game at a time. In August of 1957, our season was not yet over, and we met in the dugout before the first playoff game. Dad told us the little league team from Monterrey, Mexico just won the championship against the best from all over the United States. They did that and we could do this! It was counterintelligence at its best.

Sergio made many American friends at the baseball field that day. He was invited to come along with us, as we had a basketball game for our team called the Verona Victors. We even used the tune from the Notre Dame fight song at the halftime cheerleader rally. It was a road game, and the army bus was transporting us to the city of Vicenza. An Italian bus driver was hired since he knew the roads. Shortly after we left Verona, something happened on the bus that I would never forget. The team of fourteen players and fourteen cheerleaders with a few coaches filled the bus. Sergeant Beck was our coach, and he worked us hard and taught us well.

A song broke out from the rear of the bus. A group began to sing.

> O, I wish I were in the land of cotton, old times there are not forgotten, look away, look away, look away, Dixieland. I wish I was in Dixie, hooray, hooray, in Dixieland I'll take my stand, to live and die in Dixie. Hooray, hooray, away down south in Dixie.

That song was challenged well before it was finished by the other half of the bus. Some seats began to be switched around the bus for the challenge. And it went like this,

> Mine eyes have seen the coming of the glory of the Lord, he has trampled down the vineyard where the grapes of wrath are stored. He's unleashed the lightning of his terrible swift sword, his truth is marching on. Glory, glory hallelujah, glory, glory hallelujah, his truth is marching on.

"O, I wish I was in the land of cotton" boomed again, and then "Mine eyes have seen the coming..." interrupted once more. On and on it went this way. Sergio turned to me as we were sitting together and asked, "Charlie, que su chesa?" (What is going on here?) I told him that we are still divided along the lines caused by the American Civil War, and he became visibly saddened to witness this division.

"Stand again like you did for me that day," I told him, "and sing your song of unity. Do it now, Sergio!"

'No, not unless you stand with me."

"Okay." And up we went, many eyes wondering, *What is this now?*

Residual Civil War songs were still being sung and no end was in sight, and he boomed, with me at his side.

> Fratelli Di Italia, Italia se desta,
> Del elmo di scipio, se cinta la testa,
> Dove la vittoria, le porga la chioma,
> Che schiava di roma, iddeo la creo
> Stringiamici a corte, L, Italia Chiamo, Si!

The Italian bus driver lost it and leaned on that horn, cheering, and he wouldn't stop. The Civil War songs ceased and were replaced by cheers for Sergio and his song. He had united them with that beautiful song, for it was the song of Italy and whatever differences we had at the time. One thing was for sure—we all loved Italy. And we all loved that song!

Baseball was a big part of the story because it enabled me to teach. It became apparent with the return of the mitt that the Italian boys were beginning to love baseball as much as I was beginning to love their game that they play over here. What beautiful skills the Italian boys were capable of performing. They were as talented at their game as my friends were at our American pastime.

The footwork necessary to stop the soccer ball and redirect it in the form of a pass or a cross to a teammate was a lesson in choreography that I had become very familiar with in my position at shortstop. By the way, I had recently entered a dance contest at the teenage club, with a girl chosen by chance. We had no time for preparation, so I did not approach the contest seriously. However, the young lady I drew as a partner was indeed serious and talented. What a combination! I owed it to her to do my best, and we danced to Bill Haley and His Comets' "Rock Around the Clock." I went off into another zone. We were great and won the bottle of champagne. My friends were amazed and exclaimed, "Charlie, we didn't know you knew how to dance." My answer to them was spontaneous. "I'm a shortstop, and if a person can play shortstop, then he can certainly become a dancer."

Footwork is essential in baseball, football, and basketball. And soccer demands the same kind of dexterity I have learned in the art of turning a double play in baseball.

When I took my turn as the goaltender, I felt right at home. It felt like I was playing third base, or, as my dad liked to refer to it, the "hot corner." The ball comes at high velocity to the goalie and third baseman, and the Lords' Prayer would certainly be in order when said for these souls.

Shortstop reminds me of the position the Italian boys refer to as medio Campo, or midfielder. These are the quarterback of their respective teams. And now I have introduced a football innuendo in describing all the similarities. The positions they refer to as la ale remind me of first and third base. La ale means "the wing," as described by the body part of a bird. A bird has two wings, soccer has two wings, and we have a first and third baseman.

The wings were not the most important positions, and I could discern that by the boys who were chosen to play that position down at Piazza Bra, for I was one of them. However, they were essential for the balance and integrity of both the baseball and the soccer team concept and structure. I played third base at Yankee Stadium, and I played first base against West Point military academy in the years ahead, and now I was playing left and right wing in a dried-up old fountain called Piazza Bra.

As time went by, I had the opportunity to flavor each and every position on the soccer field. Thanks to my familiarity with baseball, I felt quite comfortable at all locations on the soccer field. I felt very lucky in this regard, for one has to have actually played in the hotly contested format of both sports to feel the similarity of the knowledge learned from each. This was a very rare and treasured opportunity for me and helped me grow into the game they play over here. They taught me how to kick a curveball and how to kick a screwball. It depends upon which part of your foot struck the ball and upon the ensuing follow through. I taught them how to pitch a curveball and a screwball depending upon which way the wrist would turn at the point of release. The spin imparted upon the ball is the common denominator and causes the ball to curve into or away from the goalposts or the batter.

These similarities amazed me as I plied my wares from each wing after I raced down the wing. The sound of the wind rushing past my ears, with the combination of my hair blowing all over the place, was exhilarating. It was like stealing second base; you go like hell and hit the dirt with a slide at second base. Here, you go like hell and pull up to cross with an in-swinger, depending upon the choice of foot. I could hit a baseball from both sides of the plate. However, I found it very difficult to strike the soccer ball with my left foot in making the correct spin occur toward the goaltender. You do not have to master switching to play baseball, but it appears to me that you must master dexterity with both feet to play soccer.

I had had the baseball go through my legs for an error at shortstop, but that was not as embarrassing as when some of the more-accomplished soccer players put the ball between my legs and then raced around me to gather in the pass and off he went. And now I was in hot pursuit of this artist, and I felt like I was going from first to third with my hair on fire! I was thinking, *Wow! These Italian kids can run, but so can I. After all, my last name is Valenti, and my favorite meal is spaghetti, and I can run with anyone!* Off I went again, and I was hoping neither one of us would trip and fall in that dried-up old fountain in Piazza Bra.

There is a difference between the two sports to be noticed more likely after the game is completed. In baseball, after the game, everything slows down and you might reach for a soda or a hotdog. Here, after a soccer game, your heart is pumping a mile a minute and you just can't sit still for a minute, or as my dad would say, you have ants in your pants. It takes awhile to unwind after a soccer match. After all, the wind has been whistling past your ears and you were running as if your hair was on fire. When you went to look in the mirror, you couldn't even recognize yourself after a soccer match. No wonder they take one-word names like *Pele, Ronaldo*, or the *Kaiser*. It's easier to remember who you are after the game. I love this sport, for as my Italian friends often exclaim, "En questa squadra, tutti suono potza," translated as "On this team, everyone is crazy."

It is a wild and crazy game, and if you want to play it the way it should be played, it would behoove you to be a wild and crazy guy. But as Dad used to always remind me, there is the wise saying "crazy like a fox." The level of intelligence involved in this sport can be found in comparison only on the chessboard—the game of chess, the game of soccer; the war of chess, the war of soccer—one and the same. Both are crazy—like the fox! The word *both* reminds me of another similarity.

Playing shortstop is not possible without your partner, the second baseman, who assists you in the choreography known as the double play and provides the team with strength up the middle. These two are the core element of the team. Soccer has partners, especially when working together in their medio campo area of the field. It takes two, baby; it takes two—me and you!

There is a glaring difference between baseball and soccer. Of course, the choice of the word *glaring* may give cause for alarm. I knew that as a baseball player, by and large, one must be somewhat introspective and calm, much like the golfer. Much of the game pits you against yourself. As Yogi Berra once said, "Ninety percent of the game is one hundred percent mental, or vice versa." Yogi always confused me and everyone else, but the point is well taken.

In baseball, one should not afford himself the luxury of celebration, at least not unduly. This can have detrimental consequences since there can be an adverse effect. First of all, you might arouse the opponent and raise him to heights he had never imagined he could muster. Secondly, if you partake in emotional excess, then you must also subscribe to emotional duress, for the former is partner to the latter. As a boating, enthusiast, I give great credence to the old adage of maintaining an even keel. Keep the boat upright, balanced, and loaded properly to prevent the dastardly capsize calamity.

Too much exuberance and too much despair are to be avoided, or down goes the ship. Now try telling that to my Italian friends, who would go out of their minds when a goal was scored. Or try telling this to a baseball team, "Now, fellas, after each out, let's raise the roof." What passes for acceptability in one sport may be looked on as absurd in the other.

And if the shot goes wide, is it necessary for a public display of your errant thrust? Try not to punish yourself. As Bob Marley would sing, "Don't worry about a thing, everything is gonna be all right." In the years ahead, this tough mental discipline was critical to the success of my famous soccer team out of Ridgewood, New York City.

If you played here in Ridgewood, you became steeled in playing soccer under pressure, while demonstrating to all who would witness the calm of a baseball player. After all, they would be taught to be that way from a baseball player out of New York City, who learned his soccer from emotional Italians in a place called Piazza Bra, near the Castel Vecchio Bridge, under which flowed the river Adige, in the town called Verona, a time long ago in a place far away.

Many memories have been rekindled in this endeavor I have undertaken—memories of growing up and coming of age back home in Verona, Italy. It truly is where I come from, and I owe that magical hamlet for all it has given to me.

It was here in Verona where I spent many a day fishing in Lago di Garda. The Italian fisherman took the piccolo Americani and taught the young boy how to catch la trutta (the trout) on a fly with a fly rod. The Verona pescadors (fishermen) also taught the young boy how to use a Mitchell 300 spinning reel to cast a number 3 Mepps spinning lure for lesser types of game fish.

Many a day, I would return home from Lake Garda to provide my catch to the concierge who was in charge of our building in front of the river Adige. Alfredo began as a grumpy sort of fellow but took a liking to me, as I would return from fishing under the Castel Vecchio Bridge a half mile up river.

"Dove va por la peche," he would ask. "Adestra, mezzo kilometer, or asinistra, uno kilometer," would be my reply, as Alfredo spoke no English. However, after a while, he was heard to say clearly in English, "Charlie, where did you go to catch these fish?" And my answer was always, "Either one half mile to the left or one mile to the right." These were my favorite spots taught to me by the Italian pescadors.

The people of Verona are kind and offer a genuine warmth not found anywhere else, and I have missed them dearly over the passing years. They taught me how to water ski and also how to ski down the side of Bosco Montico with my hair ablaze. The Italian beachgoers at Lago di Garda introduced me to the wonderful sport of snorkeling in the gin-clear waters of the volcanic Lake Garda that appeared as a teacup nestling between the mountains. Into the depths, the Italians of Verona taught me how to dive deep, hold my breath, and chase the big lake trout along the bottom. That was even more fun than a breakaway on the soccer field.

Should this memoire somehow find its way to someone in the town I grew up in, please accept my thanks for the impact you and your elders have had on my life.

"Let me have a look at that," and he took a seat beside me and said, "That chaos we saw at the park looked a lot more confusing than this diagram, but are you aware of what you have here? All I know is that this guy in the middle is the one they call *medio campo* and Alfredo said he is the best player on the field. He is the shortstop. You have far more than that information on this ice cream box," he said.

"You have done what we call a gathering of intelligence. This diagram represents each position as it relates to the formation of the team. Each position has a distinct responsibility, just like the positions that make up your baseball team. But there is a big difference, Charlie. I was trying to figure it out the Sunday at Piazza Bra and I couldn't, but with this diagram, I think you are halfway there."

"What do you mean halfway there?" I asked.

"This diagram is the intelligence needed to recognize the formation your side may choose to play. Now you need to find out the formation the opponent chooses to play against you. With that knowledge, you should win!"

"How can anyone get that other knowledge?" I asked.

"Counterintelligence," he said. "It's all about knowing your enemy and preventing him from knowing you."

I remained silent. This was getting serious.

"Are you interested in learning about these types of things?" he asked.

"Sure!" I answered, and I meant it, and he knew it in my unequivocal reply.

He told me he was taking courses for military advancement and welcomed me to study along with him provided I had addressed my homework as the priority.

"I'm all for it, Dad. Can't wait."

"Well, the apple doesn't fall far from the tree," he said as he got up off his chair and asked me to wait a minute as he went into another room. "Here, this is for you." He placed in my hand an old patch he had worn in battle during the war somewhere in Europe. I have it to this day. It is circular with red trim around a circle colored in deep blue. In the center of the blue circle is a golden-maned male lion. That lion appears to be winking, a lot like Dad would do, as one eye is open and the other eye I closed. When I asked him about the patch, all he would say was that the battle was rough and we lost a lot of men. I decided right there that I better just mind my own business as this was a sensitive issue. This was not baseball; this memory he has is far more serious and sobering. However, to a kid, it was a lion, and it was winking, and it reminds me of him. After all, he was a lion among men—strong, smart, silent, and good-looking! I must be a lion too, I thought. We must both be lions! And so the two lions submersed themselves into the world of military battle tactics on the kitchen table. Topographical maps abounded with their corresponding overlays made out of delicate onion skin paper. The lion was teaching his cub. He had enthusiasm in the way he explained every detail that was outlined before us. The only other time I ever saw him like this was when he was coaching the baseball team. Both areas require a knowledge of terrain, logistics, the opponent, and your own capabilities. It was his jungle, and I happily joined him there, for in the jungle, the mighty jungle, only the lion sleeps tonight. Everyone and everything else had better remain awake for their own good. We hunted until we had our fill, and then we slept. The two lions slept tonight.

Baseball was a big part of the story because it enabled me to teach. It became apparent with the return of the mitt that the Italian boys were beginning to love baseball as much as I was beginning to love their game that they play over here. What beautiful kills the Italian boys were capable of performing. They were as talented at their game as my friends were at our American pastime.

The footwork necessary to stop the soccer ball and redirect it in the form of a pass or a cross to a teammate is a lesson in choreography that I have become very familiar with in my position at shortstop. By the way, I had recently entered a dance contest at the teenage club with a girl chosen by chance. We had no time for preparation, so I did not approach the contest seriously. However, the young lady I drew as partner was indeed serious and talented. What a combination! I owed it to her to do my best, and we danced to Bill Haley and His Comets's "Rock around the Clock." I went off into anther zone. We were great and won the bottle of champagne.

My friends were amazed and exclaimed, "Charlie, we didn't know you knew how to dance."

My answer to them was spontaneous. "I'm a shortstop, and if a person can play shortstop, then he can certainly become a dancer. Footwork is essential in baseball, football, and basketball. And soccer demands the same kind of dexterity I have learned in the art of turning a double play in baseball."

When I took my turn as the goaltender, I felt right at home. It felt like I was playing third base, or as my dad liked to refer to it as the "hot corner." The ball comes at high velocity to the goalie and third baseman, and the Lord's Prayer would certainly be in order when said for these souls.

Shortstop reminds me of the position the Italian boys refer to as *medio campo*, or midfielder. These are the quarterback of their respective teams, and now I have introduced a football innuendo in describing all the similarities. The positions they refer to as "*la ale*" reminds me of first and third base. *La ale* means "the wing" as described by the body part of a bird. A bird has two wings, soccer has two wings, and we have a first and third baseman.

The wings are not the most important position, and I can discern that by the boys who were chosen to play that position down at the Piazza Bra, for I was one of them. However, they are essential for the balance and integrity of both the baseball and the soccer team concept and structure. I played third base at Yankee Stadium, and I played third base against West Point Military Academy in the years ahead, and now I was playing left and right wing in a dried-up old fountain called Piazza Bra.

As time went by, I had the opportunity to savor each and every position on the soccer field. Thanks to my familiarity with baseball, I felt quite comfortable at all locations on the soccer field. I feel very lucky in this regard, for one has to have actually played in the hotly contested format of both sports to feel the similarity of the knowledge learned from each. This was a very rare and treasured opportunity for me and helped me to grow into the game they play over here.

They taught me how to kick a curveball and how to kick a screwball. It depends upon which part of your foot struck the ball and upon the ensuing follow-through. I taught them how to pitch a curveball and a screwball depending upon which way the wrist would turn at the point of release. The spin imparted upon the ball is the common denominator and causes the ball to curve into or away from the goalposts or the batter. These similarities amazed me as I plied my wares from each wing after I raced down the wing. The sound of the wind rushing past my ears with the combination of my hair blowing all over the place was exhilarating. It was like stealing second base.

You go like hell and hit the dirt with a slide at second base. Here you go like hell and pull up to cross with an inswinger depending upon the choice of foot. I could hit a baseball from both sides of the plate. However, I found it very difficult to strike the soccer ball with my left foot and making the correct spin occur toward the goaltender. You do not have to master switching to play baseball, but it appears to me that you must master dexterity with both feet to play soccer.

I have had the baseball go through my legs for an error at shortstop, but that was not as embarrassing as when some of the more accomplished soccer players put the ball between my legs and then raced around me to gather in the pass, and off he went. And now I was in hot pursuit of this artist, and I felt like I was going from first to third with my hair on fire! Wow! These Italian kids can run, but so can I. After all, my last name is Valenti, and my favorite meal is spaghetti, and I can run with anyone! Off I went again, and I hoped neither one of us trip and fall in that dried-up old fountain in Piazza Bra.

There is a difference between the two sports to be noticed more likely after the game is completed. In baseball, after the game, everything slows down, and you might reach for a soda or a hotdog. Here, after a soccer game, your heart is pumping a mile a minute, and you just can't sit still for a minute, or as my dad would say, you have ants in your pants. It takes a while to unwind after a soccer match. After all, the wind had been whirling past your ears and you were running as if your hair was on fire. When you went to look in the mirror, you couldn't even recognize yourself after a soccer match. No wonder they take one-word names like Pele, Ronaldo, or the Kaiser; it's easier to remember who you are after the game. Love this sport for as my Italian friends often exclaim, "*En questa squadra, tutti suono potza*," translated, "On this team, everyone is crazy."

It is a wild and crazy game, and if you want to play it the way it should be played, it would behoove you to be a wild and crazy guy. But as Dad used to always remind me, there is a wise saying, and it is "crazy like a fox." The level of intelligence involved in this sport can be found in comparison only on the chessboard. The game of chess, the game of soccer; the war of chess, the war of soccer—one and the same. Both are crazy—like the fox! The word "both" reminds me of another similarity.

Playing shortstop is not possible without your partner, the second baseman who assists you in the choreography known as the double play and provides the team with strength up the middle. These two are the core element of the team. Soccer has partners, especially when working together in their *medio campo* area of the field. It takes two, baby; it takes two, me and you!

There is a glaring difference between baseball and soccer. Of course, the choice of the word "glaring" may give cause for alarm. I knew that as a baseball player, by and large, one must be somewhat introspective and calm, much like the golfer. Much of the game pits you against yourself. As Yogi Berra once said, "Ninety percent of the game is one hundred percent mental, or vice versa." Yogi always confused me and everyone else, but the point is well taken.

In baseball, one should not afford himself the luxury of celebration, at least not unduly. This can have detrimental consequences since there can be an adverse effects. First of all, you may arouse the opponent and raise him to heights he had never imagined he could muster. Second, if you partake in emotional excess, then you must subscribe to emotional duress, for the former is partner to the latter. As a boating enthusiast, I give great credence to the old adage of maintaining an even keel. Keep the boat upright, balanced, and loaded properly to prevent the dastardly capsize calamity.

Too much exuberance and too much despair are to be avoided, or down goes the ship. Now try telling that to my Italian friends who would go out of their minds when a goal was scored, or try telling this to a baseball team, "Now, fellas, after each out, let's raise the roof "What passes for acceptability in one sport may be looked on as absurd in the other.

And if the shot goes wide, is it necessary for a public display of your errant thrust? Try not to punish yourself. As Bob Marley would sing, "Don't worry about a thing, everything is gonna be all right." In the years ahead, this tough mental discipline was critical to the success of my famous soccer team out of Ridgewood, New York City.

If you played here in Ridgewood, you became steeled in playing soccer under pressure while demonstrating to all who would witness the calm of a baseball player. After all, they would be taught to be that way from a baseball player out of New York City who learned his soccer from emotional Italians in a place called Piazza Bra, near the Castelvecchio Bridge, under which flowed the river Adige, in the town called Verona, a long time ago in a place far away.

I went on to become a mere coach and teacher of a highly successful and storied soccer team. My dad and all our boys on Attu were fighting for their lives with one hand tied behind their back, or in soccer parlance, they had no defense—except one. The Japanese did not know this, and the orders came down to use disinformation as the defense in the form of eighty-eight-millimeter antitank artillery pieces. We were expecting to defend from an occupying force with this type of weapon, which now appeared all but useless. However, these eighty-eight must look like something they are not and let the enemy try to figure out if their risk is worth the effort to find out the truth. This concept found its way into our playbook—disinformation.

The boys on Attu worked all day and all night to scramble the eighty-eights from places near and far on the island of Attu. Huge pits were dug and reinforced with sandbags, and the eighty-eights were placed in these strategically located sites to look and appear for the Japanese eyes the next time they made that close offshore pass to appear to resemble coastal artillery capable of sinking ships!

Of course, they couldn't sink a ship; they couldn't even reach a ship. But they looked menacing as nightfall approached, and all waited on Attu for the Japanese decision. My dad would often tell me that if they wanted to, they could have come in close and blown us to bits, as he would offer in a descriptive and colorful phrase. Don't forget, he comes from the lower east side of Manhattan, and we already know what Humphrey Bogart warned the Germans with regard to their intrusion into that neighborhood in the classic movie *Casablanca*.

1943 Champions

The Japanese arrived on schedule, and they decided that discretion is the better part of valor. They believed that the impromptu coastal artillery had the same range as their own weapons and declined to engage in a shooting match. They could not risk a closer look to confirm, for in the event their guess would prove to be wrong, the consequences would -prove to be severe. A sigh of relief was heard that night on the island of Attu as the Japanese Navy sailed on by far offshore, out of range from our "big guns"!

Time and again, as the seasons assed, this battle tactic was employed by our boys here in Ridgewood, New York; a neighborhood with heart and character that may rival that of the low east side where my dad comes from. And always, after each and every game, he would ask me, "Did you win?" and always after each game, I would answer, "Sure, Dad, just like you and the boys did on Attu!"

Many of our athletes were of average capabilities on a par with the competition, and all had a burning desire to be part of such a storied team. If your skill level prevented the attempt at certain positions of responsibility, then you could help the cause by performing the duty of our "big guns." The disinformation provided by the impromptu threat to the other side was a huge contribution to my regular reply to Dad's question.

"Yes, Dad, we won! We knew the other team well, but they did not have a clue about us. Nosce hostem!"

During the summer and fall of 1943, the 159th was ordered to defend the Aleutian Island of Attu. We dug in along the coastline and watched apprehensively as the Japanese Navy cruised by menacingly. Our only deterrent would be to place eighty-eight-millimeter antitank guns where they could easily be observed to resemble coastal artillery pieces with a range to reach the Japanese. The ploy worked as the enemy thought better than to gamble the risk of coming in close for a better look. We were lucky because if they did, they could have blown us to pieces with their long-range salvos. They were so much more powerful than we were at that time during the war, but our team had to start somewhere, and we began to make our presence felt as the underdog that we were in October 1943.

Another team began to make its presence felt back home, not too far from Yorkville, in a neighborhood called Ridgewood, in October 1943. It was also an unproven underdog trying to make a name for itself against all odds. Their prospects appeared to be just as hopeless as ours. Both teams were smart enough to keep that information to ourselves. Both teams, whether they knew it or not, were practically the nosce hostem doctrine to say alive.

On October 19, 1943, the Grover Cleveland High School soccer team took the field. Perhaps they also had to use their own version of eighty-eight-millimeter artillery, we will never know. However, this we do know. After the regular season had come to a close, Cleveland was tied with Lafayette for the Brooklyn-Queens Championship, each with seven wins and one defeat. As the Japanese Navy cruised in close along the coast of Attu Island, Cleveland defeated Lafayette 3-0 to qualify for the city championship game. Of course, our fight on Attu is not comparable to an athletic event. It is simply that both events were occurring simultaneously, and there was a soldier on Attu who would bear, if he indeed would survive, a son. That son would someday be the coach of the Cleveland soccer team of Ridgewood, New York City.

In 1943, the prospects for both our men on Attu and the Cleveland team were against all odds, at the same moment in tie. Neither had a chance against the opponent they were facing. Our men were outclassed by the powerful Japanese Navy, and the Cleveland team was outclassed by James Monroe High School.

James Monroe of the Bronx had won the city championship three years in a row, from 1949 through 1942. They were the best, and no one could stop them for three years.

In the championship game played at Monroe Field, Cleveland won 1-0 when Lou Seitz, playing the inside left position, after fifteen minutes of the first half, scored the only goal of the game. And then they did what our boys on Attu were doing. They held on for dear life against all odds, and history was made by the boys on Attu and by the first soccer team from Queens to ever win the New York City championship.

The photograph shows a smiling coach, Marcy Hessel, with the soccer team that started to turn the tide. The Marcy Hessel Memorial

Trophy is displayed proudly by the Cleveland Soccer team after the undefeated championship seasons of 1970 and 1980 in the color photo in the rear. Over forty years later, the Cleveland team has been to the layoffs thirty-one times and has won nine city championships.

No other team has even come close!

Marcy Hessel passed the torch to Joe Singer, his friend. Joe Singer passed the torch to Charles L. Valenti, the son of one of our boys who fought for our freedom on Attu Island, 1943.

The story about what transpired on Attu Island during 1943 had relevance when the parts were analyzed and put to use on the soccer field. This ploy was an ingredient instrumental in our continuous success. Our eighty-eight millimeter artillery pieces were double center forwards lacking in finesse but possessing size and a degree of strength and stamina. Like the guns of Attu, their job was to keep the enemy off our back. They came off the bench frequently and were sent far downfield to occupy and pester players with far greater skills than they were capable of demonstrating. They were a cause for worry and concern as they entered the area of the opposing goal.

Two major opponents with high-caliber skills were being preoccupied by two players of a lower caliber, much like the scenario on Attu Island. Consternation entered into the picture on the opponent when they realized after a time that the hunter had become the hunted. These twins were told to relentlessly hound the sweeper and center back and deny them the ball in the attempt at reverse psychology. We were dogging them, as we liked to describe this ploy.

So now those two defenders had become compromised, and we could move in with our high-caliber guns and release salvos upon the opponent. We did what the Japanese did not do since we were assured their defense was neutralized and no harm would now come our way in a relentless assault. Midfielders led in shots and goals until the ploy was over. Of course, the word "ploy" has the inference of trickery and deceit. The defense of Attu was a ploy. Trickery and deceit are valuable weapons when one considers how their usage could transform eighty-eight-caliber antitank artillery into six-inch or ten-inch cruiser-class counterparts. It's just a ploy. It just means that we are smarter than the opponent. Intelligence should indeed have a preeminent role on the battlefield and on the soccer field.

The only difference between the ploy used on Attu and the facsimile we used was the duration. The guns remained menacingly pointed out to sea, for that was an island, and the ploy was their only card up their sleeve. We, however, possessed an arsenal of ploys, thanks to my dad. When the ploy began, it was much like the expression used in the military of fire for effect. Then, in rapid order, the ploy would be called off before the opponent could recognize it for what it was, a special operation—a special operation requiring deceit and surprise. Now you see it and now you don't.

So my dad and I would study his military advancement courses, and he would open up and relate true accounts of where he was in the war and what he had seen or heard. This is merely one of many memories he had shared with me, and with each of his accounts came something more than useful to put out on the soccer field. Today the military refers to these ploys as special-ops. Special-ops have no place on the soccer field. Now that statement was a ploy!

Many of his course required one to study various types of terrain, and I remember him pointing out obstacles on the battlefield that were natural and other obstacles that were manmade. Some of the courses I found most interesting were topographical displays of tank battles. These were steep in strategy and logistical support doctrine. If one side had the benefit of high ground, it should prove to be an advantage. If the other side had better logistical support, then they should probably prevail. However, there could be many intangibles that could affect the outcome of the battle.

Mud was one of the natural factors. Wind was another, so was the sun. These natural intangibles are factors in many of our soccer battles as well. Dad had more than once expressed sadness at one tank battle in particular. It occurred in North Africa early in the war when we were not quite as knowledgeable as the German opponent. It was the Battle of Kasserine, and we had entered into a trap set by the masterful German tank commander known as the desert fox, Erwin Rommel. Our losses were terrible in men and machine, and Dad would sadly and often repeat that they didn't have a chance and were outclassed by the opposing force on two counts—terrain and weaponry—and it appeared to him strategy was a factor as well.

He told me that General George Patton arrived to assess the Kasserine disaster and learned from the defeat. Years later, the movie starring George C. Scott appeared in theaters all over the United States. There is a part in that movie I have taken in my coaching years quite seriously, and it has been awesomely helpful. After the Kasserine defeat, Patton is seen with binoculars surveying the battlefield from high ground. He is witness to a plan he has in place, and now he is witness to a German tank division entering a trap that he has designed.

He shouts out for those nearby to hear or perhaps just for his own satisfaction some remarkable words, "Rommel, you SOB! *I read your book!*"

Rommel had apparently written a book about tank battle and tactics in intricate detail, and Patton took the tie to learn from the master. What a great idea that was, I remembered thinking at the time. I began sometime after that movie to read everything I could get my hands on pertinent to soccer dogma past, present, and future. I would be sitting in the last seat of the last row in graduate school studying everything about soccer and nothing about the course to which I was attending.

I had no idea what my plan would eventually evolve into with all of our studies regarding military tactics, strategy, and dogma. That was to come later. Now was the time for me to do what Patton did after the battle at Kasserine. I had to learn everything possible about every style employed by every country—how it worked, why it worked, why that culture chose that style to express their approach; conversely, how each had their flaws, how they could be dismantled, why one fared better against another. Years went by this way. I began to know them all. I began to nosce hostem! The handwriting was on the wall.

Up to this point, Dad had shared much of his athletic experience with me, and he had seen that it had begun to bear fruit. After a baseball game one afternoon in the parking lot outside the field, he was approached by a high-ranking officer. He came away from the conversation somewhat pleased, so I asked him what the colonel said to him.

"He told me that you have potential, Charlie."

"What does potential mean?" I asked.

"It means that people see in you a special ability," Dad said. "It means that if you apply yourself and dedicate yourself, you never know where it may lead to later in your life."

I wondered if he was talking about me or his own life. He certainly had applied himself, and his dedication to the US Army was even easy for a small boy to see and appreciate. Potential! It means that someday I may accomplish in my life what he had already accomplished in his. What a great thing to look forward to achieving, I thought. He was such a positive man and began to share with me all of his experiences as if he had long needed a close friend. I was all ears and hung on every word for two reasons: one reason was that I was so proud of him that my buttons were bursting; the other reason was that his stories were always about thinking and learning. He told me stories, and his demeanor was as calm and unflappable as Phil Rizzuto turning a double play—nothing to it—but in reality there is plenty to it, or as they say, more than meets the eye.

One of his accounts remained with me into my soccer years and had a great impact on my approach to the game. It was circa 1942, the Aleutian Islands. Master Sergeant Charles N. Valenti and his men were assigned to Attu Island in order to defend it from the Japanese who at that time were threatening to occupy the Aleutians and provide themselves with a pathway to California. The US was not in a position at that time to mount an offensive and had to take on a decidedly defensive posture. "You do what you have to do, not what you want to do" is the lesson. Components of the Japanese Navy would cruise nearby as they came down the Aleutians from their base at Kiska Island. As my dad would often tell me, they could see us, and we could see them. "We had no navy to help us since the attack on Pearl Harbor," he would recount, "but we had to do something before their logistical superiority would overwhelm us at the time of their choosing." These were learning words, and this was a teaching story. Logistical superiority would be the core of my soccer teams many years away from this crucial time in 1942, and if Dad didn't get out of this one, I wouldn't have the chance of conception, not to mention using this lesson to promote logistical superiority combined with disinformation in order to keep the enemy off your back on the soccer field of battle. "You do what you have to do with what you have and not waste time wishing your situation was better than it appears" is the lesson. The orders came down from headquarters loud and clear. The orders were we cannot possibly win against this opponent, but we can tie! In soccer, you can tie and be proud that discretion is the better part of valor. And tie we did!

Many memories have been rekindled in this endeavor I have undertaken; memories of growing up and coming of age back home in Verona, Italy. It truly is where I come from, and I owe that magical hamlet for all it has given to me.

It was here in Verona where I spent many a day fishing in Lago Di Garda. The Italian fishermen took to the *piccolo americani* and taught the young boy how to catch *la trutta* (the trout) on a fly with a fly rod. The Verona *pescadors* (fishermen) also taught the young boy how to use a Mitchell 300 spinning reel to cast a number 3 Mepps spinning lure for lesser types of game fish. Many a day I would return home from Lake Garda to provide my catch to the concierge who was in charge of our building in front of the river Adige.

Alfeo began as a grumpy sort of fellow but took a liking to me as I would return from fishing under the Castelvecchio Bridge a half mile up river.

"*Dove va por la peche,*" he would ask.

"*Adestra, ezzo kilometer* or *asinistra uno kilometer*" would be my reply as Alfeo spoke no English.

However, after a while, he was heard to say clearly in English. "Charlie, where did you go to catch these fish?" and my answer was always either one-half mile to the left or one mile to the right. These were my favorite spots taught to me by the Italia *pescadors*.

The people of Verona are kind and offer a genuine warmth not found anywhere else, and I have missed them dearly over the passing years. They taught me how to water ski and also how to ski down the side of Bosco Montico with my hair ablaze. The Italian beachgoers at Laogo Di Garda introduced me to the wonderful sport of snorkeling in the gin-clear waters of the volcanic Lake Garda that appeared as a teacup nestling between the mountains. Into the depths, the Italians of Verona taught me how to dive deep, hold my breath, and chase the big lake trout along the bottom. That was even more fun than a breakaway on the soccer field.

Should this memoir somehow find its way to someone in the town I grew up in, please accept my thanks for the impact you and your elders have had on my life.

While undertaking this project, memories have been rekindled, and appreciation is due to many who have made the memories and this story possible. I would like to take this opportunity to share with you some of these memories and thank those who encouraged the assembly of this project.

Verona, Italy, is an awesomely beautiful city, and I am fortunate to have lived there and know it as my home. The beauty of Verona did not escape me or my imagination. Verona, in my education, meant that anything is possible if one just takes the time to study, absorb the beauty and knowledge of others, and learn. Knowledge acquired here in Verona put me on the path to beating to the sound of my own music and not to be distracted by the music other people would have me play to their liking, or dance steps.

I practiced aerial reconnaissance at an early age while living in our apartment overlooking the couples walking together alongside the Adige River on beautiful moonlit nights during summer evenings. This was the *passagiata* that the Italians were so fond of, and the meaning is simply "just taking a walk."

> Down each avenue, via, street or strada
> *Andiamo passagiata*, two by two,
> *Tutti amore di Verona*.
> Thought they're grinning and mandolining in sunny Italy,
> The beginning has just begun when the sun goes down.
> Do they take them for espresso? Yea, I guess so.

> On each fella's arm a girl I wish I knew,
> *Una bella di Verona.*
> Will you meet me at the piazza, near your casa?
> For I am only one, and that is one too few,
> *Mi bella ragazza di Verona.*
> I don't know what the country is coming to,
> But when in Verona, do what the Italians do,
> So...
> *Te piace unto espresso con mi?*
> *A bella ragazza, dice si!*
> *Como bell ache la luna,*
> *La luna di Verona: per mi!*

The story of Romeo and Juliet is a powerful story known throughout the world. That story written by William Shakespeare took its inspiration right here in Verona and the couples on *la passagiata* are fully cognizant of their proximity to that story of life, love, and fate. Join me in a song about the two classic star-crossed lovers of Verona. My affinity with this story is that I identify with the misfortune and heartbreak of my particular timing in life. It seems to me that I had all the necessary skills at all the wrong times. For love, however, my timing was fine as I found my Juliet when I found my Leila, the mother of our two wonderful sons. Take with you what you will from this memory of Verona and the story of Romeo and Juliet.

> A love-struck Romeo, singing in the streets a serenade.
> Laying everybody low, with the love song that he made.
> Behind a convenient streetlight, he steps out of the shade.
> And says something like, "You and me, babe, how about it?"
> Juliet says, "Hey, it's Romeo! You nearly gave me a heart attack!"
> He's underneath the balcony. "Hey, my boyfriend's back."
> "You shouldn't come around here, singing up to people like that."

What are you going to do about it, Juliet?
The dice were loaded from the start.
When we met, you exploded in my heart.
And I forget where it says in the movie song,
When are you going to realize that it was just the timing that was wrong, Juliet?
We came up on different streets; they both were streets of shame
Both streets were dirty and both streets were mean.
Yes, and the dream was just the same.
And I dreamed your dream for you, and now your dream is real.
How can you look at me as if I am just another one of your deals?
When you can fall for chains of silver,
You can fall for chains of gold.
You can fall for pretty strangers and the promises they hold.
You promised me everything,
You promised thick and thin.
And now you just say, "Romeo,"
"Oh, I used to play this same old scene!"
Juliet, when we made love you used to cry.
I said I loved you like the stars above, and I'll love you till I die!
There's a place for us like in the movie song.
When are you going to realize that it was just the timing that was wrong? Juliet?
I can't do the talk like the talk on the TV
And I can't do a love song like the way it's meant to be.
I can't do everything, but I'll do anything for you.
I can't do anything right now but be in love with you.
All I do is miss you and the way it used to be.
All I do is keep the beat with my band as company.
All I do is kiss you, although only in my mind.
Juliet, I'll do the stars with you anytime.

> Juliet, my dear, remember when you told me, "I love you like the stars up in the sky?"
> I'll tell you now that I'll love you till I die.
> For there is a place for us like in the movie song.
> When are you going to realize that it was just the timing that went wrong?
> Now, love-struck Romeo, singing in the streets a serenade,
> Laying everybody low, with the love song that he made.
> Behind a convenient streetlight, he stepped out of the shade,
> And says something like "You and me, babe, how about it?"

And so this is the everlasting tale of the story made in Verona, Italy. It reminds us that nothing is a sure thing. Anything can happen in life as on the soccer or baseball field. What matters is what we do next. The best-laid plan for the prizefighter changes when he gets hit with a blow that puts him down onto the canvas as he lands on the seat of his pants.

"Get up," stand up, never give up, and don't worry about a thing. Everything will be all right. Draw on your inner strength, and you really can persevere. So you had a bad day, but the sun shall rise tomorrow, as goes a song from a Broadway hit, *Annie*. And remember, you shall rise with it! This was our credo in Ridgewood, New York City. Let it serve as an example to all.

## Como Bella che la Verona

How beautiful is my Verona. To me, it is the most beautiful place I have ever seen. If I would have had the choice, I ever would have left her. However, the choice was not mine to make when my tour of duty as a military dependent came to an end, after our three-year stay ran its course. If ever I would leave you, my Verona...

> It wouldn't be in summer,
> Seeing you in summer, I never would go.
> Your dawn streaked with sunlight,
> Your dusk red with flame,
> Your town has a luster,
> That puts gold to shame.
> But if I would ever leave you,
> It couldn't be in autumn,
> How I'd leave in autumn,
> I never would know.
> I've seen how you sparkle, when fall nips the air.
> I know you in autumn, and I must be there.
> And could I leave you, as it begins to snow?
> Or on a wintry evening sunlight with such a glow?
> If ever I would leave you,
> How could it be in springtime?
> Knowing how in spring, 'm bewitched by you so.
> Oh no, not in springime, summer, winter or fall.
> No never would I leave you, at all!

But we had to return to the states because we were military, and those were our orders. Destiny awaited me at Yankee Stadium as a high school phenom. Destiny had me choose to play baseball on scholarship at either St. John's or Long Island Universities as a division 1 shortstop.

Destiny made me refuse offers to play in the *grande ligas*, the major leagues, with the Boston Red Sox or the Philadelphia Phillies.

Destiny brought me to Ridgewood, New York City, where my team of soccer players went on a streak that will never be duplicated. I will never forget my Verona, but I had a date with destiny.

# Chapter 9

# Flash Forward

Flash forward to August 14, 1963, and I was playing third base for the New York City All-Star team at Yankee Stadium. Everyone wanted tickets—all my friends, my family, and teammates. Twenty thousand people filled the stands. I had come a long way from Verona, Italy, except for one thing that brought back memories of my Red Sox Little League team. It was a phone call.

After an arduous five-week tryout period requiring daily subway treks to the parade grounds in Brooklyn, I had been chosen as one of the best baseball players in New York City. And now, twenty thousand people, including family and friends, were now standing and cheering. They would not sit down.

Tom Sowinski, our pitcher, turned to me and said, "Charlie, you have to tip your cap. They won't sit down and stop until you tip your cap." So I tipped my cap while standing at third base in Yankee Stadium, and they all returned to their seats. As that famous Yankee broadcaster used to say, "How about that!"

It happened so fast, but I remembered it well. The ball was struck hard to my left. There was no time for anything but a flat out dive into the five hole, as they called that area of a baseball diamond. It was a one hopper, and it was by me, but it didn't get by my mitt as I snagged it in the webbing. A roar went up, the likes of which I haven't heard since Sunday in Verona, Italy. There was much screaming from my buddies in the nearby third base dugout.

"Get up! Get up, Charlie. You have a play!"

They were going nuts in that dugout. As loud as they were screaming, I could hardly hear them. The runner was well on his way with a base hit, and the crowd roar was subsiding to what sounded like whisper. Somehow my right knee acted as a brake, and I spun off it and found myself on both knees. There was no way, he was almost there. I fired it from my knees, and the silence was deafening until that ball hit the first baseman's glove for a photo finish out.

Yankee Stadium was now in an uproar for the second time—first for the catch and now for the determined effort to finish the play with that throw from the knees. They would not relent until I tipped that cap! Dad was there, and he saw it all. It was awesome and bewildering that all these people at this moment loved what they just saw that much. I was stunned.

Al Harper of the Boston Red Sox called to speak to my dad the next day. From the Little League Red Sox of 1957 to the Boston Red Sox of 1963—how about that! They spoke for a good long while, both being baseball men. An interest in me was expressed by the Boston Red Sox, and an offer was made to my dad on my behalf. I had already signed a letter of intent to attend Long Island University on a baseball scholarship. Lou Carnesecca of St. John's University had sat next to me on the team bus and gave me his card.

"I like your style, kid," he said. "We could sure use you at St. John's University."

"What do we do, Dad?"

The US Army draft made the decision for us. I was soon classified 1A unless there was good cause supported by proof for a reclassification. The handwriting was on the wall.

"Pride of New York"

"Versatility J-A All-Star Mark"

The draft board took baseball players and Long Island, and St. John's University took student athletes who could maintain their grades. Dad and I felt that the LIU offer was the one to take presently so that I may one day become a teacher.

He said, "If you are that good, Charlie, in four years, have a college degree."

And he was right on both counts. So before attending LIU in the fall, I spent the summer playing baseball for Lou Lamoriello in the Cape Cod Summer League for college baseball players. Lou Lamoriello is now inducted into the National Hockey League Hall of Fame, and I am so proud to have played for him. He also liked my style as a switch-hitting shortstop and gave me the nickname "Chico," and it stuck.

September came soon enough, and I enrolled at LIU in all the required courses and had room to enroll in a soccer program, making friends with Carlo Tramontozzi, who went on to assist the Azzurri Italian world cup soccer team. The years passed with me playing baseball and earning my teaching degree at LIU. Toward the end of my senior year, Dick Vining, the coach, summoned me to his office after a game.

"Charlie," he said. "The Philadelphia Phillies just called. They want to know if you will sign with them."

"Sure, Coach. I would be happy to accept their offer." Dad was right again, and indeed I was good enough!

Then came the night of the ping-pong ball draft, and my birthday came up on the eighteenth ball. If you drew anywhere from 1 to 180, the chances were good that you would be drafted. Vietnam came calling. The handwriting was on the wall.

"So good-bye to the major leagues," my dad said sadly as we were watching a Yankee game from the mezzanine seats. "Look down there on that field, Charlie. Do you see those players down there? You are as good as any one of them."

A letter from the principal, Dr. Phillip Grossier at Grover Cleveland High School was sent to the draft board since soccer was a great part of the community. The request was put into the US Army to allow the community to retain the person who is as desperately in need here in Ridgewood, Queens, NYC.

"Can you coach soccer?" was the critical question asked by the chairman, Edmund Michael. There were hundreds of people in line for this teaching position ahead of me. They had seniority, but they knew nothing of soccer.

"Where did you learn all of what you need to know since this community is very proud, mostly Europeans, and will insist on a winner. Where did you learn your soccer?" came the question again.

Thoughts of Sergio and his song entered my mind as the answer came from me with great conviction. "I learned my soccer in Italy, in Piazza Bra, near the Castelvecchio Bridge, next to the river Adige in a town called Verona."

He gave me the schedule for the games, and the rest is history. And wait till you hear about that!

It all began at Piazza Bra, a place far away a time long ago.

The college years seemed to fly by and cumulated with a bachelor's degree in education. Long Island University offered me an athletic scholarship to play division 1 shortstop for the baseball team coached by Dick Vining. I would have preferred the offer made by Lou Carnesecca of St. John's, but I decided to settle for Long Island University since they offered a degree in education. I come from Queens, New York City, and that is where St. John's is located. I remain regretful about that decision. Lou Carnesecca gave me his card and told me he liked my style. Lou Carnesecca is Italian and so am I. It would have been a better fit.

Long Island University sounded nice to hear but it is located a mile from the Brooklyn Bridge and right on Flatbush Avenue. It was a real dump, but I could not take the chance of being drafted into the army by attending St. John's, so when you have no choice, a decision comes easy. So I settled for third rate when I could have had first rate due to pressures of which I had no control. Now don't get me wrong, Long Island University isn't such a bad place, it is a terrible place!

I can remember playing third base and twenty feet to my right witnessing a robber running from the police as I am trying to concentrate on baseball. The police had his gun raised over his head and is in hot pursuit. How would you like to play baseball in a place like that?

The baseball field was located in the shadow of the dormitory building. The pitcher would be on the mound in the sunshine, and he would pitch to the batters who would be in the shade! How would you like to hit under those conditions? It was the worst field I ever played on in my life.

Every single player on the team lived in Brooklyn except yours truly. Finally, as a sophomore, I got my first chance to play and proceeded to go four for four! After the game, in the locker room, the player whose place I took in the lineup proceeded to smash his bat to bits against his locker and no one told him to stop. He was a catcher and he was a senior and he was from Brooklyn. I was a shortstop and I was a sophomore and I'm from Queens. *Too bad for you,* I thought.

So I spent four years doing time with all the Brooklyn hotshots who thought who the heck they were. However, there was one who came from Staten Island. Maybe that was his saving grace. He was special, so we took classes together in our sophomore year, and I made sure he passed the courses he had arranged to take with me, if you catch my drift. His name was Terry Crowley, and he had little patience for school, but he could hit a baseball better than anyone I had ever seen. He never saw his junior year, and the Baltimore Orioles signed him to their major league team where he performed very well, and he made us all very proud to have played with him. I liked Terry and I liked his dad too. Mr. Crowley was a baseball man from Staten Island and came to our games that season. We went to play Pratt University, and the umpire didn't show up for the game, so Mr. Crowley put on the chest protector and yelled, "Play ball!"

Wayne Sunderland was the coach of Pratt, and the score was 4 to 1 in their favor late in the game. Mr. Crowley had done a fine job, but Terry couldn't break through that day. I would kind of feel funny if my dad was sitting there behind me calling balls and strikes. I wouldn't feel relaxed. Although you may be aware of the final score from a previous page, the particulars are worth describing.

We were down 4 to 1, and the bases became loaded, and it was my turn to come to the batter's box. The count quickly got to 1 and 1, and I was looking for a pitch. The 1 and 1 pitch was a little inside, and I lined it hard into right field, but it hooked foul at the last minute. I was up there left-handed now because the pitcher was right-handed and his curveball would naturally break into my swing and not away from the swing. And so it broke in too far for me to straighten it out. I had taken off to first base only to have to return to the batter's box. When I returned to the box, I was greeted with a huge wink and a nod from the umpire! The count was 1 and 2 now, and in came the heater. Now right field at Pratt University is deeply set with a hill leading up to a twenty-foot fence. The hill is so far back that the right fielder would only venture there to retrieve a ground ball that may get that far. The fence is there to protect the cars and pedestrians. It was the right fielder who shouted through the fence to a pedestrian to fetch the ball and throw it back in over the fence. The game was over, and he came in to give me the ball, which I have to this day.

Mr. Crowley shook my hand and said, "What a shot, Charlie." With a son like he had, I guess he would know a shot when he sees one because Terry had shown him many to be sure. The coach of Pratt never forgot that shot, and his memory of that moment prevented Coach Vining and I from being reunited at Post University. I think he owed Vining for that bitter loss. He knew Vining wanted me to get the soccer position, and that alone was enough for him to make sure that I didn't get the job. Even though I was the best, he could have ever had to coach at CW Post University.

We went in to play St. John's shortly after that game, and I thought it was a beautiful field basking in full sunlight with not a trace of that ambiguous shade, and I opened up with a long triple to left field. But it was the play that occurred in foul territory that I will always remember. I was playing first base that day, and a high pop up to me was drifting to my left into foul territory. I went quickly to the ten-foot fence and stuck my spike into the chain link to climb the fence and put my mitt over the top of the fence to snag the ball for the out.

Immediately I heard someone in the St. John's dugout say, "Nice play, kid."

I looked over to see who said that. It was Lou Carnesecca. We looked at each other briefly, and he said, "Like I told you, kid, I like your style!" I never heard anyone say that to me back in Brooklyn. The house I lived in was two miles away. Boy, did this place feel comfortable to play baseball. Cold have done real well here. This is where I belonged. I'm from Queens, not Brooklyn. A tree grows best in the soil it feels most comfortable. This tree didn't grow in Brooklyn. *A Tree Grows in Brooklyn* was just the title of a book.

As the son of an army officer, I really looked forward to West Point. West Point was on the schedule, and that would be a real treat because I am an army brat and looked forward to this game more than any other on the schedule. We had a fine lunch in the very hall where General Douglas MacArthur gave his rousing farewell speech to the cadets in attendance at that time. I was eating my fruit salad with the rabble from Brooklyn when I looked across the room to the next table with awe and immense respect at the plebes sitting erect and awaiting the order for them to begin their meal. I knew this. I knew what this was—"duty, honor, country." Macarthur's words rang from the ramparts in this dining hall. These were the best of us, and I am getting the chance for a lifetime to break bread with them. No wonder MacArthur felt that on his last day as he crossed the river to the other side, he felt he would owe it all to the corps, to the corps, and to the corps.

However awestruck I was that day and however the high esteem I had for the army, in my life, first and foremost, came baseball. So when the game began, I promptly hit a three-run shot off the armory building in deep left field.

It was a right-handed bomb, and as I trotted around first base, one of the plebes in the crowd started yelling, "Charlie, Charlie! It's you!"

It was Stanley Parker, my first baseman from Little League, Italy. We hugged each other, and I said hello to all his buddies, and he told them, "I thought it was you. I told my friends I know a ballplayer who moves just like that first baseman, only he was a shortstop, so that can't be him. But when you hit that shot, Charlie, I knew it really was you. That swing is the same no matter what position you play. I would recognize that swing anywhere." It was wonderful to see Stanley after all these years—a fitting end to a wonderful day. I must remind you that everything you read here really happened. This is a true story.

Another true story is that the further away I went from Brooklyn, the better I played.

Well, apparently the Philadelphia Phillies thought, so upon graduation an offer came across Coach Vining's desk asking if I would sign with them; but Vietnam was still an issue, and although I loved the army, I had spent four years studying to become a teacher. Stanley made his choice, and I made mine. So upon graduation, I began to seek out a teaching job. I put on a shirt and tie and combed my hair to look the part. I took the patch off my team blue blazer and wore it for good luck as I interviewed for a high school job. Someone at John Browne High School suffered an appendicitis attack, and they took me as a temporary replacement. I notified the draft board. I had a job, but there was a last baseball hurrah coming my way!

I was to report to work as a teacher in September when Paul Larocca, a minor league teammate of Pete Rose, asked me to play shortstop for his summer team. He told me that Sid Gordon was the third base coach. Sid's son, Dick, was to play third base. I had Sid Gordon's baseball card. Dad knew who he was—a power hitter who had many major league seasons under his belt. This offer was too good to refuse.

I had a really good summer and received a call from head New York Yankee scout Arthur Dede. He wanted Sam Giordano, who works for him, to come down to our next double header. Sam Giordano arrived early for the first game and said he came down to take a look at me, and we shook hands. A right hander was pitching for the Hempstead Elks against Larocca's plate and went 1 for 3. After a brief respite between the second game, the Elks chose to start Bob Bartlett, their fire-balling lefty. I had played with Bob the summer before with the Elks, and he may have had a bone to pick with me, since Skip Jutze and I were the big players on that Elk team. Skip went on to catch several seasons for the Houston Astros or the Minnesota Twins; I'm not sure which team exactly.

So Skip was gone and I was gone and Bob may have resented that because what happened next never happened to me before or since. And I'm sure what happened shortly after that to Bob probably never happened to him before or since.

I was about to step in on the right side of the plate when the pitch came in so hard you could actually hear it whiz by for a strike. The umpire felt that it was a legal pitch, and everyone on my bench objected. Sid Gordon called time out to question the call, but to no avail. It was a super heater, and even though I wasn't prepared, I did see it very well and I memorized the speed and the sound. I was pissed off big time and I thought, *Bring it again and bring it now.* Before I forget the memory, bring it now, the same pitch. For this is the way of a hitter; always thinking, always playing chess, always studying the sequence. But he had to bring it now while my timing device was set. He did. He brought the express in exactly the same speed and exactly the same spot.

What happened next was the single pinnacle of achievement in my baseball career. The ball was struck with the force of a swing that only anger can generate. So there was a super pitch met by a super swing. It's a one in a million chance. It looked like a golf ball as it disappeared fully two hundred feet directly over the left-fielder's head. All three outfielders ran in to meet me as trotted around second base. They couldn't believe it. No one had ever seen anything like it ever. Pandemonium broke out from both dugouts. No one could sit down to resume the game for ten full minutes.

Sid Gordon grabbed me by the shoulders in order to hold me still and shouted in great excitement, "Look at me, Charlie. Listen to me. Listen to what I am going to say to you. I played in the big leagues for many years, and I hit 240 big league home runs. I played against Mickey Mantle, Duke Snider, and Willie Mays, and I have never seen a ball hit that far in my whole life." It came down on the fly in some other field where they saw what happened and marked the spot for measurement. The baseball traveled 575 feet on the fly, and Dick and Sid Gordon are my witness.

"Did Giordano see the shot?" I asked Sid. We both looked around and were told he had left the field a few minutes ago to scout another player. The handwriting was on the wall. I never played another inning of baseball again. That was my last swing. The handwriting was on the wall.

September 1960 arrived quickly after the summer day when Sid Gordon saw me hit the longest homerun he had ever seen in his life. I reported for duty at Grover Cleveland High School in Ridgewood, New York City. I was selected the new soccer coach and received the schedule from Mr. Ed Michael, the chairman of the Health and Physical Education Department. The first game would be played in two weeks, and I haven't even met the team. I learned to play soccer in Italy, but this would be my first attempt at coaching. The prior coach had unceremoniously departed for greener pastures, and I understood the team was in a state of disarray.

There will be no miracle in the making during this inaugural season as soccer coach. The two or three years before had taken its toll on the remnants of the school team. This was division "A" soccer, New York City. Out on that field were talented players whose parents had come to settle here from all over the world. New York City has been famous for generations as a melting pot of diversity. These players were as serious and dedicated to their sport as I had been to mine. *What have I gotten myself into?* I thought as we absorbed one loss after another until mercifully, the season came to an inglorious close. So the hotshot baseball player wasn't such a hotshot anymore; but experience is the best of all teachers, and I learned volumes from all I had seen from the high-caliber coaching and playing demonstrated by teams all over the city.

Back at Piazza Bra in Verona, Italy, the games were played for fun among many friends and one "Americani." This was different. Here they were playing for school and neighborhood pride. In addition, each player had a burning need to represent his culture. This was fierce competition. Like my dad said when we would walk down to Piazza Bra to watch the boys play and try to understand, it looked like mass chaos. This was highly organized team soccer. All the boys played for sports clubs during the year, and they lived, ate, and drank soccer. I knew the feeling, but for another sport. We met in the gymnasium after the season and made a deal that this would never happen again. I left them with a hopeful expression my dad taught me from baseball. "Wait till next year!"

Teaching at Cleveland was a joy, and I loved being able to help youngsters learn to enjoy and improve skills while interacting with other classmates. However, that season troubled me because I never had a season like that as a baseball player. This was new to me and so I studied hard at graduate school, where I attended three nights a week in pursuit of a master's degree. I took seats in the back of the classrooms three nights a week and studied soccer. It was intense studying to match what I had seen to what I could find in the books.

I soaked it all up like a sponge. My knowledge of chess provided me with an expedited way to connect with the dogma. In soccer there are wings. There are midfielders. There are fullbacks. Some players possess the skills to play only one of those positions. Some are gifted enough to play more than one and perhaps even several positions. In chess, there are knights, there are pawns, there are bishops, and there are rooks. There are knights and even a king and a queen. How medieval can you get? It is a wonderful game, or as I prefer to see it, a wonderful battle. As General George Patton would say, "God help me, but I love the smell of battle." Chess is a game of war; it is not a friendly game. It is serious and highly intellectual. My dad used to watch me play when I was a kid in the Italian chess club, and he would say, "How the heck do you know what is going on there?"

I would reply, "Just like you know what's going on out there."

The only difference between soccer and chess in a certain aspect is that soccer has someone in the "hot corner." Soccer has a third baseman. Soccer has a goaltender. My advantage over others is based on the bedrock of knowledge acquired from chess, baseball, and soccer. Do you know all three like the back of your hand? No? Poor baby, then you are no match for me, are you?

Positions. I am talking about positions. I learned their abilities and capabilities along with their limitations while taking my lumps this first season, and now I can say, "Rommel, I read your book!" The comparisons go like this. The wings on the soccer field basically move north to south in a longitudinal fashion. The rooks on the chess board move in the same fashion. The halfbacks on the soccer field are more talented and have a more deliberate manner about their mobility and purpose, or more lethal, if you will. The bishops on the chess board move in a diagonal manner that is more difficult for the eye to discern. If you have a good halfback, he may be referred to as a cut-and-slash type, much like the bishop on the chess board. Soccer has two of each and chess has two of each. However, as the battle rages out on the soccer field, you may need to, out of necessity or by design, employ two more midfielders, or halfbacks, as they are called. That would bring your total to four, if you were so disposed out of necessity. They say that necessity is the mother of invention. They also say that three is company but four is a crowd. As you like it; that sounded a little like Shakespeare, didn't it? I'm sorry if I just confused you, but that's what I do! The knights are a pair of characters in that they move in an L-shaped manner up and down, left and right, and assist the control and domination of the game predomitably in the region known as midfield or the central areas of the chess board, but there are exceptions to the rule. They also say that every rule is made to be broken. One may begin to see the awesome implications here on both genres with regard to firepower in tandem with logistical support. Wow! I saw all this out there this past season with my own eyes, and this analogy is helping to bring everything into focus.

Chess has an outstanding player. She is able to move north, south, east, or west at a moment's notice. What a gal! Her biggest problem though is one of responsibility. You see, she has to stay home and protect the king. However, if she sees the opportunity and is wise, she can actually determine the outcome of the game. Soccer has the "*libero*," a name called out frequently at Piazza Bra. *Libero* means "free," but once again, be calculating with your freedom as you are found near your goaltender at one moment and then on a rush toward the other goal tender on a special ops mission.

Earlier, I mentioned a lack of chess to equate a piece equivalent to be goal position. However, the king may be comparable. If the ball gets past the goaltender in soccer, it could be decisive to the outcome of the game. In chess, if the king is not protected, at a moment's notice checkmate may occur out of the blue and the game is over. Both require help and support from all of the other participants. So there is a similarity. Last but by no means least are the pawns. There are many of them, and they do not appear imposing in stature, but they are crucial to the outcome. A pawn may only move one square in any direction so a pawn has limitations more than any except he who wears the crown. The only difference is that he who wears the crown is king, and alas, the pawns must realize that they will never rise to that lofty post. Or will they? Look what happened to Cinderella. The substitute players are salt of the earth for the soccer team. They stand alongside me on the sidelines and cheer their buddies on. Practice without them would be impossible. There are many of them and they are vital, and they realize what MacArthur realized when he was removed from Corregidor—that Wainwright and his men were expendable. It is a tough role to fill, and these are the ones who need to be appreciated more than any aforesaid components. And don't be surprised if out of their ranks emerges some very special people who are honor bound to help the cause.

From that day I mentioned earlier at West Point, when I thought of MacArthur making his speech at the dining hall where I was having lunch, he swore never to forget the corps, the corps, and the corps. It rings true to me that I never forgot chess, chess, and chess. There is an analogy. West Point among many things is where our fine young men and women are trained in battle tactics and strategies. Much of that particular training comes from studying actual historical accounts of battles fought, battles won, and battles lost. That is how they learn, and what better example to follow than the one pursued at West Point Military Academy. If it is mandatory curriculum for them, then it is mandatory curriculum for me—and for you as well!

Now what did I see of strategies and tactics? What did I see of various styles and methods of play? What did I see, and where can I find these in the books written by those who have traveled these waters before? I cranked up my outboard. What I have seen worked so well against me that I find it worthy of imitation. Each opponent had a style that worked well and took awhile to decipher. However, we improved during the final half of the season, which indicates we all learned a lot. Maybe that's why they all showed up for the "wait till next year" speech. What did I see? Where is it in this book I checked out at the library?

Remember the library? Once I find what I saw in the book, then I will know the enemy, or as they say in Latin, I will *nosce hostem*.

The college years seemed to fly by and cumulated with a bachelor's degree in education. Long Island University offered me an athletic scholarship to play Division I shortstop for the baseball team coached by Dick Vining. I would have preferred the offer made by Lou Carnesseca of St. John's, but I decided to settle for Long Island University since they offered a degree in education. I come from Queens, New York City, and that is where St. John's is located. I remain regretful about that decision. Lou Carnesseca gave me his card and told me he liked my style. Lou Carnesseca is Italian, and so am I. It would have been a better fit.

Long Island University sounds nice to hear, but it is located a mile from the Brooklyn Bridge and right on Flatbush Avenue. It was a real dump, but I could not take the chance of being drafted into the army by attending St. John's. When you have no choice, a decision comes easy. So I settled for third rate when I could have had first rate due to pressures of which I had no control. Now don't get me wrong. Long Island University isn't such a bad place—it is a terrible place!

I can remember playing third base and, twenty feet to my right, witnessing a robber running from the police as I was trying to concentrate on baseball. The cop had his gun raised over his head and was in hot pursuit. How would you like to play baseball in a place like that?

The baseball field was located in the shadow of the dormitory building. The pitcher would be on the mound in the sunshine, and he would pitch to the batters who would be in the shade! How would you like to hit under those conditions? It was the worst field I had ever played on in my life.

However, that field on the Long Island University campus served a dual purpose. Baseball, of course, begins in the spring and consummates sometime in June. It was soccer that caught my attention during the fall semester. Long Island University athletic teams would compete under the nickname of "Blackbirds." This was certainly an appropriate name for that soccer team. They represented us very well.

I would marvel as they seemed to fly up and down that field like the blackbirds they were. They taught us baseball players a lesson in what intensity can bring to a sport. At halftime, we shared the locker room and would readily see the bumps and bruises on their legs. Parts of the field remained embedded on their arms and face! It appeared as though they truly needed this brief respite from their battle. They would always demonstrate a degree of relentless effort that could only end with the sound of the whistle.

I became proud of them, and that softened my position about Long Island University. That field was not designed for baseball, and that disappointed me. However, during the fall, it was a wonderful field on which my friends played their beautiful game. My interest was keen due to the experience of my early years down at Piazza Bra, in Verona, Italy. My repeated attempts to have my baseball teammates watch were met with a result just as fruitless now as they were then back in Verona, Italy. Once again, my teammates didn't realize what they were missing.

As mentioned earlier, Carlo Tramontozzi became a good friend. I think he liked the way I played shortstop, and I know the reason. He played medio campo and la ale the way I played shortstop. We are both Italian, and we played like only Italians can play. We played with heart and emotion. He went on to coach St. Francis University in New York City for many successful seasons, in addition to assisting the Azzuri. I would model many of our players at Cleveland over the years after Carlos—he was not a big man but was very versatile and could do many jobs. I would need this type of player in the years ahead.

And then I made an acquaintance with the type of player I would never have in all my years down the road. A classic center forward who could move about the field with the speed and grace of a gazelle, Dov Markus had the size, speed, tenacity, and cunning of the true goal scorer. "Hey, Charlie, how did you guys do?" he would ask about the baseball team in that heavy Israeli accent that seemed to fit the part he played.

But as good as Dov was, he needed a partner, just as certain as I needed a second baseman. And he was fortunate enough to have the perfect partner in Dieter Ficken. Each of these was a handful in their own right, but as a combination, they complimented each other exponentially. Dieter was the classic "technical" soccer player. He was quick, agile, fundamentally sound, and equally adept at logistics of attack or defense. He was the type of player around which you could build a team. I was fortunate to have that type many times in Ridgewood in the trials and tribulations of the coming years.

Dieter went on to coach for many successful years at Columbia University in Manhattan, New York City. A few years ago, he coached at CW Post University. I went to see a game one fall afternoon. After the game, I approached him and said, "Hi, Dieter, it's Charlie. Do you remember me?" And his immediate response was, "Sure I do. You're the baseball player." We spoke of old friends, and we spoke of soccer. There were ideas of mine that began to become interesting to him, and at the end of our meeting, he mentioned that one could never learn enough.

Now there was yet another Blackbird that indeed seemed to be the leader of that soccer team. I knew Joe Machnik as a fearless competitor and would seek in my goaltenders his attributes during the ensuing years. He now serves as a commissioner for the worldwide soccer organization known as FIFA.

I would be fortunate to have a goaltender like Joe Machnik. Eugene DuChateau went on to play pro soccer for the Roughnecks, and he was the best goalie I ever saw. I even had the luck of a Dieter Ficken–type named Bill Easteadt to captain my team at Cleveland. He would eventually go on to become the best soccer coach CW Post University ever had with many winning seasons.

The point raised here is that I had a visual side to help me in player development at the key positions. These "Four Horsemen of the Apocalypse" became the blueprint I needed to build, as an architect would, my powerful team of Ridgewood, from the high school known as Cleveland, in the big apple known as New York. To the "Four Horsemen," I can only say,

> Forget all your cares and woes,
> Singing low, here we go,
> Bye Bye Blackbird

No one seems to know
Or understand me,
Oh, what hardluck stories
They all hand me
I'll pack my bags
If you light the light
I'll be home late tonight
Blackbirds Bye Bye!

Every single player on the team lived in Brooklyn, except yours truly. Finally, as a sophomore, I got my first chance to play and proceeded to go four for four! After the game, in the locker room, the player whose place I took in the lineup proceeded to smash his bat to bits against his locker, and no one told him to stop. He was a catcher and he was a senior and he was from Brooklyn. *I'm a shortstop and I'm a sophomore and I'm from Queens. Too bad for you*, I thought.

So I spent four years doing time with all the Brooklyn hotshots who thought who the heck they were. However, there was one who came from Staten Island. Maybe that was his saving grace. He was special. So we took classes together in our sophomore year, and I made sure he passed the courses he had arranged to take with me, if you catch my drift. His name was Terry Crowley, and he had little patience for school, but he could hit a baseball better than anyone I had ever seen. He never saw his junior year, and the Baltimore Orioles signed him to their major league team, where he performed very well, and he made us all very proud to have played with him. I liked Terry, and I liked his Dad, too. Mr. Crowley was a baseball man from Staten Island and came to our games that season. We went to play Pratt University, and the umpire didn't show up for the game, so Mr. Crowley put on the chest protector and yelled, "Play ball!"

Wayne Sunderland was the coach of Pratt, and the score was 4–1 in their favor late in the game. Mr. Crowley had done a fine job, but Terry couldn't break through that day. I would kind of feel funny if my dad was sitting there behind me, calling balls and strikes; I wouldn't feel relaxed.

We were down 4–1, and the bases became loaded, and it was my turn to come to the batter's box. The count quickly got to one and one, and I was looking for a pitch. The one and one pitch was a little inside, and I lined it hard into right field, but it fouled at the last minute. I was up there left handed now because the pitcher was right handed and his curveball would naturally break into my swing and not away from the swing. And so it broke in too far for me to straighten it out. I had taken off to first base, only to have to return to the batter's box. When I returned to the box, I was greeted with a huge wink and a nod from the umpire!

The count was one and two now, and in came the heater. Now the right field at Pratt University was deeply set with a hill leading up to a twenty-foot fence. The hill was so far back that the right fielder would only venture there to retrieve a ground ball that may get that far. The fence was there to protect the cars and pedestrians. It was the right fielder who shouted through the fence to a pedestrian to fetch the ball and throw it back in over the fence.

The game was over, and he came in to give me the ball, which I have to this day. Mr. Crowley shook my hand and said, "What a shot, Charlie!" With a son like he had, I guess he would know a shot when he sees one because Terry had shown him many to be sure. The coach of Pratt never forgot that shot, and his memory of that moment prevented Coach Vining and I from being reunited at Post University. I think he owed Vining for that bitter loss. He knew Vining wanted me to get the soccer position, and that alone was enough for him to make sure that I didn't get the job. Even though I was the best for it, he could have ever had to coach at CW Post University.

<<<MISSING PAGES 170-177>>>

The comparisons go like this. The wings on the soccer field basically move north to south in a longitudinal fashion. The rooks on the chessboard move in the same fashion. The halfbacks on the soccer field are more talented and have a more deliberate manner about their mobility and purpose, or more lethal, if you will. The bishops on the chess board move in a diagonal manner, which is more difficult for the eye to discern. If you have a good halfback, he may be referred to as a cut-and-slash type, much like the bishop on the chess board. Soccer has two of each, and chess has two of each. However, as the battle rages out on the soccer field, you may need to, out of necessity or by design, employ two more midfielders, or halfbacks, as they are called. That would bring your total to four if you were so disposed out of necessity. They say that necessity is the mother of invention. They also say that three is company, but four is a crowd—as you like it. That sounded a little like Shakespeare, didn't it? I'm sorry if I just confused you, but that's what I do!

The knights are a pair of characters in that they move in an L-shaped manner up and down, left and right, and assist the control and domination of the game predominately in the region known as midfield, or the central areas of the chessboard, but there are exceptions to the rule.

They also say that every rule is made to be broken. One may begin to see the awesome implications here on both genres with regard to firepower in tandem with logistical support. Wow! I saw all this out there this past season with my own eyes and this analogy was helping to bring everything into focus.

Chess has an outstanding player. She is able to move north, south, east, or west at a moments notice. What a gal! Her biggest problem though is one of responsibility. You see, she has to stay home and protect the king. However, if she sees the opportunity and is wise, she can actually determine the outcome of the game. Soccer has the libero, a name called out frequently at piazza Bra. Libero means "free," but once again be calculating with your freedom as you are found near your goaltender at one moment and then on a rush toward the other goal tender on a special-ops mission.

Earlier, I mentioned a lack of chess to equate a piece equivalent to the goal position. However, the king may be comparable. If the ball gets past the goaltender in soccer, it could be decisive to the outcome of the game. In chess, if the king is not protected, at a moment's notice, checkmate may occur out of the blue and the game is over. Both require help and support from all of the other participants. So there is a similarity.

Last, but by no means least, are the pawns. There are many of them, and they do not appear imposing in stature, but they are crucial to the outcome. A pawn may only move one square in any direction, so a pawn has limitations more than any, except he who wears the crown. The only difference is that he who wears the crown is king, and alas, the pawns must realize that they will never rise to that lofty post. Or will they? Look what happened to Cinderella.

The substitute players are salt of the earth for the soccer team. They stand alongside me on the sidelines and cheer their buddies on. Practice without them would be impossible. There are many of them, and they are vital. They realize what MacArthur realized when he was removed from Corregidor—that Wainright and his men were expendable. It is a tough role to fill, and these are the ones who need to be appreciated more than any aforesaid components. And don't be surprised if out of their ranks emerges some very special people who are honor bound to help the cause.

From that day I mentioned earlier at West Point, when I thought of MacArthur making his speech at the dining hall where I was having lunch, he swore never to forget the corps, the corps, and the corps. It rings true to me that I never forgot chess, chess, and chess. There is an analogy. West Point, among many things, is where our fine men and women are trained in battle tactics and strategies. Much of that particular training comes from studying actual historical accounts of battles fought. Battles won and battles lost. That is how they learn and what better example to follow than the one pursued at West Point. If it is mandatory curriculum for them, then it is mandatory curriculum for me. And for you as well!

Now what did I see of strategies and tactics? What did I see of various styles and methods of play? What did I see and where can I find these in the books written by those who have traveled these waters before? I cranked up my outboard. What I have seen worked so well against me that I find it worthy of imitation. Each opponent had a style that worked well and took awhile to decipher. However, we improved during the final half of the season, which indicated we all learned a lot. Maybe that's why they all showed up for the "Wait till next year" speech. What did I see? Where would it be in this book I checked out at the library? Remember the library? Once I'd find it in the book, then I'd know the enemy, or I would nosce hostem.

# Chapter 10

# Ridgewood N.Y.C.

Ridgewood has many tree-lined streets, and spring was in full swing when I first saw this beautiful community. Graduation from Long Island University brought me to this hamlet because they were in desperate need of a soccer coach. Blossoms from the trees were falling everywhere you looked. Even the blossoms were swept clean shortly after they hit the ground. *Could this be Camelot?* I thought as I entered Grover Cleveland High School for the first time to meet Chairman Edmund Michael for a job interview.

What do the simple folk do? Well, they sure keep the neighborhood looking good! Ed was a big man, and he, along with legendary coach Joe Singer, invited me into the office, and we sat at a round table. Ed immediately reminded me of King Arthur, and his elderly sidekick, Joe Singer, had all the appearances of Merlin. Could this be Camelot? I thought.

The church bells outside the open window were making their contribution as I began answering their questions. King Arthur needed a soccer coach and sent his heralds riding throughout the countryside. His orders were to tell every living person far and near that there is simply not in the world a spot where ruled a more resplendent soccer team than here in Camelot! Joe Singer had been the legendary coach. I haven't felt this way about a place since I left Verona, Italy. It is so distinctly European, and I knew I will bond to this neighborhood. I had already taken a liking to King Arthur and I was feeling that Merlin was taking a liking to the "kinder," as he was referring to me already with his consultations with his King.

Finally, the big question. "Where did you learn your soccer as this is a very proud community and will insist upon a winner. So where did you learn your soccer?"

"I learned my soccer in Piazza Bra, near the river Adige, which flows under the nearby Castelvecchio Bridge, through the town of Verona, in the magical land called Italy." A time long ago, in a place far away.

This was a neighborhood new to me but old in many ways. It felt somewhat similar to what I had known while living as an army dependent in Verona, Italy. I felt very comfortable in this part of New York City.

The season as coach flew by in a flash; however, I began to familiarize myself with all the streets and avenues in the area. It was decidedly European, and it was a pleasure for me to hear Italian spoken by old men at the outdoor cafe where some of my colleagues introduced me to sharing baked ziti and red wine after school on special occasions. There were church bells to be heard here during the school week, reminding me of Verona, Italy. Many languages were spoken in this area, and each of the European ethnic groups lived harmoniously on certain blocks where they felt most comfortable to be among their countrymen. These blocks were kept immaculate and were broom-swept daily by the prideful people who occupied the dwellings. There was a genuine warmth here that I thought I would never find again. I was one of these people, and I felt right at home here. I felt lucky and fortunate to have found such a wonderful place—or did it find me?

The deli across the street from school was owned and operated by an elderly woman fondly referred to by everyone from students to teachers as Mom. Roast beef with lettuce, tomato, and American cheese with salt, pepper, and mayo was the standard order my colleagues would request. The athletic director I worked for was a wonderful man who possessed great patience and kindness. Edmond Michael and I got along very well right from the beginning, and perhaps Mom, across the street, was partly responsible. If something came up where we did not see eye to eye, we tended to lock horns a little. The next day, I would pop up at lunchtime and knock on his office door.

He would answer with a serious face, and I would say, "Okay, Ed, what do you want for lunch. I'm going across the street to Mom's."

And Ed would say, "Get me a roast beef hero with lettuce, tomato, and American cheese, with salt, pepper, and mayo." And all was forgotten. Twenty-four-hour limit existed on any disagreement. We all had a job to do and some of us were headstrong, like yours truly. But with him as our fearless leader, we all did a splendid job teaching the youngsters to work together toward common goals and having a sense of humor while attending to our assigned task. The entire department had a riotous sense of humor, and the students loved us; this to the consternation of the more serious types, which populate every faculty. It was like Ed was King Arthur and the rest of us were his magnificent knights, and we all would help the rest of the population. We would even be chosen to protect the principal if a disturbance appeared to be brewing. I was chosen to stand outside his door just in case, because I was known as the baseball hotshot and was the fastest of the department. It is a good thing they chose me because I played linebacker for my neighborhood football team and threw the neatest cross body block on a belligerent student who got a little too "friendly" with the principal during class change in the hallway. I was starting to make my mark on the place.

I had a lot to live up to and first realized this when I saw the many championship soccer teams decorating the halls of the school. These teams were of a time gone by; however, their old coach was still teaching in the department. He was in all of the pictures.

Joe Singer was famous as a soccer coach. His teams were legendary, and a book called A *Goal for Greg* was published as a result of the notoriety. He gave me a copy after my second season. He referred fondly to me as the "kinder," which in German means the "kid." I felt that I had let him and the school down that first season as I do not believe in excuses.

I asked him for advice, and he replied, "Charlie, I have seen you play basketball with the students and with our basketball team after school. You know a lot about how to play that game. Use what you know about basketball and apply it to soccer. You will find it has a place out there."

I used football skills to protect the principal and now was advised to use basketball skills to assist the soccer team. I like the way they think around here, kind of like my dad, unorthodox but cool!

What Joe Singer didn't know happened during my senior year at Long Island University. The basketball coach at LIU was passing through the gymnasium and stopped abruptly as I was horsing around with my friends while playing three on three. Sergeant Beck had taught us well back in Verona, Italy. Baseball was the only sport I every took serious, so the ball would be pushed through my legs, behind my back, left-handed, right-handed, followed by a dipsy-do layup under the basket up and over my head with a big laugh attached. Two points!

"Time out!" Roy Rubin yelled, and the game came to an abrupt halt. He was a big man and known to be a stern disciplinarian.

"You shouldn't have fooled around," my buddies told me. "We feel sorry for you now."

"Charlie," he bellowed. "I need to speak to you for a minute."

I know, they are right! I'm in for it now.

"Listen," he said softly so no one else could hear. The marks were just posted and most of his basketball team had just failed off the roster. "Can you do me a favor and finish out the season for me?"

"Coach, I never played college basketball. Those guys are six foot eight—eight inches bigger than me."

"Just do what you do, and you'll do just fine. Help me out, *okay?*"

"Sure, Coach." The next night, we were bussed up to Bridgeport University, and I was dressed up in a shirt way too big for me. I sat on the bench, but I didn't mind; it looked rough out there. These guys were as big as trees.

Five minutes into the second half and one of the boys turned his ankle, and then I hear my name.

"Charlie, get in there for him!"

I don't know if it was from sheer fright or what you may choose to call it, but by game's end, I had contributed twenty-two points, and LIU won the game. The big guys took to me and made noises that sounded like *beep beep* after the Road Runner cartoon character they thought I resembled in my mad dash to score as many points before the final buzzer. Isn't that what basketball is all about? I finished the season for Roy Rubin and then went back to my final year of college baseball. Roy Rubin went on to become the basketball coach of the Philadelphia Seventy-Sixers. I dropped him a line after I learned he got the job, wishing him good luck and assuring him that if need be, I am ready to help him once again at a moment's notice. *Beep beep!*

Basketball philosophies worked for Joe Singer. He must have been a magician to even think of the idea. However, he was the elder here and reminded me of Merlin. He was wise.

Even big Ed listened when Joe Singer spoke. The pair, when taken in context, really did offer a King Arthur and Merlin combo. Joe Singer's suggestion was taken under advisement, it crossed my mind. What about football and even hockey? Could those be used to help us here as well? Oh, don't be ridiculous. From my baseball experiences, I know what pressure feels like, and after that first season, I was feeling it big time. This neighborhood sees soccer as a way of life, and I was getting the feelings that if I don't turn this thing around, I might not see this neighborhood again for the rest of my life. Years later, we had a saying around here: "If you play for Cleveland, then you have to love the pressure."

By the time the spring semester approached, the grade advisers in the building were acutely aware that there was someone in the building to whom they could send any non-English-speaking student. Either I could speak to the student directly if the student was Italian or Spanish, or I could summon one of my players to interpret if the student was German, Yugoslavian, Romanian, or Polish, as these were the predominant languages spoken by the foreign students at that time. I would arrange to assign a buddy to the newcomer to show him the ropes for a while and make for a comfortable adjustment. Eventually, all would learn to speak English, and then we threw them out of the next. I say "we" because the soccer team and I are growing together, and the sense of family has settled in among all of the newcomers. The reward for helping came down the road in the immense interest being built up from the outpouring of goodwill demonstrated by my players. Many saw our way and wanted to join our ranks. Something was building here. I had never known this type of thing before. With baseball, it was a cut-throat environment where you were only as good as your last game. If that were true here, then we wouldn't be much good for yourself or anybody else for that matter. But it is not true here.

Send them to me, I'll take care of them, don't worry about a thing. As time went by and the years would pass, I often wondered if I was taking care of them or they were taking care of me. Perhaps, at the end of this story, you can be the judge of that. I think I know the answer, and there is no "I" in the word team.

Have no fear, the pied piper is here! And the pied piper began to learn more and more that spring, and who was his teacher? His teachers were the Polish, the Germans, Italians, Yugoslavians, Romanians, Spanish, and even some from the Caribbean. They all had something to tell me or something to show me about the game they loved. Something was building here. Everyone was chipping in, and I was downloading as fast as my gigabytes would allow. My hard drive was constantly receiving new data to process. Could my software possibly accept all this information? We shall see! All this, and computers weren't even invented yet.

Ridgewood has many tree-lined streets, and spring was in full swing, with blossoms everywhere you look. Even the blossoms were swept clean shortly after they hit the ground. Could this be Camelot? What do the simple folk do? Well, they sure keep the neighborhood looking good. This place reminds me of Piazza Bra. Indeed, especially when the bells of the churches make their contribution. So, "a tree grows in Brooklyn." Well, this tree didn't grow at all in Brooklyn, but he's growing just fine here in this place.

During this first year here in Ridgewood, I had learned that this place gives a person pause.

> These are the legal laws.
> Here it never rains until after sundown.
> By eight in the morning, fog will disappear,
> The winter is forbidden until December,
> Due to laws made a distant moon ago here.

> The snow may never slush upon the hillside,
> By nine PM the moonlight must appear.
> The summer often lingers until September,
> Although I kind of like this time of year.
> This all may sound a bit bizarre,
> But here it is how conditions are.
> In short, there is simply not,
> A more congenial spot,
> For happily everaftering,
> Than here in Camelot.

I haven't felt this way about a place since I left Verona, Italy. It is so distinctly European, and I am bonding to the neighborhood, the students, and to the school. I have taken a liking to the "kinder." The rest of the department sitting at the round table have all welcomed me as one of them.

King Arthur needed soccer coach and sent the heralds riding through the countryside. His orders were to tell every living person far and near.

> That there is simply not, in the world a spot,
> Where ruled a more resplendent soccer team,
> Than here in Camelot!

It was to that call I answered and have been promptly met with a season of two wins and twelve losses. My armor had been tarnished. I remain confident that I am the one and only person for this task, and I am happy the king has chosen me, for in far off Queens, New York City, I heard his call. After the king chose me, I knew I would give it my all.

> I knew in my soul what you expect of me,
> And all that and more, I shall be.
> A knight of the table round should be invincible,
> Succeed when a less fantastic ma shall fail,
> Impossible deeds will be my daily fare.

But where in the world is there in the world
A man so extraordinaire? *Se Moire!*
*Se Moire, se moire*, I'm forced to admit
It is I, I humbly replied,
That mortal who these marvels can do,
*Se moire, se moire*, it's I
I never lost in battle or game
I'm simply the best by far
When swords are crossed, it's simply the same,
One blow and they drink at the bar.
*Se moire, se moire*, so I wildly fit.
And here I am with that talent untold
Exceptionally brave, amazingly bold
To sit at the table round.
The soul of a knight should be a thing remarkable
His heart and mind as pure as morning dew.
With a will of self-restraint,
That's the envy of every saint,
He could easily work a miracle or two,
Whoever he is, he ought to be unstoppable.
But where in the world is there in the world,
A man so untouched and pure?
*Se moire, se moire*, I blush to disclose,
I'm far too noble to lie,
That man to whom, these qualities bloom,
*Se moire, se moire*, it's I!
I never strayed from what I believed,
I'm blessed with an iron will,
Had I been made the partner of Eve,
We'd be in Eden still,
*Se moire, se moire*, the angels have chose,
To fight their battles below,
And here am I, as cute as a pear,
In orderly clean, with virtue to spare,
The godliest man I know—*Se moire!*

"Welcome to my table," said King Arthur. Merlin told me in a dream that you would come and that you would be the greatest knight at the table.

And so this is how my interview came to pass, and that was how my first season would come to pass. But Merlin had a dream, for King Arthur and Merlin had already taken me under his wing. Merlin had told me to use all my knowledge of American sports on the soccer field next season. He assured me that his dreams are not to be taken lightly. I told Merlin the same thing I told the King: "Merlin, *Se Moire*. Merlin, it's me!"

And the church bells were resounding in the neighborhood as the blossoms were falling. The streets were being swept clean and school was let out for the summer. My fellow knight, Ron Mauro, and I went to have some baked ziti a few blocks away at Knickerbocker Avenue. We listened to the church bells and talked baseball, for he was the baseball coach at the school, and I grew to love him dearly; baked ziti, church bells ringing, a bottle of Chianti, and even a red-and-white checked tablecloth as we ate outdoors at the local cafe. What a sweet ending to my first year as a teacher.

> It's here, it's here, that wonderful time of year
> Where every maiden, wholesome or not, merrily appear,
> It's time to do a wretched thing or two
> And try our luck this precious day,
> At Knickerbocker Avenue...
> (Wow, this wine is getting to me, Mauro. Can you drive me home?)
> Here it never rains 'til after sundown,
> July and August cannot be too hot, in short––
> There's really not a more congenial spot,
> For happily ever aftering, than here in Camelot!

The summer of 1970 was a wonderful time spent at the beach with my beautiful wife, Leila, and our newborn son, Ted. Ted was born on December 22, 1969, and Leila kept asking me for my suggestion with regard to his name, if indeed he would be a boy. I offered only two choices for her: one would be Mickey, after Mickey Mantle of the New York Yankees; the other choice was Ted, after Ted Williams of the Boston Red Sox. Leila chose her son to be named Ted, and so he would become a ballplayer in his own right as the years passed. He would always wear the number 9 on his player jersey in honor of his namesake, Ted Williams. He would hit the ball farther than anyone had ever seen during his athletic years. The adventures of Ted and Charlie will appear sometime in the future in the book called *Saturday's Paradise*. We teamed up as a father-and-son combination and enjoyed many a summer in a town called Easthampton, on Long Island, New York. Here we would fish, clam, and trap lobsters; but that is a story for another time, and my second son, Chris, would be a great part of that tumultuous time in our lives.

The point raised here though is that being married and giving birth to a child did not matter to the US Army draft board. When September 1970 arrived, I returned to Grover Cleveland High School, eager to atone for the unfortunate result of the past season. I inherited a worn-out and broken-down jalopy from another coach who had departed for greener pastures. I felt sure that if I failed to make the school and neighborhood proud of their soccer team, then I too would be grazing in the same field with my hapless colleague. So you may begin to realize that this was not an ordinary situation. Much was at stake. I made many friends here in Ridgewood already. I had a responsibility to them, to the team, to the school, and to the neighborhood. I had a responsibility to my wife and my son. This wasn't just a game coming up this season. There would be no free lunch; I had to produce in order to keep my job. I had to keep my job, and I knew of only one way to sing for my supper. I had to teach and coach a miracle!

And the song I would sing to the students and players when school resumed in September 1970 resonated throughout the community of Ridgewood and all of the beautifully diverse cultures found here in this hamlet—"let's tell all the world. join in!"

> Everybody,
> The next stop that we make will be in England,
> Tell all the folks in Russia and China too.
> Don't you know that it's time to get on board.
> And let this train keep on riding,
> Riding on through,
> Tell all the world, join in,
> It's our love train, love train.
> Tell all of your brothers over in Africa.
> Tell all the folks in Egypt and Israel too.
> Please, don't miss this train at the station.
> Because if you miss it,
> I'll feel sorry, sorry for you.

That train left the station, and not a soul on the train ever looked back. We were about to make history. The address of that station remains today 21-27 Himrod Street, Ridgewood, Queens, New York City. The name of that train was the Grover Cleveland Express, and there would be no stops along the way. Hold on tight, everybody, and join in for the wildest ride of your life! I was the conductor, and they all believed in me even though they all knew I had never operated a train before. How was that for faith? "All aboard!"––and it was standing room only.

Throughout the spring, I had many meetings with the players, and we exchanged wisdom from many lands, including the wisdom offered by baseball knowledge from right here in America. Much enthusiasm had been accumulating in that off season. Hope spread through the neighborhood of Ridgewood, to students yet to attend for the first time, and to others who hesitated to join our ranks due to failures of seasons past. For these students, there was no history with which to base a foundation for success, but now there was promise. Now there would be a chance for us to regain the honor and respect of a time long ago; a time when Grover Cleveland Soccer meant something special to New York City. Now it was time to make our own history.

We trained and studied as if we were men possessed. More talent miraculously appeared hand delivered to me at the training facility accompanied by an interpreter. All were eager to learn what I learned from Claudio, Paolo, and Sergio while serving my apprenticeship at Piazza Bra. All were eager to teach me what they knew. We were on the same page, and that page was on fire!

The season opened up in mid-September. By the end of the month, the entire neighborhood was stunned. We were six wins and zero defeats and a resident of first place. We had become the talk of the town, giving rise to the slogan "From worst to first!"

The beat went on, for it indeed was a beat and hum you identify with a smooth-running automobile engine running and purring on all eight cylinders. We were ten victories and zero by the second week of October when I received a letter in the mail that took my breath away. It was from the Selective Service advising me that I was to report for induction into the armed forces immediately!

If this were a novel, then perhaps you would toss this book aside right now and declare the story to be preposterous. So I am disclosing the providence of this part of the story in the pages that follow, because seeing is believing. Dr. Phillip L. Groisser was so notified. As the principal, he had to seek out another soccer coach for the neighborhood.

## Special Notice

The Army is authorized to retain you at the Armed Forces Examining and Entrance Station for up to three days to complete its examination. You should inform your family, employer or others concerned of this possibility.

If you wish the Armed Forces Examining and Entrance Station to consider any medical documentation you have not previously given your local board, you should have it in your possession when you report.

One of the reasons for retaining registrants three days is to complete eye tests of those who wear contact lenses if they have worn the lenses within 72 hours of examination. If you wear contact lenses, you may avoid the possibility of being retained at the Armed Forces Examining and Entrance Station by removing them 72 hours before examination date.

October 16, 1970

Selective Service Board #65
41-25 Kissena Blvd
Flushing, N.Y.

Re: Charles L. Valenti
Regular – Health Education
File #382901
S.S.#50-65-43-846

Gentlemen:

Mr. Valenti has been assigned to our school as a regular teacher since September 1969, and is still on our staff.

Inasmuch as there is a shortage of teachers in his field, losing him at this time would be a serious blow to our instructional program.

Therefore, I am requesting that if possible Mr. Valenti be deferred from active military service at this time.

Very truly yours

Philip L. Groisser
Principal

PLG/atb

October 16, 1970 from Philip L. Groisser

The boys on the team were not advised of this turn of events since all agreed that they already had the weight of a heavy piano to carry on their back and were receiving tremendous support from friends, family, and faculty. Only the physical education department became aware of this development, and tension began to settle into our daily teaching chores in the building. My wife was teaching elementary school, and her mom was babysitting our son, the slugger. No one must know. The principal had his secretary generate a request to the draft board and sent it out. No one must know. What was going to happen? No one knew.

Back down to the training field with the boys. Back to work. Don't rest on your laurels; work, work, harder, harder. They noticed something different in me. For now I was coaching for my wife, and I was coaching for my life, and there was no way in hell that anyone was going to beat us this year!

And so we don't go home until dark. We stayed and practiced. No one missed a practice. They stayed with me, and I loved them for that. The beat went on. By Halloween, we were thirteen wins and zero defeats. There was no answer from the draft board. The pressures were intense. For the boys who were desperately trying to make their own history, the pressure was enormous.

For my own situation, coupled with this miracle season, I became aware of a godsend that I hadn't used in a while. I set the mechanism. It was the mechanism I set a few years ago in Yankee Stadium on August 14, 1963. There was no one at third base to help me then, and there was no one here to help me now. So be it, for I am a baseball player out of New York City, and if anyone can get through this with no help from anyone, it will have to be that hardnosed Italian baseball player. But I did have help from Dr. Philip L. Grossier. When will they answer that letter? Why was it taking so long?

The beat went on. Each week in November, there was one citywide playoff game scheduled. We were fourteen and zero by the end of the first week. By the end of the second week, we were fifteen and zero. There was no answer yet from the draft board. We were on a mission, and it was as if we were all wearing blinders like the horses in a parade, for it surely felt like a parade.

The third week of November required one last victory in order to reach the city final, and by the end of the week, we were sixteen and zero. For the first time in years, Cleveland would be in the city final. It would be against a fine team from Brooklyn named Eastern District High School. We were to play at a neutral site behind the Queens Center Mall in the borough of Queens.

We could not beat them. We could not break through no matter what tactic we chose, but they could not beat us. There was a strength in our fiber that may have come from my pushing them so hard to escape from something outside the soccer field. They just refused to lose, and the game, along with the required overtime periods, came to an end.

The commissioner, Mr. Allen Phail, met with both coaches at midfield, as the officials waited for instructions. We could end the contest with a shootout right now, only if we both, as coaches, agreed to this solution. The Eastern District coach said he couldn't take much more of this and agreed. I asked what was the alternative. The commissioner replied it would be to come back tomorrow and play the entire game all over again. My answer was the same one Humphrey Bogart said to his piano player in the classic film called *Casablanca*— "Play it again, Sam!"

We returned the next day for an encore. There were teachers who just couldn't come back to watch another episode for fear of developing an ulcer or heart palpitations. However, one teacher pinned a badge on my chest for the final game. It was from the movie he attended called *Star Wars*. The medal said, "May the force be with you."

Gaspare Sciacca scored at the thirteenth minute of the first half. It remained one to zero as we came off the field during the halftime break. What to do now? We need not score, and yet they must have two.

"What do we do now, boys?" I asked.

Robert Sommer, our distinguished team captain, had the idea.

"Let's play a double stopper," he advised. It was something from Piazza Bra. Sergio and Paolo would combine with a one goal lead as a team behind our last line of defense. They were our best players at Piazza Bra. All would call out, friend and foe alike, *"Gioga catenacio!"* They play the locked gate!

"I heard of this, Bob," I said to him and the team. It is called *"catenacio."*

*"Si, Valenti, chiama catenacio,"* chimed in Gaspare.

"Who of the last two will be the *libero*," I asked the captain.

"That will be me, Vee," he said with conviction.

*Boy, how they can step up when you need them*, I thought.

And so we took to Piazza Bra for the second half of the city championship with one goal and forth minutes to hold onto the lead. For today, we were told there would be no third game. The shootout would be mandated in the event of a tie.

Val Milos and Joseph Costa flew up and down the wings tirelessly. Mike Nicovic fought fiercely in support of his wing partner. Val was Croatian and Mile was Serbian, but they fought this day as brothers. Greg Songal and Rheinhold Schucat, my two outstanding Germans, held strong at midfield while my stout Spaniard brothers, Joe and Alex Morreira, fended off one attack after the other. John Pasler teamed up with the two brothers. Norbert Jonke and John, two more Germans, assisted the captain in clearing the ball after another away from our outstanding French goaltender named Eugene DuChateau, who went on to play with the Tampa Bay Roughnecks. How can I remember their names after all these years? How could I forget? The final whistle blew, and we finished seventeen and zero!

The season we made history was finally over. Dr. Phillip Groisser generated yet another request to the draft board dated November 30, 1970. There must have been much encouragement from those who knew the situation for him to be so persistent. His letter came back "Approved." A follow-up letter from the draft board dated December 7, 1970, confirmed the issue.

BOARD OF EDUCATION · NEW YORK CITY

## Grover Cleveland High School

2127 HIMROD STREET · BROOKLYN N.Y. 11237 · TELEPHONE: 967-9800

DR. PHILIP L. GROISSER, PRINCIPAL

November 30, 1970

Selective Service Board #65
41-25 Kissena Blvd.
Flushing, N.Y.

Re: Charles L. Valenti
Regular - Health Ed.
File #382901
S.S.#50-65-45-846

Gentlemen:

Mr. Valenti has been assigned to our school as a regular teacher since September 1969.

Inasmuch as there is a shortage of teachers in his field, losing him at this time would be a serious blow to our instructional program.

Therefore I am requesting that, if possible, Mr. Valenti be deferred from active military service at this time.

Very truly yours,

Philip L. Groisser
Principal

PLG/atb

APPROVED

Deferment requested to Sept. 30, 1971

Status: Reg. Tr. ........ For. Ed. .........

Deputy Supt., Division of Personnel

REGISTRANT TO BE NOTIFIED BY APPRAISAL

To Grover Cleveland High School (November 30, 1970)

Selective Service System
LOCAL BOARD NO. 65 B
41-25 Kissena Boulevard
Flushing, New York 11355

Mr. Charles L. Valenti
151-48 21st Ave.
Whitestone, N.Y.

_____(Local Board Stamp)_____

Dear Sir:                                                Dec. 7, 1970

Your Order to report for: -                    Re: SSS No. 50 65 48 346

    (X) Armed Forces Physical Examination

    ( ) Induction

has been:

    ( ) Postponed until _____ 196__

    (XX) Cancelled

for the following reasons:

( ) You are a student satisfactorily pursuing a course of study.

( ) You are a married man living in your home with your wife.

( ) You are a married man and a father living in your home with your wife and child or children.

( ) You are a member of a Reserve Unit of the Armed Forces and are satisfactorily participating in your reserve obligations.

(XX) Other: - Is a teacher, verif. of teaching status received.

YOU ARE REQUIRED BY LAW, to keep this local board advised at all times of any change in your address; your physical condition or the physical condition of any claimed dependents; your occupation (including student status); your marriage status; your family status in relation to any claimed dependents; any change in your military status.

                          BY DIRECTION OF THE LOCAL BOARD

                          _____
                          Clerk

SSS-NY City
FL #;
October 1, 1966

From Selective Service System, (December 7, 1970)

King Arthur beamed with a smile from ear to ear as he lit the first of his many victory cigars. Merlin, the old prince of seasons past, nodded in approval that the "kinder" had used his idea of American sports on the soccer field. Merlin now happily passed the torch. Church bells resounded throughout the neighborhood as Ridgewood celebrated the arrival of her new prince, who remained welcome for many years to come.

> For here, it never rains until after sundown,
> July and August cannot be too hot,
> N short there is simply not,
> A more congenial spot,
> For happily ever aftering than here,
> N Camelot!

It was here in Ridgewood that I so "wildly fit." It would be here in Ridgewood with all the "talent untold." Boys exceptionally brave and amazingly bold. It was here in Ridgewood that I would sit at the "table round."

Loyal supporters like my "distinguished" captain Robert Sommer would see to it that "impossible deeds would be my daily fare." His letters to Congresswoman Rosemary Gunning and to the superintendent of schools, Mr. Wilner, ruffled a few feathers that needed ruffling now that a different kind of school principal was inflicted upon the faculty. So my boys knew that if we needed help, we would go elsewhere. We knew our enemy because we were students of the "Nosce Hostem." The letters are to follow and served to demonstrate that no one was to adversely affect "our prince." Because he promised us that, "he knew in his soul what we expected of him, and all that and more he would be." They knew that a knight of the table round should be invincible. The boys insisted that I succeed where a less fantastic man would fail. To that end, they would always be there for me, and I for them. But it was members only.

They knew that I had "a will of self-restraint, the envy of every saint, and could easily work a miracle or two." When swords were crossed, it was simply the same, one blow and they drink at the bar. The soccer players of Grover Cleveland all knew that I never strayed from what I believed because I was blessed with an iron will.

With those beliefs and their eagerness to adapt their sport to complexities found only here in America, the members-only club presented Grover Cleveland with a gift.

That undefeated season was the history and yardstick by which future generations of Cleveland teams would use to measure themselves. This feat would happen again when the angels would choose us to fight their battles below once more. That story will unfold in this sequel entitled *Nosce Hostem*.

But for now, here is how we went from "worst to first." If we were able to do it, then so can you. However, you must remember that as a coach, the soul of a knight should be a thing remarkable. That, my fellow knight, is up to you.

### The Passenger Manifest

The Grover Cleveland Express:
Departure: September, 1970
Destination: History

The following pages The Manifest

This is a manifest on the first train that left Ridgewood many years ago. These boys and girls were loyal supporters. The belief they somehow had in me to pull off a miracle was the source of strength and conviction that would become a force of energy for all of our athletes. They were special people from a special time in a place called Ridgewood. They loved their community and took pride in their soccer team.

That train ride gave the students a taste of something sweet. Something dear to their heart had happened along from a faraway place called Piazza Bra, in Verona,

Italy. They made up their minds that they would keep me right here with them where I belonged.

These wonderful and loyal supporters went on to graduate, and that meant that they had to leave me behind. However, if they are reading this, let me tell them now what they had left behind.

They left behind an undying sprit that would permeate their school for generations. They left behind the ideal that one really could strive for perfection. They left behind the notion that "You can do this, so do it!"

They left behind, for us to have as a gift, something very, very precious. They left behind the feeling that you will win, and you will win for us.

And so we always and forever will, and we could not have done it without you. Every time we took the field, you were all there right alongside. How can we thank you enough?

### An American Approach to Soccer

# Chapter 11

# Three Coins In The Fountain

There were three coins in the fountain, through the ripples how one shined. Is it mine, is it mine, is it mine?

How can I make it mine? How do you make something be yours? By putting your signature on it? Or by owning it outright? I had been chosen to coach this soccer team from Ridgewood as part of my job as teacher of physical education at Grover Cleveland High School in the community of Ridgewood, New York City. We had had some success during my first five years here. However, I was feeling uneasy about the uncertainty that I feel about our prospects going from one year to another. Much depended upon many factors over which I had no control. For example, which players were to return next season? What new players will join to help us in the next season? Will injuries determine how the pendulum will swing?

And here we were at the practice field each and every day, going over the same old boring details we have been so accustomed to for the past five years. How could I make this boring, unimaginative routine be mine? Soccer is a wonderfully exciting game. Why was I not excited? Why were the boys feeling the same way?

I couldn't motivate myself to promote ideas and concepts formulated by others. I had had just about enough of this! I had studied all the systems employed throughout the world and am well versed in their attributes and liabilities. I had even studied behavior patterns in all the different and wonderful backgrounds that my young athletes from our melting pot of Ridgewood possess. I had studied my own strengths and weaknesses in those departments as well and realize there is need for improvement within myself.

I had been aware for some time that we had been in this mindset, and I wished I could do something about this soccer trance in which we found ourselves immobilized. Immobilized?

*Where* have I heard that word before? Oh no, don't even go there. Stay right here in this perpetual comfort zone, where we all feel comfortable doing exactly what others have told us, that this is what we must beat to, whether we like it or not. In this circus, everyone spontaneously has an idea and then acts upon that idea. No one knew of that idea ahead of time as the soccer ball was struck. Now the ball arrives onto the foot of your teammate, you hope. Let us all witness what his great idea will accomplish.

The first idea was a German idea. It was followed by an Italian idea, and then perhaps more contributions from our Polish and Romanian players. It got real good when our Yugoslavian forwards disagree on their idea and pulled up short to exchange roundhouse punches with one another! I learned from the boys that one is Serbian and the other is Croatian. *Oh, that's just fine!* We were indeed immobilized. Where had I heard that word before? I was thinking seriously about going there. So what if it doesn't work. It can't possibly be as ridiculous as this comedy of errors. The whistle blew. "Time out!" and "sit before me in a tight circle so that you may listen up."

"Have any of you ever heard of Popeye?" I asked.

Several hands were raised, and one boy responded proudly, "Yeah, Vee."

"He's the cartoon sailorman on TV."

"Right!" I responded. But the only cartoon around here is me and you for the way we play soccer *and the way I am coaching along with it!*"

As Popeye, "'I took all I can stand, and I can't stand's no more!' Did you ever hear Popeye say that?"

"What do you mean, Vee?"

"Boys, tomorrow, we mobilize! That's what I mean!"

And so somewhere during the midpoint of that fifth year, Popeye had enough. The boys by now were feeling for me, and since we were all bonded closely as a team, they agreed to do whatever *mobilize* means.

I know from accounts told to me by an intelligence officer that once the order goes out to mobilize, there is no turning back. So we all left the past behind forever and dared to go where no soccer player has gone before. "Mobilize, boys" just means that I have some new ideas about soccer that I want to teach you.

Finally, I was free to train my men the right way! I would introduce concepts, finally, that would protect my team in times of stress. Finally, I can begin to train them in the art learned in the school of military intelligence. There are many weapons in this military arsenal that no one on a soccer field has ever seen. There are so many opportunities for counterintelligence measures that I may not even know where to begin. These concepts, on the field of soccer, I can sign my name to and call my own. Now I would be able to make this way of playing soccer be mine. The fountain will bear the wish of my coin. The coin of soccer! These ideas will make it mine, make it mine, make it mine!

# Chapter 12

# Special Operations

We never subscribed to luck here in Ridgewood. Instead, we were believers in the design that we cleverly took from the word of intelligence and counterintelligence. My athletes at Cleveland were extremely talented and intelligent, and I write these pages for them. I owe them at least that much. They were A students. Many couldn't speak English right away, and for that, their intellect was in question. However, when fellow students or teachers found out that one of them was a member of our famous soccer team, the respect meter hit the ceiling. They couldn't cut class. They couldn't be absent from school. For here, they were truly someone to be proud of; here they were big men on campus. You see, it works both ways.

During our training sessions for a specific opponent, a sophomore was heard to exclaim, "What is this?"

A senior was heard to reply, "We don't know what this is, and we have been doing this for three years. All we know is that he knows what this is, and if we do this, we win!"

Luck is the residue of design.

We often were training for a specific opponent and would design a specific coordination more complex than the choreography found in the school dance classes. It would be for a special time in the game. A coordinated plan or design for a special time during the game? Dare I call that a cha-cha? A waltz? The tango? Or shall we now agree to throw political correctness out the window and call it what it is, special ops. Does that sound military? Well, if it does, that's because that is exactly what my boys would soak up like a sponge as we went deep inside enemy lines. Nice guys don't win ball games, so if this scares you, don't feel too bad. You should have seen the faces on the other team as we rushed in, did the job, and then retreated. Nice guys finish last, so we took no prisoners!

The boys on the team never heard the mention of something called special operations. My colleagues never heard any mention of this, and the sportswriters who covered the games were never informed of this tactic. The only clue that we left behind was innocuous. Everyone playing in or attending the game realized that something just happened, but no one except my boys knew exactly what had occurred. The mission may have succeeded or it may have failed, but everyone just saw something and then it was gone. We would withdraw rapidly so as not to leave any information behind. The speed with which we used the special ops tactic was matched only by the speed of our withdrawal.

If the other team is able to recognize the tactic, then they will doom it to failure. If they memorize the tactic, then you must not use it again on this day. Instead, another tactic must be chosen, but all have the same thing in common—speed. Speed is the great equalizer, Dad would often declare, for if you operate with speed, it will cover up your vulnerabilities and serve to disguise your intentions.

Speed, however, requires great energy expenditure, and special ops must be chosen wisely and at precise moments. Overreliance on this tactic will drain your team of the energy necessary to see the contest through to a successful conclusion. On the contrary, a successful special operation that results in a goal will lift the adrenaline level of the team to a level here to for unknown.

Caution must be the prerequisite to a special op. There must be no doubt that you have the element of complete surprise; therefore, these events must be chosen wisely. One choice may be an outflanking maneuver and another option might be an overload done with the attempt to obtain momentary numerical superiority. It only takes the time of a few heartbeats, and there the ball rests in the opponent's goal. It happens faster than I can type about the tactic.

The military chooses these same tactics wisely and with precision so as to ensure a high degree of success and the safe return of their men. The mission must be defined so that no doubt exists in the mind of any team member undertaking this perilous action. The attacking force must act quickly, in unison, and with conviction. The remainder of the team must be at the ready to cover for a special op that has gone wrong. You see, a special operation involves only a small group of the team. This group is assembled at a moment's notice by switches so as to capitalize on their individual expertise. The degree of difficulty must be measured and assessed before the special force is signaled to begin rapid deployment. This is how it is done in the military, and this is how it was done here in Ridgewood, New York City.

When reporters asked about spurts in the action that would determine the outcome of the contest, the answer would come as forthright as possible. However, it was secrecy I adhered to in order to maintain the integrity of Nosce Hostem. So no one ever heard of the word "special op"—not even my boys. It was simply just a play that came to my mind; just a play that came to the mind of a physical education instructor, that's all it was.

However, there were some who knew there was something going on here that just didn't meet the eye. During one of our hotly contested games, a referee ran past our bench with whistle in hand and pulled up short, for he felt compelled to say something to me. In his European accent came the assessment that he had been marveling it, perhaps because we probably sent in one or two special ops too many. The discerning eye of a trained professional saw something only a soccer purist would truly be able to decipher and appreciate. And so he breathlessly blurted out his discovery, and I was happy he was out of earshot from the opponent.

Richard Kihm exclaimed, "I have seen all of the college teams in the area, and I must tell you that your team counters better than any team I ever saw."

And off he went in hot pursuit of our counterattack. Secrecy must be paramount, for what would the league do if it became known that I am teaching my boys to go in "hot," do the job, and get the hell out quick! Oh, this is not pedagocally sound. I can just hear them now as they loosen their bowtie, calling me in for disciplinary action. Creativity is my province. A letter in your file is their province.

Special operations have merit and find their occasion for usefulness in many stages of a contest. Therefore, these particular events that will occur during certain parts of a game must be prepared for, and training must accompany this preparation so as to leave minimal the chance for failure.

The selection of a special op is undertaken after much thought and information has been assimilated. There is a time during the game referred to as halftime. It is at this juncture that one has the opportunity to meet behind closed doors with his team. These minutes are precious, since there are no timeouts in this game except for the one you have right now. Quickly, assemble, rest sit down, and listen up. I see their strengths, and these are them. I see their weaknesses, and these are them. This is what we will do about what I have seen. Now, questions; and finally, what have you seen? Hands go up, suggestions run rampant.

This is good stuff! The team is pulsating with thought, and I am loving it, for I am their teacher, and this is what we do. Teacher has only one set of eyes, but before me I have the eyes and ears tantamount to an entire US Army signal corps. The information garnered is enormous. We are in an exercise of interpretation and full disclosure of the opponent.

This is not the time or the place for recrimination or even for jubilation. This is a full-fledged debriefing! From information gained by virtue of this debriefing, we are better able now to select a preplanned array of special op missions that are to be taken in rapid order so that this opponent will be dispatched in rapid order, immediately and straight out of this locker room! Can you imagine the level of confidence with which this team now takes the field for the remaining half? If we were losing, we now have the plan to win. If we were winning, we now had the plan to secure the victory. This conviction belonged to us now more than ever since we now had their blueprint. We have made our assessment, we have our intelligence, we have our counterintelligence, and now it's a go!

The team captain and the two co-captains remain behind as the boys take to the field to resume the battle. There is a chain of command, and consultation must be addressed immediately.

# Chapter 13

# Curveballs and Screwballs

We consult briefly about the possibility that all does not go as planned. If that occurs, then these are the contingencies. If time is becoming our enemy, these are the contingencies. If time is in our favor, these are the contingencies. Is this understood? Do we have agreement? Good. Then you each know exactly what to do when a contingency may occur, and you have the authority to relay orders to the team depending upon which of these contingencies prevail.

The second half resumes. Which special ops do we use? Well, we trained for each and every one, so this decision will be made by the coach and then relayed to the rest of the team by our field leaders. These leaders have been selected not by popularity. One must be from the last line of defense, one must be from our midfield, and the other must be from the attack line. This, so that transitions may be consummated rapidly.

1980 undefeated city champions

One may begin to realize how it was possible for the boys from Ridgewood to carry on for ten full years of division-A soccer in New York City without allowing a single team to beat them by more than one goal! These boys came to believe in something bigger than themselves. They were smart in many ways. They never heard of Branch Rickey or even the Brooklyn Dodgers, but they knew that luck is the residue of design. These boys were diligent in their approach to representing their beautiful and proud community of Ridgewood. Their work ethic was simply amazing, and when they took to the field, they truly played like the band of brothers that they were.

Their confidence grew with each passing year along with their fame. All believed that they had a friend out there on the battlefield. That friend was the design of a way to play the game that was stumbled upon by the "Ghost and the Darkness."

My soccer teams met with success experienced by many in the first five years. We had our moments in the sun along with our share of rainy days. We became more and more powerful with the passing of the years because of the doctrine that became invincible. This doctrine was woven tightly together from the fine fabric of two distinctly different cloths. This is the doctrine that resulted in the famous streak of an unheard of run spanning ten consecutive years of never losing a regulation game of soccer by more than one goal! How could that be possible? Have the Azzurri ever put together a streak equal to that? Has Juventus, Real Madrid, Manchester United? Has Brazil, Germany, England, or Argentina? Does anyone know of any team of any sport of any time that has done this?

Well, my boys out of Ridgewood, New York City, did just that. And they did it against division-A Public Schools Athletic league talent. These opponents played club soccer for Inter-Giuliana, Gottschee – Blavweiss, and other numerous sports clubs. Our opponents were trained and accomplished by fine soccer coaches from all over the world. Indeed, the athletes themselves were from all over the world; trained by former coaches, fathers, brothers, uncles in all the best ideas and strategies available worldwide. And we, from Ridgewood, New York City, put them all on a streak that will never be matched. We were Italian,

German, Yugoslavian playing alongside the two components of Serbian and Croatian for our own common cause. We were Romanian, Polish, Spanish, and we came from Haiti, Jamaica and the Orient. Where in the world except here, in New York City, could such an army be assembled?

The 1980 undefeated championship season would be the second undefeated championship of New York City in recent memory, if actually ever done twice by the same school ever before. So what was the beef? Is this not something for the Pubic Schools Athletic League to be proud of in their own right? I have a few questions for you.

As we attempted to take the field in 1983 for yet another city championship, our opponent wore black shorts and orange shirts. Why did you permit the use of a ball colored in orange and black dots when this was a neutral field and the ball customarily is black and white dots on a neutral field. We met with the officials at the start of the game in order to agree that only a neutral ball may be used in this game. However, the opponent did not respect fair play and threw an illegal ball into the field. Why did you allow that transgression upon my boys? Are you aware that when my goaltender saw that ball thrown onto the field, he rushed out of his net to alert the official, when an opponent promptly put the ball into that open net and decided the New York City Championship on a travesty of the rules. How could this have been permitted? Reader, please refer to the scrapbook section at the rear of the book in order to familiarize yourself with some very suspicious activity that the Public Schools Athletic League participated in with collusion from the PSAL Soccer Officials Association. There were many reporters there on that day who witnessed this disgrace.

We could not help the fact that from 190 through 1985, we won almost every damn game we played in New York City! Shouldn't that have made you proud of my boys from Grover Cleveland High School? Why instead did you create an obstacle? Could it have been that a belief existed that no team could beat my boys from Ridgewood fairly? Reader, consult letter in scrapbook section dated November 22, 1983, addressed to the soccer commissioner and signed by every one of our players. His decision was no decision, indicating that it was all right with him that we got screwed. Nice going, Commissioner! This information can be reviewed, as I have mentioned, in the rear scrapbook section, and you can be the judge if something was not quite above board.

A year later, the night after our first playoff victory, I received a telephone call from an official who resided in Ridgewood. At the request of anonymity, he was saddened to disclose that the PSAL Soccer Officials Association met the night before and the centerpiece, to his dismay, was how to prevent the Grover Cleveland Soccer Team from continuing to dominate New York City Soccer. It was city championship time in 1984. A year had passed when the illegal game of 1983 occurred. Now how can the PSAL and the Soccer Officials Association screw us this year?

Well, before the big game, my boys asked me to submit a list of five officials that they felt had an adverse agenda. This list was sent to my chairmen, who agreed and sent it into the PSAD office. The promise was accepted that these officials would not be selected. (Alva DeFreitas was on the list.)

Why then was Alva DeFreitas allowed to referee that city championship game? I requested withdrawal from the contest after my boys saw this turn of events. It was suggested that this may be looked at as insubordination, and so we were forced to take the field. So many questionable calls were made by this official whom none of us trusted or wanted. Soon the game got out of hand with fouls and fisticuffs. The game was aborted with four minutes remaining, as we had finally had enough of this Public Schools Athletic League bullshit. Why did you allow that official to be present when my boys from Ridgewood said he could not be trusted? And so you all reared your ugly face once more. How far up the ladder does this go? we all wondered. Stay with me and you may once again decide for yourself.

1985 arrived one year later, and so did my Ridgewood boys. You could set your watch by us because we were that good. Please refer to the scrapbook section and specific letter dated October 16, 1985, addressed to Mr. Ronald King, director of the Public Schools Athletic League. This time, during a regular season game, a referee decided to change his mind about a yellow card he had issued. He decided to make it a red card long after the event had ended, and we all left for the day. Have you ever heard of such a thing? What was that all about?

And what does the good old boy commissioner do about that? Please refer to the scrapbook section and the response dated October 17, 1985, and once again, you may decide for yourself. Andreas Borcelli has in his repertoire a beautiful song that I finally felt compelled to sing. The Prince of Ridgewood was one, and it was "Time to say Goodbye" forever.

My boys of Ridgewood and I had no equal, and we proved it to everyone. This created jealousies among many. In the scrapbook section, please refer to what I am providing for your perusal in the form of a list. This is the list that has only one friend out of well over one hundred people who can influence the outcome of a soccer match. Can you find that one friend? Where did he live those many years ago? Is he the one and only person on that list who lived where we proudly come from? You be the judge!

My dad, Major Charles N. Valenti, was a career Untied Stated Army intelligence officer. He was my best friend and my teacher. Who the hell did you think you were dealing with? He taught me that as an intelligence and counterintelligence student, I must never discard anything that perhaps the enemy might pick up and use against me, or better yet, that may someday serve a purpose of my intent and interest. We are students of the "Nosce Hostem"; that is why you were no match for us, even if you did number in the hundreds. At least, our fine and proud opponents treated us with dignity and respect. On behalf of all our boys from Ridgewood, I thank them all for the gentlemen and sportsmen that they all were.

However, I hope the powers that be were happy when I decided that my boys would be punished no more if the prince was gone forever. I loved them that much.

And so, like an old soldier, I did not die.

I simply faded away.

Public Schools Athletic League, you broke my heart.

Or maybe not.

...(He Who Dares, Wins)...is the motor or the British special forces. So I dared to write a letter to the New York Cosmos. Of course, it went unanswered. After all, what could I possibly know that they don't already know? They had the great Pele, Franz Beckenbauer, Giorgio Chinaglia, Werner Roth, Shep Messing, Carlos Alberto et al. over the years, and we thrilled to their performance. However, lately, things had taken a turn since the departure of many of those premier athletes.

So what have I got to lose? I thought. Surely they would at least lend me an ear and hear what has made my team so consistent. Who knows, maybe they could even learn something.

But there are none so blind as those who will not see! Perhaps they actually read my correspondence and were intimidated by the prospect of having to hear details pertinent to playing an old game in a new way. Perhaps the reader thought it might even work. Most likely, he or she thought I was crazy––"crazy like a fox!"

For who among you of such high stature learned every American sport proficiently? Who among you would dare to put American concepts out on your foreign field? Scary, it just might work. Oh no. "We must stay with the tried and true." That was the statement made to me at a sit-down with the Red Bull organization in 2007 at their New Jersey office.

Who among you coached a soccer team for ten consecutive years in a first division without losing a single game by more than one goal?

And now, finally, this letter may be viewed by the soccer community, and let us hear what they think about the folly of my ways. It gets real simple. Do you need to win? Or don't you?

And where are you out there? You know where to find me. Put that in your pipe and smoke it! Jimmy Piersall, the baseball player, once said, "Fear strikes out."

And I am fearless––like a fox!

Cosmos letter next page.

Mr. Charles Valenti
150-42 26th Ave
Whitestone, N.Y. 11357
October 1, 1984

Mr. Peppe Pinton
Managing Director
New York Cosmos
301 Rt. 17 North
Rutherford, N.J. 07070

Dear Sir:

This correspondence is in reference to matters that are of an urgent mutual concern. Although our backgrounds may be diverse, perhaps we have arrived at a juncture that may serve as a common denominator. You are searching for a method to sell a product and I may have the method for which you have searched. You wouldn't have purchased part of the New York cosmos if you didn't firmly believe there must be a way of promoting interest and ticket sales. I wouldn't be contacting you now if I didn't firmly believe that I may have your answer. As surely as time is running out in search of an illusive idea, I am certain I have the idea whose time has come.

Would you have the courage to blend your background with mine in order to enable your product to reach the hearts of the American sports fan? Would you demonstrate flexibility and deviate somewhat from tradition in order to sell soccer in America? Will you allow the Cosmos to make an American cultural commitment to the game? An affirmative response to these questions can set forth procedures that will put people in the seats.

Being that we are in the media hub, it is apparent what the success of the Cosmos means to the success of the North American Soccer League. It is toward that end that I would like to submit material developed to make soccer appeal in a cultural aspect to the American sports enthusiast. We have seen what this cultural aspect has done to fill football, baseball and basketball arenas through the country. Soccer can be added to this list by infusing concepts of certain sports that are rooted deeply in the American psyche and culture. These concepts would require reinforcement supported by a program to educate the public in identifying the remarkable similarities between soccer and other popular spectator sports.

These actions, if undertaken properly, may result in a powerful cultural commitment to the game on the part of the Cosmos management and team. I have developed such a program while coaching at Grover Cleveland High School. The combination of traditional play with the infusion of American concepts has yielded the reward of a remarkable and visually stimulating game reflecting the best from both worlds.

The concepts are unique in many ways. I have been fortunate to be proficient in every major American sport and yet six of my early years were spent in Italy as a military dependent of a U.S. Army major. As a result, military tactics and philosophies, combined with proficient knowledge of American sports, tempered by an understanding of the foreign way of thinking, has brought me to the point where I am today.

This approach has enabled me to stimulate foreign and American athletes to achieve a record of 110-39-15 in "A" division play since 1970. My teams have not lost a single game by over a goal in eight years!

Based on that record and the crucial method from which the record has accumulated, it is hoped that you will not dismiss this correspondence lightly. I sincerely hope that you will match my initiative by arranging for a meeting at your offices so that we can discuss in greater detail what I have to offer your organization.

                    Yours in soccer,

                    Charles L. Valenti

To Mr. Peppe Pinton from Mr. Charles L Valenti

# Chapter 14

# Order of Battle

- Four defensive backs
- One designated as *libero*
- Two midfielders
- Both remain in center
- Two group one wing support
- Two group two wing support
- Two group one attackers
- Two group two attackers
- One group five teams right (sp. ops.)
- One group five teams left (sp. ops.)
- One group three directs right
- One group three directs left
- One corner kick right
- One corner kick left
- 1st group five sharpshooters
- 2nd group five sharpshooters
- Goaltender primary
- Goaltender support secondary
- Group one reserves offense
- Group two reserves defense

These become the assigned units in the mobilization structure relative to the order of battle necessary to mount a consistent and sustained effort. Measures have been taken to provide for troop strength and reserve support. Reserve support paramount in the flanking areas, therefore, pairs are assigned and rotate at the flanks. Special operation units are assembled as a team of five for triangulation purposes; one special ops team for right flank attack, the other for left flank attack.

Sharpshooters or snipers consist of the corner kick and eleven-meter shootout corps.

Artillery units consist of the direct or indirect group left and group right pursuant to field position at point of attack.

Who said this was only a game?

Mobilization requires the gearing up of many different parts and pieces that are not currently together into a well-oiled, disciplined fighting force. In the military, jeeps serve a specific purpose. Tanks serve another purpose. Artillery pieces serve yet another purpose. If all are used in a coordinated fashion, there will be no doubt or confusion as to what role each will play to benefit the success of the mission. Each piece of equipment must be used in a certain manner in cohesion with the rest of the force. There are limitations of each. There is also great discipline in the use of restraint in knowing when not to engage or where on the field of battle that certain pieces of equipment should never enter, no matter what!

So which of my players are more suited with their particular skills to fill their role in the mobilization? Who is the quickest? Which work best in pairs? Who are the most powerful, and where do they fit in? Which can adapt from a situation that transforms the mindset of the team from attack to a more defensive posture? Which one or two can fire quickly at a moment's notice, and who can launch artillery salvos from a distance?

A fast jeep can run the lines with the speed of the wind. The tanks can control the midfield as long as they dare not venture into areas they were forbidden to enter. Artillery salvos must come from those chosen to defend, first and foremost. Is there a group that could be mobilized at a moment's notice in order to enter into the enemy's camp in triangulation?

Of these attributes, which may have a secondary skill? Perhaps an ability to launch the ball something between the quick shot and the artillery salvo? In soccer parlance, we often refer to that as a "chip" shot useful for the indirect kick. Which artillery piece has the secondary ability to bend the ball into the goal area from a corner kick from the right side? And which artillery piece has the ability to bend the ball from the left side?

Training these various types to become mobilized entails that all function in their own specialty while working with the interests of the group as the paramount objective in mind for all. We coaches recognize this as teamwork. The military recognizes this as survival. The most critical factor involved in ensuring the survival of the soccer team out on that field is the ability of these various units to work comfortably together. Tanks can't run with jeeps. Artillery pieces can't run at all! Fast-moving shooting pieces cannot launch salvos. Each has a role specific, and all must be trained to know where they are on that battlefield in relation to one another. Once the training reaches that level, then the training in triangular mobilization can begin to be implemented. In order to move effectively into the opponent's camp in a degree of strength, the mobilization must penetrate in groups of three; anything less will only break down and open up into a counterattack at your peril. The group of three mobilizes with the ball and moves upfield. There is a point vehicle supported by two trailing vehicles; each are supporting the flanks of the pointman. The three proceed upfield in a methodical manner. As they progress, they are to support each other's flanks and maintain that triangle at all costs. Once this small mobilized force loses the triangulation, the situation becomes untenable, and this unit must break off the assault, retreat orderly, and regroup. They must not remain upfield for rest and relaxation as this would be to the detriment of the entire team. Even the full-fledged retreat should occur as each player falls back orderly and finds new triangulation partners along the way.

General Patton's Third Army was in hot pursuit of the retreating German Armies in France during the war in 1944. The German Army retreated orderly through the Falaise Gap into Germany so that it could live to fight another day. It accomplished this by guarding its flanks while buying time for the main body to retreat. After escaping into Germany, the Falaise Gap was closed, and the Army was saved from destruction for the time being. If the discipline and the triangulation breaks down, the entire retreat may break down. The principle of mobilization in this scenario implies that you will choose where and when to fight, not your opponent. There can be no cohesive attack when you are mobilized for retreat. Only foolhardy, undisciplined skirmishes will occur, and who knows what that may lead to.

In order to begin the mobilization process, one must know exactly what he is mobilizing against. Advancing foolishly into a heavily fortified area on a wing and a prayer is gallant but dangerous. The British forces, in their gallant attempt to take the bridge at Arnhem, learned that it was a bridge too far. The Thirtieth Corps under General Montgomery had been furnished with intelligence information in the form of aerial reconnaissance. Aerial photographs revealed a large Panzer Division hidden in the area. What else may be supporting that group, the planners in their eagerness chose to ignore. The mission met with an unfortunate end. The less for us as a soccer coach is that you just do not mobilize and go in there unless you know exactly what is in there and how to handle the situation.

Allow me to make a point here. As a student of military philosophies, mobilization is a basic tactic we may employ. In the effort to learn and then teach these philosophies, we may learn from actual military struggles like the two I have used. This, throughout this book, will not imply a position of being on one side or the other. The examples of history can only bring credit upon all the men who fought these great battles. They all have something from which we may learn, and we must respect these proud men no matter what our personal preference is, or they all had one thing in common. They were obeying their orders and doing their duty the best way they saw fit. I believe that as a coach or leader of men, like my dad, that is the least we can do for the charges that believe in us. There is honor on the field of battle—and don't forget that the soccer field is also included in that assertion.

Now the question may arise as to who or what we are mobilizing against. In the world of soccer, this is really not that hard to assess. The battle plans employed by the opponents are obvious to the point of extreme boredom. The selection of battle plans are stifling in their predictability. The choices available are so archaic that they should be used for a nursing home league, with all due respect for the elderly. The elderly have wisdom beyond their years, and when an old person speaks, everyone should quiet down and listen. They have been there and done that, and I'm sure even they would agree to welcome new ideas.

These selections are what the opponent has at his disposal. He may choose to employ the god old bore me to tears 4–3–3—four defenders, three midfielders, and three attackers. Or he may select the 4–4–2—four defenders, four midfielders, and two attackers. Another predictable plan would be the 4–2–4, with four defenders, four attackers, and only two midfielders. There are several other variations to these bound by the numbers styles, and each one is worse than the other, as all are predictable by the very nature of the formation selected. Each lunges and parries at the other until the game is decided by an error or a skill advantage. I believe that the game of soccer deserves better than that.

However, if they keep serving this food to me, one thing is certain: I'll never go hungry for long! Each has severe limitations accompanied by extreme predictability.

On the battlefield, those two features can only result in one outcome. Perhaps a full measure of gratitude is due the opponent for granting such a full measure of disclosure, simply by the rigid and inflexible method with which he chooses, or is forced to do battle. He may as well don a red coat, like the British did in our Revolutionary war. They sure looked good, but look what happened to them when the colonists attacked guerilla style attired in camouflage.

The boys at Cleveland were mobilized to train against these "tried and true" dominoes. It was right there at this juncture when we began our ten-year run whereby no team of any style could manage to beat us by more than one goal. How is that for the proof of the pudding? The proof of the pudding is in the eating, and we sure had our fill of all the "expert styles currently employed."

If it walks like a duck and quacks like a duck, then it's a duck. We knew these styles well and fully expected everything these opponents could deliver. Their numerical disclosure gave us much of the intelligence we needed to mobilize to our strategic and tactically advantageous positions, where we would lie and wait for the ducks. Our triangulation offered an added benefit in that enfilading fire proved too formidable.

The German Army, during WWII, employed enfilading fire during their steady retreat north up the Italian peninsula. Machine gun nests would be set up in triangular shooting positions that proved almost impossible to advance upon.

Our troops landed at the Anzio beaches in 1944 and had to face this defense as they progressed north to Rome and pointed north in pursuit of the retreating German Army. In our defense, we would set up triangulated positions in order to obtain the soccer ball and counterattack with a rapid deployment deep into the heart of the opponent's stronghold.

There was no worry that we would run short on fuel as the German Army did in their push to reach the port city of Antwerp in January 1945. By lying in wait, fuel or energy expenditures were kept at a minimum. This energy was needed for the full-fledged assault that would come as the battle would dictate. Never was the issue to be forced. Our counterintelligence operations were always begun by the impetuous and impatient folly of the opponent. This all came from field manuals that were printed during August 1944 and carried through France and Germany in my dad's back pocket. Every action takes place, and our mobilization is the planed reaction. Our intelligence was discovered many tendencies that our opponents all wish to employ, and then we mobilize and use our counterintelligence to go in and dismantle their entire structure. They would fall apart at the onslaught that they would signal through their predictability. We were rested and waiting; they were tired of their relentless attack into our enfilading fire. Eventually, the battle of attrition would be in our favor, and the jeeps would move swiftly up the line, flanked by our tanks, and supported by our relentless artillery salvos from our big guns. Sounds pretty, doesn't it? Mobilize. Where did I get that idea?

Superimposed on each diagram of the opponent is the countering system that will send the other coach scurrying to the library! Each of these visual sides will give you a bird's-eye view of events as they are about to unfold. You will have in your possession every critical aerial reconnaissance photograph necessary to dominate and *now your opponent*. This innovative technique was presented to me years ago by an officer in the G2 Intelligence section of the US Army. It involves the use of *overlays* indicating where to position your players in order to maximize their efficiency against each and every particular opponent.

This is a technique used by the armed forces to formulate plans of battle against known enemy fortifications and capabilities. It is based on the premise that you will *know your opponent* in time of conflict, but he will not know you. In appreciation for providing me with the technique not available in any library or store, I'd like to say thanks to that officer, my dad, Major Charles N Valenti, US Army, retired.

When organizing a team, it is natural for most coaches to concern themselves with the style of play they wish to develop. This decision accomplished, the coach will be able to select players to fill certain positions in order to build that style. However, much has been written about the folly of dictating a style to players who may not have the talent to perform efficiently under the restrictions or demands of a certain system. Therefore, the coach is caught in a quandary of trying to fit players into a certain system without sacrificing the efficiency of the style or the player. Suggestions prevailing with regard to this problem indicate that the successful coach must not be rigid in his demands and expectations. He must adapt the style to the quality and talent of his players; in other words, allow the talent to dictate the style.

With this concept in mind, the coach may need to alter his style from one year to the next, depending upon graduation losses and newcomers. This will necessitate the adapting and learning of new roles by returning players. There is justification in building each team as a separate entity according to available talent. However, the coach subscribing to this theory must be prepared to look forward to good and bad times ahead. Much of the good times will depend simply on the comparable talent of your team as opposed to others. You will have winning and losing seasons according to the swing of the pendulum. Your success will run in cycles as will those of your colleagues. You will be just as predictable and inconsistent as most of your opponents. Attaining consistency will be out of your reach.

## Sustaining Consistency Requires Creativity

There is a way to develop a team so that it can replenish itself with newcomers without sacrificing the ability to win consistently or changing your style. The faces wearing the jerseys will naturally change over the years, but the personality and system of the team can remain unchanged. Players will come and go, but the capability of the consistent winner will prevail over opponents going through cycles. The result has offered me and the Cleveland team one challenge after another over the years, depending upon which team happens to be at the peak of their pendulum swing. Consistency means that you are there each year to accept the challenge when playoff time arrives.

Each opponent will look the same, train the same, and go through their cycles with a great deal of regularity. In applying reverse psychology, if you don't look the same or train the same, you will be unpredictable, since you certainly won't play the same. There will always be that uncertain feeling in your opponent as he comes to play your team. The uncertainty will be a part of every game as they futilely try to understand what they are up against.

## Why You Are So Hard to Understand

Due to the evolution of soccer systems, there are only a few modern ways to play the game successfully. All of these methods are very well known and understood by most present-day coaches. Therefore, when the opponent lines up and employs a certain style, he will look to see which of the proven styles you are selecting to counter him with during the game. Thus armed, each team proceeds to nullify the other with this information.

By placing your players in locations where there are no opponents, you are creating a system the opponent cannot understand. He has no basis from which to draw from experience in order to deal with and counter this strange approach. You are unlike any team he has ever faced, and it is indeed a confusing encounter. However, your team sees nothing new, since they have seen the style employed by the opponent many times as the season progressed. They have been trained to play against that style daily and are always prepared to dismantle it and are very rarely surprised. The opponent will be assisting you by locating all of his players in each of the expected areas.

The method to this system will bear fruit as all of your players in the unexpected localities coordinate to form a highly effective, well-trained, cohesive unit on the field.

State of the art soccer formations usually employ four defenders. To complete the picture, one will usually see three midfielders and three attackers. This is a very popular style currently employed. This team expects to play against others of the same style. This would indicate that the four defenders are to cover three, leaving one free to assist if the occasion arises. The midfielders are marked on a man-to-man basis, and the three attackers must somehow find a way through four defenders. Each team thoroughly understands the other as they lunge and parry until a skill advantage prevails and the game is decided. This makes for a very dull contest, with little creativity, initiative, or imagination.

## Positioning Each Player for Maximum Efficiency

Placing your players where the opponent will not expect them is arrived at by deductive reasoning. The four defenders employed by the opponent are usually set up three across with a sweeper roaming free behind his teammates, preferable behind the middle defender who is called the stopper. However, on occasion, you will see four across in the backfield. At any rate, it will become apparent that if you attack with three forwards, each will be covered, and they will still have a man advantage. In addition, each of the three forwards will be attacking down a slot occupied by a defender and therefore playing right into the hands of the opponent.

With the help of aerial reconnaissance, you will see this opponent clearly and without an obstructive view. The recon will provide you with a mental picture of your opponent and indicates what you are up against so far as that system is concerned. Using the overlay provided with each recon will once again give you a mental picture. However, this picture has much more important information since it is providing you with an overall account of where each player on your team is located in relation to each of the opponents. You now have what amounts an aerial reconnaissance photograph capable of indicating the best course of action for you to employ. There will be many more recon missions in the ensuing games; each will help you to identify the opponent and locate your own team in each of the seams the particular opponent has been kind enough to provide.

Suppose you consider where your players might be located to make for uncertainty in the mind of those four customary defenders. By placing a center forward on the left of the middle defender and another center forward on the right of that same defender, you are, to say the least, doing something very unexpected. Naturally, this concept is nothing new and has been known as the double center forward technique of attack. To be perfectly frank, nothing you will find between these covers could be considered new when taken separately and analyzed. However, as the big picture begins to unfold, you will begin to realize why Cleveland is expected to win each encounter. This expectation is usually shared by teammates and opponents alike.

Instead of seeing one center forward as usual, now they see two. The center fullback, named the stopper, has always been assigned the task of stopping the center forward without being distracted or confused by other attackers in the immediate area. His decision was programmed and planned in all his previous practice sessions and games. He is now in need of assistance to deal with two attackers and must secure this assistance from the player who is nearby and has been programmed to do just that, the sweeper. The problem for your opponent is that his sweeper is supposed to be a free man who can come quickly to the aid of any three defenders in addition to his goalie. Now the sweeper must take a man, thus effectively neutralizing him and his capabilities of playing a free zone coverage known so affectionately as *libero*, meaning "free" in Italian. Since one of your forwards infiltrates between the outside left fullback and the center fullback while the other does the same on the opposite side, you can see that even without the ball, they pose a serious threat to your opponent and must be marked accordingly. They must be marked tightly down the middle, yet they are a threat to go outside as well. Because of the latter possibility, the outside defenders must keep a watchful eye on them and will tend to pinch the middle in concentrating coverage in that regard. This is especially so because there is no one else in the immediate area for the outside fullback to cover. Naturally, this has been achieved by design.

## How to Achieve Numerical Superiority at Midfield

Not only do you desire the distraction of four defenders by two attackers, you have laid important groundwork for what will follow. By referring to the recon mission and overlay provided, you may come to the opinion that all heck is about to break loose. This diagram is in reference to the attack phase of my system as opposed to the defensive phase indicated earlier. By looking at one, then the other diagram, you will get the idea what is about to occur just as if you had your own home movie of the entire process. Of course, it is the overlay that should occupy our interest; all else regarding your opponent will remain pretty much the same. From the tadpole to a frog, metamorphosis is about to occur dramatically.

Up to this point, you have been playing without wings, using a style that has found limited success among world-class teams over the years. By referring to the overlay, you can see this tyle for what it has been called, the 4–4–2. Little success must indeed be expected if the team employing this style remains bound by the locations of those numbers. Creativity, like sunlight, is necessary to make the seed blossom into the flower.

Since you have been playing without wings, there has been a numerical superiority buildup in your favor at midfield. The withdrawn wings have been disguised as midfielders and intentionally employed as such so that a four to three numerical superiority is attained in that critical area. With this advantage established, it is reasonable to assume that control of midfield will follow. Small wonder that any local honors are bestowed upon Cleveland midfielders annually, including the selection of our own Panta Ardeljan as all-American at the midfield position.

It has been a matter of opinion among many that the game is decided at midfield. However, some will argue correctly that goals cannot be scored from midfield and therefore do not subscribe to this theory that it must be controlled. But if you want to dominate consistently and develop a ball control team in order to maintain your superiority over many years, you had best not attempt this by skipping midfield play à la the American kick and run travesty we see all too often. Even a team with a low level of skills can learn this system. You will see that your individual player is not on his own and that by playing in pairs, he has oral support and others close by who will serve to enhance his skills with their own on the road to building the confidence level of each other and that of the entire team. The concept behind my system depends heavily on obtaining possession of the ball. This cannot be done without winning the midfield area. As a result of midfield domination and ball control, you will find that you can't get hurt while the ball is resting on the foot of your players.

Therefore, numerical superiority at midfield is paramount to the success of the ball control team. Since most of your opponents employ three midfielders, it can be very important to have the countered by four of your own. For example, the center midfielder of your opponent will usually be one of their best players, and well, he better be in order to make this style work effectively. My ideas have always enabled me to double-team that extraordinary player with two adequate players of my own and come out of the issue much to the advantage. While this midfielder is being double-teamed, the other two employed by your opponent are drawing man-to-man coverage by the outside halfbacks who will become wings when needed. To go a step further, if one of his outside partners receives the ball, that layer will now draw the double coverage since he is of greater danger due to that excess baggage he is carrying about. This extra man assigned to double up on the outside midfielder will come from the inside as he drops off their center midfielder and leaves this lesser throat covered by one of his teammates. The same situation may develop to the other side and would be handled accordingly. This will result in control of midfield and eventual domination of the game.

While the battle is ensuing at midfield, it should be noted that everything is just fine on your last line of defense. Your opponent has elected to choose the style that permits him to attack with three forwards. You will have the situation well in hand once again due to your numerical superiority. Each of their forwards will find that they are covered by a defender who is backed by a sweeper of your own. Who said your enemy never had a good idea? He certainly does at times, and we might as well learn from every available source if being highly consistent is what we are striving to achieve.

So you have seen the importance of numerical superiority at midfield and on defense. I'm sure you will agree that this is indeed a tough defense to penetrate. If you are not sold on it yet, just think how you might feel trying to go about penetrating this defense yourself. It should be noted here that out of the 150 league games that I have coached, the Cleveland team has applied sixty-two shutouts—not bad for a team that plays offense almost all the time. But there are many fine teams coached by many knowledgeable opponents, and there will be times during the game when the opponent is coming on strong and the issue is in doubt. When the opponent mounts tremendous pressure on your team and comes up empty-handed, you have dealt him a blow from which he may not recover; your team will have added confidence in this system knowing that it is capable of taking the best punch your enemy can deliver and still be able to come out of the issue smelling like a rose. The very style you are employing will be regarded as a friend in time of need. It will take care of you under pressure and see you through the trying times of each hard-fought ball game. It must be advertised and sold as such to your team, for it is they who are the foot soldiers, and it is they who must believe. Confidence and morale are built up immeasurably in the process of employing this system.

## **Developing the Offensive Spirit**

All well and good for defense, but how do we go about doing some damage of our own? When do we apply the pressure and force the issue to the other side? Obtaining numerical superiority to contain the opponent is fine, but once committed thus, how can we expect to have the capability to score? The key to this problem lies in the process of transition. Once the ball is picked off and is under the control of a teammate, everyone on the team changes from the tadpole to the frog. The metamorphosis changes defenders to attackers, and so we are now reminded of the popular concept of total team soccer. This is the concept many would love to play if only they knew how to teach it to the players without losing the games in the process. Remember the old Indian movies with the cavalry charges? Well, in a way, it's something like that, only the nickname of my Cleveland team is "the Indians," and this time we get to do the routing, and so will your boys when this method is mastered. Believe me, this is a fun way to play, pardon the grammar. At any rate, someone turned off the red light and switched on the green. "Get the women in the wagons and the wagons in a circle!"

Here is where the offensive spirit of the team becomes a critical factor. Enthusiasm abounds at the sight of the ball being played by a teammate. It is time to move rapidly in a coordinated effort to the very mount of the opponent's goal. It is time to bring the game into the camp of the enemy. All the energy that has been stored by each individual must be released at this opportunity. This mental outlook is so important since the lack of it may doom the offensive effort to failure and lead to a dangerous counter attack by the opponent.

## How to Feint, Penetrate, and Support

Usually, the transition of ball possession will take place at midfield, and the following transitional stages will occur. Due to the prior penetration by your double center forwards, the opponents' stopper and sweeper have been preoccupied. The same holds true for the two outside fullbacks who have followed a natural tendency and have come out away from their goal so that they may take up closer proximity to the play. The feint is a very clever tactic with a very definite intention in mind. It is used to freeze the opponent in place where he is strong so that he cannot apply that strength toward stopping your true intentions as they develop. Therefore, the primary objective of your two center forwards has been accomplished. This philosophy must be relayed in a most convincing manner to those who will play these positions, for they must be content to do a lot of damage without touching the ball in the process. They are very valuable people. In addition to all of this, the sweeper can hardly be considered as such, since he has his hands full with a man to mark. If the opponent drops a halfback to cover a center forward, they will maintain their sweeper, but they better get a shovel because they will need to dig in and stay for a while, having overcommitted badly to a defensive posture.

The siege is about to begin.

Your outside midfielder has raced up the line and is receiving a through pass from one of his partners inside. He has run with much speed and abandon since he will be in no danger of going into the opponents' end offside. This has all been provided for, thanks to that feint, which forced the two defenders to mark closely while encouraging the two outside fullbacks to move away from their goal in order to close the distance between them and your nearest attacker. They would like to play also and have begun to feel deprived and underprivileged, not to mention a little lonely.

Therefore, your outside midfielder has gone in as a wing behind their defense and is onside, thanks to the other two defenders occupying space even further downfield. However, since the sweeper and stopper are busy covering the feint, they cannot move to stop the wing, who is moving in quickly with the ball. If they do choose to send an emissary out to greet your winger, they do so at great risk. If this proves to be the case, then your winger must pass the ball to an unmarked center forward since the opponent has elected to leave his partner with a two-on-one disadvantage right at the mouth of the goal. Otherwise, the winger has competed the outflanking maneuver with precision and the outside fullback is in hot pursuit on his trail. As the wing pulls up to measure his centering pass, much has already occurred behind him that will serve to support this as a full-fledged assault.

# Chapter 15

# The Calculated Risk

Returning to the fray finds us with four of their defenders pinned down by four of our attackers as a free man trailing or two center forwards comes upfield unmarked. A centering pass to him will bring wonderful results with the ensuing shot from the ten-meter area or thereabouts. Another possibility is a pass back to the midfielder, who can then advance the ball to the unmarked trailer. There are endless varieties and options due

..................................................................................

"Charlie, while with the men of the 106th (Golden Lions) in Germany during that spring of 1945, I became aware of certain definite conclusions based on statements and facts. Most importantly, serious consideration was given by any echelon in the entire command in the west to the possibility of a strong German attack through the 'calculated risk' in the Ardennes."

"What facts and conclusions did you discover, Dad?"

"Charlie, the nature of the divisions occupying the front, the written statements of intelligence officers that I had privy to, unconcern for secondary defensive positions in the Ardennes and an utter denial that in their wildest dreams, our intelligence officers did not give consideration to this location for the German attack. However, there were some intelligence officers who did believe the possibility of a German attack, which would risk the entire German future. One of our intelligence officers believed Germany would be so foolish to attempt an attack of that magnitude and risk her entire future in the process.

It didn't make sense to presume. Charlie, to save face, there were some military people of rank who stated that they did believe an attack was imminent. If they did, they concealed their knowledge as well as the Germans did their troop movements. The German cover or camouflage plan, *Wacht Am Rhein*, had exceeded its fondest expectations. We were completely, utterly fooled."

I was amazed of the knowledge he had explained and yet marveled at the cleverness of the German attack. They fooled everyone. I'm sorry, but I really like that aspect for two reasons. I like to win and insist on it. However, to be able to fool everyone and then win, to me, is superb. What a lesson I have learned here for the years ahead. The lesson of the "salient" coupled with this lesson of camouflaging your intention is simply masterful and will be brought to the forefront of our meticulous planning at Cleveland High School in the soccer battles to come. Meticulous planning requires many ingredients, so for a moment, let us review how the German strategy had succeeded so well and became one for emulation.

It always impressed me that the German Army at that stage of the war was the underdog. Many assumed in the intelligence community that they were on their last legs and didn't have a chance. *Well, wouldn't there come a day when my team would find itself on its last legs and wouldn't have a chance?* I thought. To go a step further, why wait for my team to even reach that dire circumstance? Why not gain from this knowledge and use these battle tactics while we are fresh, strong, and full of energy? That way, we could simply overwhelm our opponents early and put them away before they even realized what the hell had just happened to them. We use knowledge provided by an army intelligence officer not as a last resort; instead, it was our protocol, and we came right out of the box with the whole meticulous plan. They didn't have a chance, for now there was a "Golden Lion" that the German Army failed to encircle and capture at the Schnee Eifel. That "Golden Lion" was me!––and there was another one with me all the way. Dad's friends didn't have a chance, and now these two lions would make sure that our opponents wouldn't have a chance. Call it revenge if you wish—it matters not to us––for it is a jungle out there on that soccer field. And in the jungle, the mighty jungle, only the lion sleeps tonight. Everything else had better remain wide awake. Oh, how could he have possessed such arrogant confidence, you ask? A review of the German plan that we emulated may answer your query. Dad continued.

"First, Sixth Panzer Army was brought west of the Rhine, where it sat in front of Cologne, in plain sight for all to see! Was I not logical that it would be used to defend the approaches to the industrial Ruhr Valley? Had not the Germans always reacted bitterly to any attempts to push east of Aachen, the first major city put under attack by the allies?"

"Secondly, new Volksgrenadier Divisions were moved into the deep forests of the Ardennes. Was it not probable, thought the Germans, that some of them will get in there without being detected at all? And cannot we presume that the Americans will assume that the divisions they may spot are simply relieving other divisions that have been there for some time? This habit had already been closely observed for three months prior and gave rise for no cause to be alarmed."

Let me pause here for a moment in order to bring everything into perspective. "Time out!" as they say in the jargon of the sports world. As a teacher and coach, after my fifth year, I needed to break out of the same old boring routines. Covering your ass with the submission of ridiculous lesson plans to please someone called the principal was Neanderthal in every sense of the word. I needed to learn, not to regurgitate pedagogical baloney in order to please a man who could never teach in front of a classroom. So they make such men principals, and we become subject to their nonsense. Instead, I must immerse myself into the world of military intelligence if for nothing else than to stave off the onset of Alzheimer's! Finally, I was learning something worthy enough to teach to my students. These lesson plans I could truly identify with, and with the knowledge gained, the only principal I recognized in the building named Grover Cleveland High School was me! So be aware that each and every word of the passages I am revealing to you now has been carefully scrutinized by me throughout the years and meticulously applied to my wonderful battlefield of soccer. Agee with Gen. George Patton, for I too have come to love the smell of battle. God help me! If he talks like an intelligence officer and thinks like an intelligence officer and writes like an intelligence officer, then he is an intelligence officer! And so, I was an intelligence officer disguised as a physical education instructor while coaching that wonderful band of brothers from Ridgewood. Now that you can see where I'm coming from, let us return to my study.

So, as aforesaid, there was no cause for alarm as this situation had gone on for three months, and the situation appeared to be static. The 106th and all other outfits camped out in the vicinity felt secure that the intelligence received warranted a sense of complacency. However, just before the attack, the Germans suddenly shifted their Panzer Division south in a series of night moves and hid them in the woods during daylight hours.

"We will be ready for the attack, which the Americans will not expect, and we will attack before dawn! At dawn, the America sentries will be surprised, and confusion or panic will work to our favor. And while Eisenhower tries to figure out our intentions and then argues with Roosevelt and Churchill, we will drive forward and cross the Meuse River before he can turn on us."

Camouflage, surprise, power, and even predictability about the mindset of the leaders—all under the cover of the least expected time of such an attack. Nothing short of brilliant! What a way to open up a "salient," I thought. And then would *Wacht Am Rhein* emerge as *Herbstnebel* (autumn smoke), and in that proverbial cloud of smoke, they would suffocate the entire northern group of allied armies. German deception at its best had outfoxed us. We were shocked and rocked onto our heels. The 422nd and 423rd Infantry Regiments of the 106th Infantry Division were overrun and encircled, leading to their capture. This amounted to eight thousand men. Each had a patch on their arm. The patch was a "Golden Lion." They didn't have a chance! Dad would resume.

"The theory of the 'calculated risk' has been reviewed by many with the passing of the years. It is certainly true that the Ardennes sector was rugged, had poor roads throughout, and was remote from any strategic objectives. These were the very reasons that Eisenhower had thinned out this sector, and that was the reason the Germans attacked there."

I remember Dad telling me that the Golden Lions of the 106th Infantry Division had just arrived at their position four days before the German attack. They told him that when they arrived, they were cold and wet and disheartened after a miserable truck ride from Normandy. The weather had been rainy all the time. The shelters were full of water, and many of the men already had trench foot because of their continuously wet feet from the ride, wet shelters, and lack of dry socks. Because of these problems, a state of rehabilitation was in order. The Germans began to react violently to American patrol activity, and this was an indication unheeded that something unusual was about to occur. In addition, five of our men crossed the line on patrol, and none of them came back alive.

"That was a clue gathered during the crucial period, and I believe our intelligence officers were not fully alert. Several factors helped build this intelligence blind spot, Charlie."

More important bits and pieces of factual information started coming my way now, and all were diligently applied in the approach my soccer team would adhere to in the coming years. Here he began to delineate the pitfalls of neglect that I could relate to down the road ahead and do my best to predict and avoid. He went on.

"First was the general overconfidence of the time. Overconfidence is the harbinger of disaster. Second was a certain smugness of the intelligence officers who are supposed to be pessimists by training." I'm receiving this loud and clear, and the knowledge alerts me to focus even more clearly on this last observation that he had made about being a pessimist. I always thought that was a word used to describe a negative feature and therefore thought of myself in that manner. However, being his sidekick over the years had rubbed off on me. So pessimism can be a virtue? Pessimism can alert you? If you wish to think like an intelligence officer, then you had better make room for your pessimistic side to contribute, and when it does, you must not disregard that message. If you do, it may be at your own peril.

Now you have heard of that commercial, "When E. F. Hutton Speaks," everyone within earshot suddenly freezes whatever they had been doing, and all ears are at attention to hear what E. F. Hutton was about to espouse. Well, it's like that when Dad speaks. Listen and pay attention for something is coming through here from an intelligence officer; a bona fide intelligence officer who is "E. F. Hutton" to his son!

"Third, Charlie, was a more fundamental weakness in our intelligence organization."

Priceless stuff on the way, I anticipate.

"The function of an intelligence officer is first to collect, then evaluate, and finally to disseminate to other levels of command information of the enemy." Great stuff, I thought! The only difference for me would be in the singular. I would evaluate, disseminate, and collect, and then decide how to put the information out on the soccer field where we could use it (to overrun the opponent.)

"When in a conflict, Charlie, one must disseminate enemy intentions while including a reference to your plans."

Yes, I thought. This sounds like good old "Nosce Hostem" to me.

"You see, our actions directly affects theirs. For example," he continued, "it was very difficult to say what the Germans may do if we do not first say what we intend to do, but this is exactly what our intelligence officers were doing. To discuss German intentions in the Ardennes without analyzing the weakness of our positions there, our present and pending intentions elsewhere is to overlook the true situation."

More for me here, this is contingency planning in order to anticipate what may happen before it does and what you then will do with the contingency plan predisposed and meticulously arranged to maximize your chance for success. As Jack Nicholson said in a classic line during one of his acting roles on the big screen, "It's like playing with the devil in the pale moonlight!"

"An intelligence man who only considers the German potentialities without assessing our own aims and desires soon is no longer an 'intelligent' man." These words to the wise are sufficient. I heeded these words.

This conversation began to have a life of its own and was picked up wherever we had left off as he continued to fill me in with every succeeding visit. A discussion of the ideas preempting the attack on the morning of December 16, 1944, offered the opinion that perhaps this was an act of desperation handed down by leadership for the German cause. But we had been fighting an unpredictable enemy for three years. We had been watching our friends fight them for two years before that. We had followed the pattern of conquest and surprise through Poland, France, Russia, to Stalingrad, Norway, the Balkans, and Italy. And yet we had not learned that we were dealing with a desperate opponent."

Interesting, I though. Would it be possible to put forth a scheme on the soccer field that would appear to all to resemble an act of desperation; and yet not be an act of desperation at all but simply a well-planned action unrecognizable by the very appearance of irrationality. This sounds wild; I may never be bored again. This was right up my alley. Good luck, all you sane soccer teams!

"Charlie, the acts of desperation should not have been new to us because we had been subjected to the German intuition before, first in France, at Mourtain, when the German forces rallied to bite off the tail of Patton's fast-moving armored tentacles, and later by a series of three sudden attacks that were unexpected and unheralded at various points along our west wall line."

Attacks that are unheralded? That means to me there was no warning. Attacks that were unexpected? This means, the opponent is looking elsewhere for you, and you have fooled him Wonderful, this goes into my personal field manual immediately.

"In each of these cases, he struck hard and cunningly from a surprise buildup of forces." That gives me the impression I may disguise an attacking force until the very last minute in order to overwhelm a sector of the soccer field that we so desired preemptively. And we'll have fun, fun, fun, until Daddy takes the 'T-bird' away, if I may borrow a phrase from that Beach Boys song. Only Daddy isn't going to take this "T-bird" away, and if you look closely, I believe it's him driving it!

"You know, Charlie, so astonishing were these attacks that they prompted the alert intelligence officer of XIX Corps to report these attacks in November and conclude: "The German's selection of the swamps west of the Meuse as a spot to employ two of his best mobile divisions alerts us to the fact that the enemy cannot be trusted always to act according to the book. He remains a clever, aggressive foe." Is he talking about the Germans, because I have the feeling that this sounds a little bit like me. It's kind of like a personality thing.

"This officer then cautioned his readers to combat this by alert observation posts, listening posts, air observations, aggressive patrolling, and defensive preparation for a variety of eventualities. He advised rapid and complete dissemination of each bit of information to the next higher echelon can frequently produce the picture of lurking dangers and avoid disaster."

"We failed to heed the message of this one intelligence officer, a lesson that anyone will find obvious if only they examine the record. We were lured to sleep, as we had been before at Pearl Harbor, and once again we were saved—this time not only by our own resilience and ability to bounce back from a shock, but also by the real weakness of the German arms."

But this would be no solace to the men who awoke in the Ardennes on that fateful morning. Roaring cannons along an eighty-mile front served as the alarm clock for thousands of sleeping American troops that murky morning. It electrified men who felt safe in the assurance that theirs was a rest area commanders and their staffs tumbled out of bed to eye with wonder the flashes of the distant artillery and listen to reports from their outposts. Through the early morning dark could be seen German infantry moving forward slowly. Behind them rumbled the tanks, ready to roar through the gaps cleared by the infantry.

"Surprise, Charlie, had been complete and devastating. Caught unawares, overwhelmed by the weight of the German attack, uncertain about German intentions and objectives, front line divisions could only give out an array of confused reports. So suddenly did the tide turn that the returning flow of information from corps, giving the biggest picture, was vague and uncertain. During these first critical hours, it was every man for himself."

Dad went on to explain much more of the intricacies of that battle. I took from his revelations much. However, in order to keep things at a minimum here, I have related only the bits and pieces that became relevant. This has not been an effort to recount a battle; that type of work is left to historians. This has merely been an attempt to reveal to you what I, as a coach of soccer, have gleaned from information with regard to how that battle was fought from the perspective of both sides. Fear and intimidation were dished out and received by both armies, and I took from it what I could put to use offensively. Dad went on to tell about another feature employed by the German Army in that effort.

"There was a section of the Sixth Panzer Army under the command of Dietrich that exercised a very effective counterintelligence tactic."

I became all ears for this new feature he was about to reveal.

"An elite Panzer division called the Liebstandare under the leadership of Kamfgruppe Peiper had a trick up their sleeve––and a very effective one at that. That section I am referring to was known as the 150 Panzer Brigade under the command of Otto Skorzeny."

What tactic? I had to know.

"Have you heard of the Trojan horse, Charlie?"

"Sure," I answered. It was a trick that the Greeks used to hide their true intentions as they also hid many men in the giant gift of a wooden horse that would be taken inside the victor's walls. When everyone fell asleep after the victory party, the troops exited the horse and opened the gates for their army to enter and win.

"Well, Otto Skorzeny was the German master of counterintelligence, and his 150 Panzer Brigade employed the Trojan horse tactic on December 17, 1944."

"How?" I asked, on bated breath.

"Deep inside Germany, much of our captured equipment had been put to use outfitting Otto and his men."

"You mean they wore our uniforms?"

"Not only did they wear our uniforms, they also had our weapons and even some of our tanks."

"What good was that if they spoke German?"

"They didn't. They grouped in teams of four. One member of each group was fluent in perfect English while the other three were somewhat less competent in that regard."

"What did they accomplish?"

"Plenty. They changed all of the signposts to confuse us and even left fake maps to be found on their way to take the bridges at the river Meuse so that their Panzers could break out on their road to the objective of the Belgium port of Antwerp."

"Were they in contact with their armored groups?"

"Yes, and as they slipped through our lines, they relayed our position and deployments, including strengths and weaknesses. It was a type of espionage."

What an idea, I thought, and stored this away with everything else until I would mobilize my Ridgewood army someday.

"These groups of four men to a jeep were known as Kommandos and were trained to cause confusion by disrupting communications, misdirecting traffic, changing the signs on infields, and generally upsetting an already confused and disorganized enemy." This indeed sounds like something I could eventually put to use!

Confusion, diversions, irrational behavior, desperation, unheralded attack, camouflage, trickery, power, speed, psychological warfare, and now, espionage—what a battle this was. Truly one for the ages! As they say, it is "all in a nutshell." Everything I need to know in the future is right here encompassed within the scope of the very battle that has been, uh, a sore spot for Dad. I believe I can make this knowledge be a sore spot for a lot of people.

And so we would assemble on an off day when we had no game scheduled. We would dress up like Otto Skorzeny's men in casual street attire and look for high ground to conduct an aerial recon mission on the enemy. Other opponents would have a game scheduled, so this was our opportunity to practice espionage upon our opponents. All is fair in love and war!

There was a tall building with a parking lot overlooking the soccer field where on a given off day we would appear high above the fray. Like Skorzeny's men, we were always in my 280ZX in a group of four. Each of the four team members accompanying me on this scouting mission was furnished with a pencil and paper. Each was given a specific assignment to issue a full report on enemy trends, failures, and capabilities witnessed during our "bird's-eye view of the contest down below. Four such missions, and we had book on every player on every team in the league! We knew their formation, their best players, their tendencies. Heck, we even had the number of each of their jerseys. I believe we even had their shirt size! We observed the tendencies of the coaches. Who was like Patton? Who was like Montgomery? Who was like Eisenhower? What are his strength and flaws? We knew more about these men than their respective principals did! And on game day, we took them apart at the seams!

> *Se moire, se moire*, the angels have chose,
> To fight their battles below,
> So here am I, as cute as a pear.
> Inorderly clean, with virtue to spare.
> The godliest man I know.
> *Se moire!*

*Okay*, boys, get back in the car, and let's get the hell out of here before they spot us! And off went the Kommandos of Grover Cleveland High School. Back to Ridgewood to where we all felt safe to evaluate, disseminate, and relay on to the rest of our troops the priceless information obtained from our aerial recon mission from behind the enemy lines.

With this information, we can prepare our attack. We will know where to deploy our tanks and what areas to project our salient upon each of these foes. Where will a diversion be best attempted, and which is more susceptible to an outflanking maneuver? What areas of their field must we not enter? How do we get them to come out and leave the passing lanes to us?

Which opponent may succumb to our power and which to our speed? Can we use a combination of both? What are their energy capacities, and do they measure up to our own? What plays have we seen that we may anticipate and draw them into an offside trap? Where are they strong, on the right or the left? Do we challenge the midfield, or do we bypass and flank?

How do we select various artillery salvos by way of our selection of direct and indirect kicks? Which of the opponents is high-strung and which are cunning? Is the goalie strong to his left, right, or easy prey to a chip shot up high?

It goes on and on and on and infinitum as the endless supply of information keeps accumulating in our intelligence community. With this knowledge, we return to Dekalo and Seneca Avenue where the Empire State Building and our Twin Towers inspire us to plan intricate and meticulous measures of counterintelligence taught to us by the "Golden Lions"––the Ghost and the Darkness.

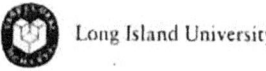 Long Island University

C. W. POST CENTER
Greenvale, New York 11548

Mr. Charles Valenti
Athletic Department
Grover Cleveland High School
2127 Himrod Street
Ridgewood, New York 11237

February 21, 1984

Dear Mr. Valenti:

Our present soccer coach has formalized the fact that he will not be returning to C. W. Post next fall. We will miss George Vargas and his many fine qualities, but must start our earnest search now for the right person to fill that position. We believe it to be a position with as yet unfulfilled potential.

The public notice of the job opening will be in the newspaper within this week from which time we will allow a maximum of 10 days to receive resumes and applications. Since I already have a number of quality people interested in the job, the interview process will start very shortly.

My secretary, Betty Crane, or I will call those whom we would like to interview to set up appropriate times within the next several days. Students will be involved in that process, for several reasons- it helps them to grow, it makes them feel like part of the process, and they may ask insightful and pertinent questions. They can also answer questions about the program from a different perspective than mine. I hope candidates will not mind the process.

Please call my office (516:299-2288) if you have any questions.

Sincerely,

Wayne Sunderland
Director of Athletics

WS:bc

Now I have provided a glimpse into what may be called the bookends. By that, I mean a reference to the beginning and the end of the journey. The journey began long ago, in a place far away called Piazza Bra, in Verona, Italy. There began a birth of knowledge learned from young Italian soccer players. That experience was strongly augmented by military philosophies shared through studies with my dad, an army counterintelligence officer. Through it all wafted the flavor of baseball and the love Dad and I shared for that game. So those are bits and pieces of how it all began.

The decision at CW Post to select a former pro soccer player as coach placed the writing on the wall. And when an Adelphi assistant assumed the position I had believed would be mine, the writing became focused a little more clearly. Finally, when first I was asked to coach at Adelphi and then that was rescinded even as that person now went on to coach CW Post––the last straw had been reached.

The handwriting was on the wall, and the message was clear. It was similar to another message from sometime in the past. My dad said I was just as good as any of them down there on the field at Yankee Stadium that opening day as we sat up in the mezzanine. Vietnam came calling, and I had to walk away from baseball. Now these events reminded me of that bitter pill of years past. It tasted the same, and the result once again was the same. It was time to repeat the past and walk away this time from soccer.

I would not be allowed to know how good I could have been on the major-league baseball field, and now I will never know how good I could have been as a soccer coach on the college level. These decisions were made for me by other people.

So that is the beginning, and it is followed by the end. However, it is what happened in the middle and how it came to pass that merits the writing of this story. What makes this story worth writing is that it is true. This story is as true as the catch I made in front of thousands at Yankee Stadium. It is as true as the left-handed home run I hit to beat Wayne Sunderland and Pratt University that had a part in denying the soccer position.

This is a true story of what a man is capable of achieving if every one will just leave him alone and let him be himself. This is the story of all my boys out of Ridgewood, New York City, who believed in me religiously, even though they wondered where my religion came from. They never missed a practice, there was too much religion to learn, and time was at a premium to learn such new methods to play an old game.

"What is this?" the sophomore would exclaim in the middle of training.

"You don't have to know what it is," the senior would answer. "We don't know what it is, and we've been here three years. All we know is that he knows what this is, and if you do what he says, we will win. That's all you have to know, kid."

Now we arrive at the end of the story. It is about what we did and how we did it! It was out there for all the newspapers and all the coaches to see, and it went on for ten years, and no one could stop us. We took them all on. The Italians, Germans, South Americans. All of their styles and tactics and none had the measure of the boys from Ridgewood. How could that have happened? It did, and it is true, and no style in the world was our match because we dominated all comers from all over the world.

That could only happen in the melting pot known as New York City, and it did happen, indeed. Now the book publishers were taking notice that something unusual had been occurring on the soccer field in Ridgewood, New York. Parker Publishing Company, Inc., sent a letter my way on January 24, 1983, indicating that my successful coaching career suggests possibilities that they would like to discuss with me. They wanted me to consider writing a book for them, drawing principally from my own background and system of play.

Parker Publishing Company expressed the interest that I emphasize the areas to which I credit my success as a coach. I met with my counselor—Dad. The major was proud to read the letter and yet showed signs of concern. "This," he said, "is a double-edged sword. If you go ahead with this, then you will compromise your mission."

In the military, when the word *compromise* is uttered, it refers to the folly of divulging secret information to the enemy. We agreed that this would be unacceptable and passed on the offer since this information had to be withheld, as I had the ambition of coaching at the college level. College would be fair game in the very near future. Everything we had collaborated on must remain top secret and at the ready to dismantle all the teams at a higher intellectual level. At least, that's what they think of themselves until we take them all to school!

Vantage Press, Inc., also encouraged the pursuit with a similar proposition. Todd and Honeywell, Inc., looked at a preliminary manuscript and wanted to go ahead with the project, but I still expressed reluctance for the same reasons. Gottshee-Blaweiss wanted my services as coach of the local club team, and I declined their offer.

We decided to wait for the right offer, then go in hard with all of our proven secrets and leave no man standing. However, as time passed, we kept winning, and the colleges just kept hiring one foreigner after the other, as you have learned in the preceding pages. Even New York University had it down to two final choices and chose an Italian coach from Italy. Oh, I guess I was too all-American.

# PARKER PUBLISHING COMPANY, INC.

*Executive Offices*

West Nyack, N.Y. 10994

January 24, 1983

Mr. Charles Valenti
Soccer Coach
Grover Cleveland HS
Ridgewood, NY 11385

Dear Coach Valenti:

Your successful coaching career suggests possibilities that I would like to discuss with you.

As you may know, Parker Publishing Company is the division of Prentice-Hall that publishes, among other works, books for coaches--primarily at the high school level--who want to improve their coaching techniques.

I want you to consider developing such a book for us, drawing principally from your own background and system of play, emphasizing those areas to which you credit your success as a coach. Our many coach-authors have found such a writing experience highly beneficial in terms of professional recognition and advancement and in the codification of their own knowledge of the game.

You will have the backing of Parker Publishing Company, the nation's largest and most experienced publisher of books by and for coaches. The time schedule for completing the manuscript will be kept flexible; you simply develop your subject in stages and eventually connect each stage to form the finished manuscript. A successful background in coaching is the most important prerequisite for authoring these books, not writing experience. And, of course, the royalties from the published book will give an additional source of income.

Please write to me at your earliest convenience so that we can discuss the next step in this exciting project.

Sincerely,

Jack Leach
Sports Editor

JL/vs

# Vantage Press, Inc.

BOOK PUBLISHERS • 516 WEST 34TH STREET • NEW YORK, N.Y. 10001 • TELEPHONE (212) 736-1767

Dear Author:

Thank you for your recent inquiry about our publishing program.

I am pleased to send you our illustrated guidebook which explains how to get your book published through Vantage Press, the nation's largest publisher of books by new authors.

Since 1949, more than 10,000 books of all types have been published under our program -- fiction, non-fiction, poetry and children's books, as well as books on many specialized subjects. Quite a few of our authors have placed two, three or more books with us.

Vantage Press has attracted authors prominent in a variety of fields and in many walks of life. These include leading figures in the law, in medicine, the theatre, finance, education and religion, as well as homemakers and retired people.

Many of these authors have found that book publication not only offered deep personal satisfaction, but led to greater prestige in their chosen fields as well as in their community.

If you are seriously interested in having your book placed on the market, and wish to have us read it free of charge and submit a publishing proposal to you, simply do this:

Slip your material into the enclosed manuscript envelope, add the proper postage, and mail. (Postage rate: 69¢ for the first lb., 25¢ for each additional lb.) Within three or four weeks after receiving your material we shall let you know if we wish to publish your book. If we do offer to publish your book, we shall also send you a report which will...

        (a) outline the advertising and promotion we
        shall give your book, and (b) describe the
        physical specifications of the finished volume.

Please note that a publication fee is required, the amount of which depends on production and other costs associated with your particular work. This fee, which in many cases is tax deductible, covers our entire service. There are no additional charges.

After reading our literature, if you think this unusual publishing service may be for you, send us your manuscript (with no obligation, of course). We shall report back to you shortly after receiving it.

                                    Sincerely,

                                    Walter Kendall
                                    WALTER KENDALL
                                    Associate Editor

WK/tlh

P.S. Please fill in and return the enclosed business reply card promptly. We shall appreciate knowing that you have received our guidebook and manuscript envelope.

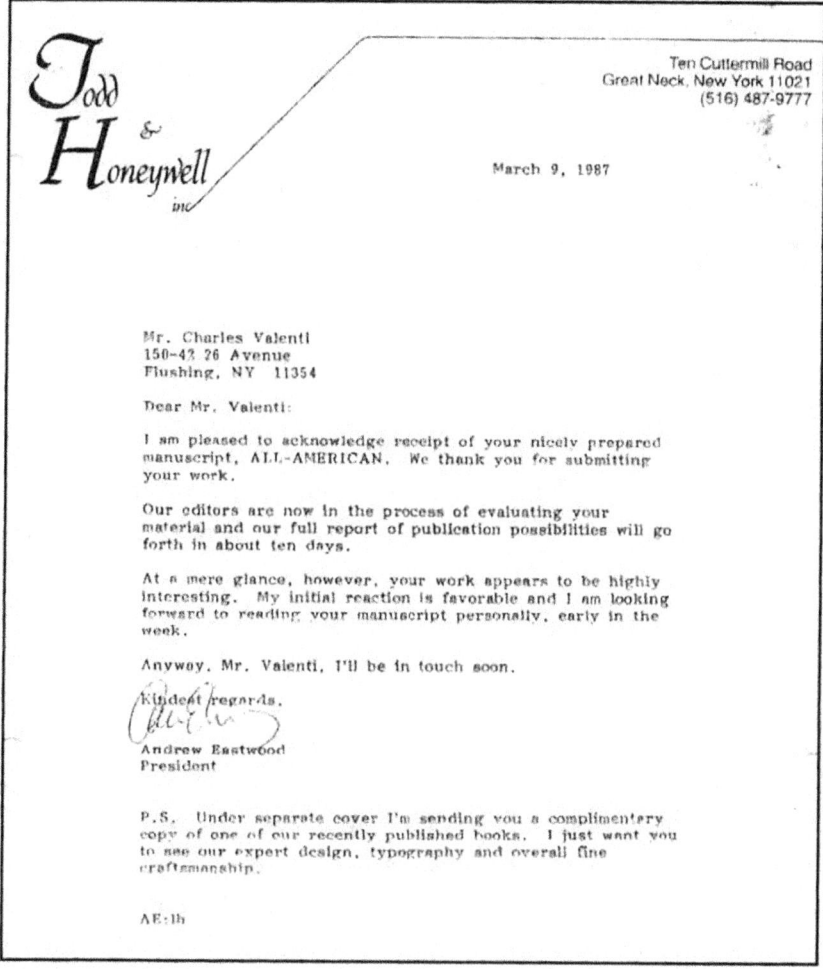

The Todd and Honeywell offer came in 1987, and the years passed as that grew yellow around the edges and resembled parchment paper. However, in the fall of 2007, I learned that an old colleague of mine had left his coaching position as head soccer coach of Adelphi University. He now moved on to the Red Bull professional soccer organization. Bob Montgomery was now in charge of the Red Bull Academy. I stopped in to pay him a visit and to extend my congratulations. We spoke soccer and the business of ticket sales and fan interests. Some of my ideas were discussed and my old manuscript was resurrected for his review.

He mentioned that his duties included overseeing the development of six academy teams within the Red Bull organization. I offered to coach the worst of the six teams. I asked only for thirty days of intense preparation so that I could prove a point. I guaranteed that after the thirty-day training period consummated, my team would then defeat each of the other five teams in any order he chose. Bob took it under advisement and reviewed the manuscript; however, he felt more comfortable with the Red Bull way of doing things.

The tried-and-true method would be the choice for the Red Bull organization. Doesn't this sound kind of familiar? Oh, I guess I'm just too all-American! "He who dares wins!" This is the motto of Britain's Special Forces. I believe in that motto, and I dare to proclaim the following: indeed, all I need is eleven good and dedicated men and thirty days, and I will beat anyone that would dare to take the field against us! Put that in your pipe, and smoke it!

On June 27, 2012, I received a phone call from Tate Publishing. The caller wondered if I ever finished my manuscript since we had discussed the possibility back in 2010. When my reply was in the negative, the gentleman expressed disappointment and bid me farewell.

On June 28, I received a phone call from the same person, and we spoke soccer for a full hour. The Euro Cup soccer play-offs had captured our imagination, and we were now birds of a feather. Finally, toward the end of our disagreement over who would prevail as Euro Cup champion, he said to me spontaneously, "Why don't you do it? Just do it? You seem to know an awful lot about soccer."

He felt Germany was the best team, and I advised him not to look past the Azzuri, of Italy. The two juggernauts were to face each other that weekend. Before saying good-bye, I indicated that if my Azzuri could beat Germany, then maybe I just might do it!

Final score: 2–1 in favor of Italy.

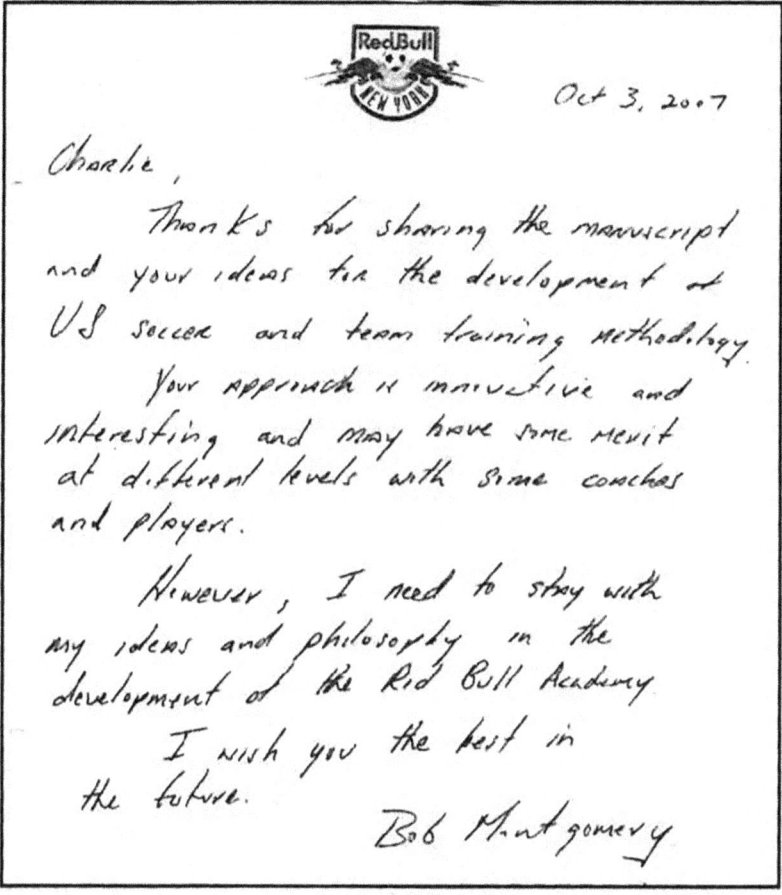

The team had attracted many fans from near and far due to their exploits over the years. College coaches came to the games to recruit talent and became fans. Principals of other high schools came to see a game and became fans. Teachers in the building came to see their students play and became fans.

We inspired the imagination of the newspaper reporters, who became fans. We even made fans of people I hadn't seen in years. One day, while driving home from school, I was stopped at a light and the driver next to me motioned for me to lower my window. It was an old friend from my baseball days. He and I exchanged greetings, and then before the light turned green, he said, "Keep them going, Charlie! Keep that streak going!"

We knew we had a lot of people interested in our team; however, can you imagine the surprise to hear that Geraldine Ferraro called the school to congratulate the team on their efforts in representing her district in such an exemplary manner. We were very proud of Geraldine Ferraro as she went on to seek the vice presidency of the United States of America. Geraldine Ferraro was the first woman to attempt that high honor. Surely, we found another one of us cut from the wood of that same dense tree you can only find in Ridgewood, New York City.

### *Grover Cleveland High School*

---

**BOARD OF EDUCATION • NEW YORK CITY**

*Grover Cleveland High School*

3127 HIMROD STREET   RIDGEWOOD, N. Y. 11237   TELEPHONE: 381-9900

MYRON L. LIEBRADER, Principal

February 12, 1981

Mr. Charles L. Valenti
Grover Cleveland H. S.
Ridgewood, NY 11237

Congresswoman Geraldine Ferraro
312 Cannon Building
Washington D. C. 20515

Dear Congresswoman Ferraro:

The boys have been informed of your interest in the accomplishments of All-American, Panta Ardeljan, and the team he captained to an undefeated city championship.

Throughout the season, we were happy to represent our community of Ridgewood in the Public School Athletic League. When the playoffs ended, we were proud to represent our borough of Queens in the championship game on November 23, 1980. Ever since that date, we have been honored to represent our City of New York, as it's finest high school soccer team.

We realize your schedule is very busy, and your time is at a premium. However, we would consider it a further honor to have you as our guest for the awards presentation. On behalf of the boys and myself, I would like to extend an invitation for you to be our guest at Awards Night held in Grover Cleveland High School on Wednesday evening, May 30.

At any rate, I would like to offer my sincere thanks on behalf of the boys for the interest you have shown in the accomplishments they worked so hard to achieve.

Sincerely,

Grover Cleveland H. S.

Charles L. Valenti

Soccer Coach

## **NOTABLE NOTES**

Overwhelming. Perhaps that is the only way to describe Grover Cleveland's performance yesterday against Sarah Hale. Cleveland controlled play, created seemingly endless opportunities and converted them into scoring chances almost at will. Cleveland spent the early going deciding which mode of attack suited their offense. Cleveland lured Hale into a false sense of security, over loading its mid-fielders and forwards to the left side, combating Hale midfielders who were clogging the middle and allowing one forward to loop around midfield and break open runs down right wing. Cleveland utilized the openings well. As it moved the overload from one side to the other, it created scoring chances on each wing. When the opportunities failed to produce goals, they produced throw-ins and corner kicks—which produced goals.

––Mike Halpern
Hale Coach, November, 1983

They're well coached and they play so well too. I think they could have beaten a lot of college teams today.

––John Valenti
*Newsday*, November, 1983

The team concept is so simple that it is scary––all 27 players get in the game, and they all know just what is expected of them. The concept, the theory, the strategies are all fine and dandy. They key is to make it work as well on the field as it does on the blackboard. Cleveland's soccer team did just that, capturing the P.S.A.L. A championship with a textbook perfect shutout. Just like on the blackboard. Only Cleveland does it on the field, too."

––Paul Needell
*New York Daily News*, November, 1980

It's unfortunate that there weren't more P.S.A.L. coaches at George Washington High School Astroturf stadium a week ago. They missed out on watching one of their own league's member schools put on what most of the numerous college coaches in attendance termed the finest team performance in recent memory as Grover Cleveland won the "A" championship over tough but outclassed Theodore Roosevelt. For the Queens school, it was their ninth "A" title, making them the league leader in the country's oldest and largest (77 teams) scholastic soccer program that goes back to the turn of the century in 1906. There was no denying Cleveland this year in a near picture-perfect display of high school soccer at its best.

*Soccer Week Journal*, December 1980

It can be said that in winning the P.S.A.L. title, Cleveland played an almost flawless 60 minutes of soccer. Cleveland's brilliant execution of fundamentals––something that Valenti stresses during both practices and games––was never more evident.

––[Note: Insert source here.]

# Crown Cleveland

It's unfortunate that there weren't more PSAL coaches at George Washington High School's million dollar Aumueff Stadium a week ago Sunday. They missed out on watching one of their own league's member schools put on what most of the numerous college coaches in attendance termed the finest team performance in recent memory as Grover Cleveland won the "A" Championship 2-0 over tough but outclassed Theodore Roosevelt.

For the Queens school, it was their sixth "A" title, making them the League leader in the country's oldest and largest (77 season) scholastic soccer program that goes back to the turn of the century in 1906. Roosevelt had hoped to add its third trophy to its wins in 1971 and 1972, but there was no denying Cleveland this year in a near picture-perfect display of high school soccer at its best.

The Queens winner experienced only an eight minute period late in the first half when the direction of the game could have changed. At that point, they already built a 1-0 lead, with co-captain Paris Ardeljan scoring the initial goal on a 35 yard breakaway when Roosevelt gambled on an offside trap. Reading the play ably, Lesley Ferdinand chipped the indirect free kick quickly over the Roosevelt defenders to Ardeljan who took off on what reminded one of an NASL shootout situation. Goalie Miguel Gallardo came straight out about twelve yards to challenge, but the Cleveland senior midfielder confidently hit the mark on a hard shot into the net.

Cleveland added its second score at 19:30 when Ardeljan converted from five yards out on a low field-level cross from freshman winger Andy Bartley, who had drawn out the Roosevelt sweeper into the far right corner.

Two minutes later, Roosevelt was awarded a direct free kick, but Francisco Delgado's attempt to convert and put his team back in the game went high over the crossbar. That failure to capitalize, plus several near misses took some steam out of Roosevelt in the second half, with Cleveland icing the game with just 2:06 remaining, Milton Cueva scoring on a pass from Ferdinand.

Cleveland had won the Queens West division with a record of 9-0-1, the tie coming in their second game with second place finisher, Newtown, 2-2. Cleveland defeated Bayside, 2-0, in the first round and Newtown, 1-0, in the quarterfinals. A bye in the semis then moved them directly into the finals.

Roosevelt had to win three playoff games to get there after winning the Bronx division with a record of 6-2-0. They did so by beating the Manhattan first and second place finishers, Brandeis, 2-1, and Washington, 3-0 and followed with a semi-final victory over Brooklyn winner, South Shore, on penalty shots.

Cleveland was scheduled to face the CHSAA city champs, Mt. St. Michaels, last Friday at John Adams for the New York City title, but that game was rained out. The Mount had beaten Holy Cross for the Catholic League championship on penalty shots. The new date and location can be obtained by contacting Jim Mackay, PSAL Soccer Administrator, at (212) 852-0192 or 852-....

LONG ISLAND UNIVERSITY / THE BROOKLYN CENTER
**Department Of Athletics**
Brooklyn, N.Y. 11201 / Phone: (212) 834-6237

November 25, 1980

Mr. Charles Valenti
Soccer Coach
Grover Cleveland High
 School
Ridgewood, New York 11237

Dear Coach Valenti:

    Congratulations on an excellent season, and an impressive win against Roosevelt High School. Your team played excellent soccer, executing beautiful combinations, keeping the ball on the ground with a mixture of short and long passes. I congratulate you on a super job. Many of my fellow colleagues agreed that Grover Cleveland is a well coached team.

    I spoke to Panta's father, and we're going to meet at Long Island University to discuss his educational plans. As you wrote in your recommendation, he is an excellent player.

    As an alumnus I am sure you are well aware of our rich tradition of our sports programs, and in particularly, soccer. With student athletes such as Panta who excells in both the classroom and the field, we will be able to continue our program on a nationally competitive level.

    Best wishes.

                                      Sincerely,

                                      Arnold Ramirez
                                      Soccer Coach

AR:cm

### Franklin Delano Roosevelt High School

5800 - 20th Avenue
Brooklyn, New York 11204

Telephone: 256 - 1346

ALAN IRGANG
Principal

AARON M. MILLER
JOHN SISTI
Assistant Principals

November 5, 1981

Mr. Charles Valenti
c/o Grover Cleveland High School
2127 Himrod Street
Ridgewood, NY 11237

Dear Charlie,

    Please accept my sincere congratulations on your success this year with the Grover Cleveland High School Soccer Team. A superior soccer team just doesn't happen by chance. Your ability to train and mold high school students into a top performing group, year after year, is indicative of your expertise as a coach.

    The students of Grover Cleveland High School, and especially the Boys' Soccer Team, are very fortunate to have you as an advisor, coach and friend. Keep up the good work.

Sincerely,

ALAN IRGANG
Principal

AI:cfs

**BOARD OF EDUCATION • NEW YORK CITY**

## Grover Cleveland High School

2127 HIMROD STREET • RIDGEWOOD, N.Y. 11237 • TELEPHONE: 381-9800

MYRON L. LIEBRADER, PRINCIPAL

November 26, 1980

TO: Mr. Charles Valenti

Dear Mr. Valenti:

The season record is now 12-0-1. Of course the 12 includes the final game of the season, which was the game against Theodore Roosevelt High School for the city championship in soccer.

You can well be proud of the accomplishments of the young people under your coaching. Particularly commendable was the outstanding performance of Leslie Ferdinand who helped Grover Cleveland achieve a shut out.

The feeling that existed on the part of the boys at the end of the game was a once-in-a-lifetime thrill, especially for the seniors who were members of a city championship team on the last possible occasion.

Please commend the youngsters for their outstanding performance in bringing back the Marcy Hessel Memorial Cup to Grover Cleveland.

Very truly yours,

Myron L. Liebrader
Principal

MLL:jwg
CC: Mr. Michael

BOARD OF EDUCATION • NEW YORK CITY

## Grover Cleveland High School

2127 HIMROD STREET • RIDGEWOOD, N. Y. 11237 • TELEPHONE: 381-9600

MYRON L. LIEBRADER, PRINCIPAL

December 8th, 1980

Dear Mr. Valenti:

Now that the Soccer Season is officially over, I must take the time to congratulate you and your team for the superb accomplishments of finishing the season with an undefeated record, winning the New York City Championship, and winning the Soccer Metro-Bowl.

I have witnessed few teams that have displayed such outstanding teamwork and belief in each others skills. You have melded together a real "MELTING POT" of players into a well tuned coordinated team.

Please accept my thanks and the thanks of the school for bringing these honors to Grover Cleveland High School.

Very truly yours,

Edmund Michael,
Assistant Principal-Sup.

cc. Mr. Liebrader
     File

**BOARD OF EDUCATION • NEW YORK CITY**

## Grover Cleveland High School

2127 HIMROD STREET • RIDGEWOOD, N.Y. 11237 • TELEPHONE: 361-9600

MYRON L. LIEBRADER, PRINCIPAL

November 1, 1982

Mr. Charles Valenti
Health Education Department

Dear Mr. Valenti:

The performance of our young people at the soccer game which I witnessed on Friday was exceeded only by your own desire to involve all the students and to exercise superior sportsmanship. The three goals that our team scored in the first half of the game gave you the opportunity to have all members of the team participate in the game, and you certainly took advantage of this opportunity. I know that this raises team morale.

In addition, when plays were called by the referee regarding an out-of-bounds call, and the youngsters seemed to question the call, you said, "Let's play the game." This transmitted your feeling to the team, that while the referee may not be correct, it was "just one of those things." I think we have to realize that when the plays are miscalled against us, they are probably also miscalled in our favor at other times, so that in the course of a season, things balance out.

Please extend my congratulations to the team on their performance. The ability of the team to "bounce back" after losing the first two games of the season, and to capture a play-off berth must be recognized. I know it is through your outstanding coaching efforts that they have achieved this high level of performance. We both look forward to the play-offs.

Sincerely yours,

Myron L. Liebrader
Principal

MLL:dc

CC: Mr. Michael

THE BOARD OF EDUCATION
OF THE CITY SCHOOL DISTRICT OF NEW YORK
DIVISION OF PERSONNEL
65 COURT STREET
BROOKLYN, N.Y. 11201

Edward Aquilone
EXECUTIVE DIRECTOR

596-8121/22/23

May 3, 1983

Mr. Myron Liebrader
Principal
Grover Cleveland H.S.
2127 Himrod Street
Ridgewood, N.Y. 11385

Re: Charles Valenti

Dear Mr. Liebrader:

This is in reply to your letter of April 29, 1983, requesting that Mr. Valenti be permitted to continue as coach of the school soccer team.

There is a definite prohibition of any gainful employment for a pedagogue while on sabbatical leave. This statement also appears on the sabbatical application which Mr. Valenti signed.

In light of the above, I must inform you that an exception to allow Mr. Valenti to work while on sabbatical must be denied.

Very truly yours,

ALICE C. STASINSKI
DIRECTOR
OFFICE OF TEACHER STATUS

ACS/me

**BOARD OF EDUCATION • NEW YORK CITY**

## Grover Cleveland High School

**2127 HIMROD STREET • RIDGEWOOD, N.Y. 11237 • TELEPHONE: 967-9600**

MYRON L. LIEBRADER, PRINCIPAL

November 15, 1983

Mr. Charles Valenti
150-42 26th Avenue
Flushing, New York 11357

Dear Mr. Valenti:

A super game! Your efforts working with our young people brought you a reward that was probably beyond your dreams when the season started.

The triumph yesterday over Bryant shows what a good coach can do with a good team.

We look forward to the City championship once again.

Sincerely yours,

Myron L. Liebrader
Principal

MLL:dc

cc: Mr. Michael

BOARD OF EDUCATION · NEW YORK CITY

## Grover Cleveland High School

2127 HIMROD STREET · RIDGEWOOD, N.Y. 11237 · TELEPHONE: 967-9600

MYRON L. LIEBRADER, PRINCIPAL

November 21, 1983

Mr. Charles Valenti

Dear Mr. Valenti:

Your willingness to volunteer to serve as coach of our soccer team during your sabbatical is certainly appreciated.

I was pleased with the reward that you have been receiving, that of victory after victory, right up to the city championship.

Your inspiring speech to the team at halftime encouraged them to come back, even after a goal was scored against them to tie the score. The boys played well, were high-spirited, and gave much of themselves.

The fact that we lost by a single goal, despite the youth of the team, must be recognized. As we used to say with the Brooklyn Dodgers, "Wait till next year."

Sincerely yours,

Myron L. Liebrader
Principal

MLL:dc

cc: Mr. Michael

The "Halftime Speech" of Nov. 20, 1983

This is your game . . .

I hope you win - I hope you win for your sake, not mine. Because winning is nice. It's a good feeling, like the whole world is yours. But it passes, this feeling. And what lasts is what you have learned. And what you learn is about life. That's what sports are all about — Life. The whole thing is played out in the afternoon. The happiness of life, the miseries, the joys, the heartbreaks. There's no telling whether they'll toss you out in the first five minutes, or whether you'll stay for the long haul. There is no telling how you will do. You might be a hero or you might be absolutely nothing. There is just no telling. Too much depends on chance. On how the ball bounces. I'm not talking about the game, I'm talking about life. But it's life that the game is all about. Just as I said. Because every game is life, and life is a game -a serious one, dead serious. But that is what you do with serious things - you do your best. You take what comes. You take what comes, and you run with it. Winning is fun sure, but winning is not the point. Wanting to win is the point. Not giving up is the point. Never letting up is the point. Never letting anyone down is the point. Play to win sure, but lose like a champion. Because it's not winning that counts. What counts is trying.

— Author Unknown —

BOARD OF EDUCATION • NEW YORK CITY

## Grover Cleveland High School

2127 HIMROD STREET • RIDGEWOOD, N.Y. 11237 • TELEPHONE: 967-9600

MYRON L. LIEBRADER, PRINCIPAL

January 4, 1984


Mr. Charles Valenti
150-42 26 Avenue
Flushing, New York 11357

Dear Mr. Valenti:

I was pleased to receive the plaque that you sent me in recognition of my contribution to the soccer team.

The contributions that you and Mr. Comanducci made far exceed those that could be expected. Your willingness to volunteer, while on sabbatical, certainly was the most significant contribution to the welfare of the students. We look forward to many more victories!

I am still waiting for the plaque attached to the trophy to be engraved. Please apprise me of the procedure.

Sincerely yours,

Myron L. Liebrader
Principal

MLL:dc

BOARD OF EDUCATION • NEW YORK CITY

## Grover Cleveland High School

2127 HIMROD STREET • RIDGEWOOD, N. Y. 11385 • TELEPHONE: 381-9600

MYRON L. LIEBRADER, PRINCIPAL

June 5, 1984

Mr. Charles Valenti

Dear Mr. Valenti:

Thank you for joining us last evening in honoring our soccer team, despite the fact that you have been on sabbatical leave.

The young people were especially pleased by your presence, and I was delighted that you were able to give due recognition to them for their accomplishments.

We look forward to your return.

Sincerely yours,

Myron L. Liebrader
Principal

dc

**BOARD OF EDUCATION • NEW YORK CITY**

# Grover Cleveland High School

2127 HIMROD STREET • RIDGEWOOD, N.Y. 11386-1299 • TELEPHONE (718) 381-9600

MYRON L. LIEBRADER, PRINCIPAL

November 20, 1984

Mr. Charles Valenti
Soccer Coach

Dear Mr. Valenti:

I enjoyed attending the final soccer game of the season between Grover Cleveland and George Washington High Schools, and was pleased to meet with you and your family on this occasion.

Our young people played to the best of their ability, and they should feel satisfaction in their achievement in reaching the citywide finals. Experience teaches us that even as we strive to the utmost to achieve success, it is sometimes beyond our grasp. Good sportsmanship decrees that we accept the results with grace.

Please commend the team for an outstanding season, and an excellent final performance of which they can be proud. I agree that it was a hotly contested game; there is no doubt that in such rivalries all are motivated to perform at a high level.

As we said when I was young and the Dodgers were in town, "Wait 'til next year!"

Sincerely yours,

Myron L. Liebrader
Principal

MLL:jwg

cc: Mr. A. Minkoff

BOARD OF EDUCATION • NEW YORK CITY

# Grover Cleveland High School

2127 HIMROD STREET • RIDGEWOOD, N. Y. 11385 • TELEPHONE: 381-9600

MYRON L. LIEBRADER, PRINCIPAL

November 29, 1984

Mr. Charles Valenti
Physical Education Department

Dear Mr. Valenti:

Let me extend my congratulations to you for the success of Grover Cleveland's soccer team this year. When we spoke earlier in the term, you expressed reservations about the team's performance since most of last year's team members had graduated, and you were dealing with a young group of athletes.

Your success in winning the Queens Championship and reaching the City Finals in a tough A Division is a testament to the kind of work you do in inspiring and motivating your team.

I am sure that your athletes developed a great deal of experience from their successes, and next year they will return determined to win the City championship.

Sincerely,

Sydney Farber
Assistant Principal Guidance

SF:dp

cc: Myron L. Liebrader, Principal
    Arnold Minkoff, Assistant Principal

???. My wife, an Italian ragazza who is quite beautiful, has been a faithful supporter of mine. And by the way, it is only fitting that a shortstop must have a beautiful ragazza. Don't you agree?

Ted has two children, who have taken an interest in this project. Christina, my granddaughter, "E una ragazza moulta bella," and thanks to her as my secretary sorting out bits and pieces of an old manuscript, an idea has become a reality. Her brother, Ted Jr. asked if he could have a copy of the book to take to school as he finds much humor between these pages and wants to make his friends laugh. I took that as positive reinforcement.

And of course there is my dad, Maj. Charles N. Valenti, whom I was so fortunate to have for a father and a best friend. He was my professor, he was my ???

BOARD OF EDUCATION • NEW YORK CITY

## Grover Cleveland High School

2127 HIMROD STREET • RIDGEWOOD, N. Y. 11237 • TELEPHONE: 381-96(

MYRON L. LIEBRADER, PRINCIPAL

May 10, 1985

Dear Mr. Valenti:

I was delighted when you told me Grover Cleveland was in first place with a 3-2 victory.

When is the World Series?

Very truly yours

Myron L. Liebrader
Principal

MLL/atb

??? the story, and the other ??? another book called *Nosce Hostem*.

MY DAD - US Army Team

## 532D MILITARY INTELLIGENCE BATTALION

DISTINCTIVE UNIT INSIGNIA

COAT OF ARMS

Distinctive Unit Insignia. Description: A Gold color metal and enamel device 1 1/8 inches (2.86 cm) in height overall consisting of the shield adapted from the coat of arms and blazoned as follows: Checky Azure (teal blue) and Or a horse rampant Sable fimbriated of the second. Attached below, an arcing Teal Blue motto scroll doubled to the sides inscribed with the words "NOSCE HOSTEM" in Gold letters.

    Symbolism: Teal blue and yellow are the colors formerly used for Military Intelligence Battalions. The black horse alludes to Stuttgart, Germany, the place of organization of the unit. The horse and checky field combined, symbolic of a chess board, refer to the strategic and tactical functions of an intelligence unit.

    Background: The distinctive unit insignia was approved on 22 December 1959. It was amended to update the description and symbolism on 2 January 1987.

Coat of Arms.
    Blazon:
        Shield: Checky Azure (teal blue) and Or a horse rampant Sable fimbriated of the second.
        Crest: None.
        Motto: NOSCE HOSTEM.
    Symbolism:
        Shield: Teal blue and yellow are the colors used for Military Intelligence Battalions. The black horse alludes to Stuttgart, Germany, the place of organization and present location of the unit. The horse and checky field combined, symbolic of a chess board, refer to the strategic and tactical functions of an intelligence unit.
        Crest: None.
        Background: The coat of arms was approved on 22 December 1959.

What an ominous sounding pair of words are these two. When taken separately, they appear to have a meaning or a definition of an ambiguous nature. For instance, nosce in Latin, simply means "to know." Hostem, in Latin, simply means "your enemy." Taken separately, they appear just as neutral and non-offensive as any other word. However, when combined as equal parts of a team, these words become an extremely powerful proposition.

For example, a few years ago, a movie appeared at many local theaters here in the United States. The movie portrayed Michael Douglas and Val Kilmer as the two big-game hunters hired by a railroad company in India. Progress in laying the track had come to a standstill due to a lion that found the workers to be easy prey. The fatalities began to accumulate to totally unacceptable proportions. Truth be known, one fatality is indeed totally unacceptable. So these two men were hired to put an end to the attacks by the lion, which would always occur under the cover of darkness. There were many witnesses to this nocturnal event, and people who had been working to lay the track were now four deep on the train leaving the workplace. Panic has shown itself in the justified fear exhibited by the mass exodus.

The name of the movie is *The Ghost and the Darkness*. Naturally, when one finds that these two superb actors are playing alongside each other, one wonders which one is the ghost and which of the two is named the darkness. For when there are two characters, confusion becomes part of the equation. So who is who and which is which? Already, things have become much more complicated, to say the least.

With all the workers almost evacuated, the hunt begins. The two men have a cavalier attitude since they are both accomplished big-game hunters with plenty of kills to support their resumes. It is agreed they will make short work of this lion, and a wager is made as to who will be the better of the two. For when there is two, there is confusion, and the wager becomes the issue, as focus is lost upon the lion.

The actor portrayed by Michael Douglas is sure the next day of only one certainty: he will not win this wager, for the lion now has only one hunter left to deal with and now there is less confusion. The hunter portrayed as Val Kilmer must now avenge his partner. The odds, however, have dropped to even money. The odds are even. The odds are one to one. But the advantage must be with this clever lion since he has proven superior already. The hunter has become the hunted.

They finally come face to face when a villager is attacked and the lion is seen standing on the victim's rooftop. He takes aim; however, the lion has placed the sun behind himself as the shot is taken. Then there is a blur of a shadow as the hunter is knocked to the ground. Another shot is fired, and finally, the confusion comes to an end.

There were two lions! Both are in a museum today, and the inscription under the glass case reads, "The Ghost and the Darkness." They are now part of India's history because of the terrible toll they took upon human life. However, they are wild beasts, and hunting prey is how they survive. The reason for enshrinement at the museum is to respect what they had done. Individually, each was quite formidable in his own right. Each was a male with the same appearance, and either one could wreak havoc as an individual. They were put in the museum because of the havoc they were responsible for as hunting partners. They were a team, and they were unstoppable.

While attention was being drawn to the Ghost by the rail workers, the Darkness would strike. When attention was drawn by the Darkness, the Ghost would strike. Under the cover of confusion and disinformation, it was assumed that there was only one lion. One could be dealt with, but not two working in tandem as a team. No one had ever heard of two male lions behaving in this manner. They stumbled upon something, and so have we!

Nosce hostem is the partner to All-American. Each, when taken separately, is a handful. However, when all-American concepts are combined with nosce hostem doctrine, the result is, for lack of a better word, *invincible*!

Just as the Ghost was partner to the Darkness, each was a separate entity. All-American and nosce hostem are partners; however, each is a separate entity. As such, it is not possible or even appropriate to combine both in the same book. All-American must be digested first on its own merits. Time must elapse for this assimilation to run its course, or confusion would be introduced by introducing two remarkable concepts at one time, and I do not wish to confuse the reader. I only wish to help the reader confuse his or her opponent—as I had.

Besides, who among us really wishes to dive into a four-hundred-page book? If you read *All-American*, then you are halfway there. If you haven't, and you are only reading to nosce hostem, then at the conclusion of this doctrine, you also will be halfway there. It felt unsettling to feel that way before a game. It meant the issue would have a little bit too much of what I call intangibles.

When all-American concepts accepted help from the nosce hostem doctrine, the intangibles were all but eliminated. Now my boys and I could enjoy the game. Now we were well armed and well versed. We had prepared for each opponent separately and had trained specifically for that opponent. The weaponry we took from our all-American arsenal, and the preparation was made available from our nosce hostem classified information.

This was how we did what we did here in Ridgewood, New York City, while the Cosmos nearby were crumbling. These pages are not being compiled to infer that this is the way one should coach soccer, it is merely the story of how I coached soccer. Nosce hostem is the second part to that story.

We know what to do as a team from ideas discussed in all-American. For, it is our intent to know what you wish to do as a team when we meet. We wish to know you very well, all your strengths, weaknesses, and habits. We will analyze these particulars and then devise a plan for you. And then we will train specifically for you and execute that plan. Does that sound military? Well, it is, and this was how I was taught to think by a G2 counterintelligence major named Charles N. Valenti. Nosce hostem is the seal of his intelligence detachment in the US Army.

Once again, an innuendo arises with respect to an effort attempted by two entities, a unified effort by two working as one to achieve the interest shared by both. One entity, called all-American, comes from the experience of an American athlete. The other entity, called nosce hostem, comes from the experience of a career US Army major. The first would liken itself to the Ghost since my opponents never did have a clue what my boys were doing as we subjected them to one American sport tactic after another, and it all remained a mystery. The second would liken itself to the Darkness since these tactics operated in the clandestine world of the cloak and dagger. The major belonged to the society called the cloak and dagger. This is the world of obtaining information secretly and using that information you obtained to destroy your opponent, without him even knowing you were in his camp!

So now I am beginning to tip my hand by divulging information, by revealing to you who was the Ghost and who was the Darkness. Each was an expert; both were a team. As did the two lions, we ran wild for over fifteen years as we consumed the prey called the Public School Athletic League. However, unlike the two lions, we were never mastered or even understood. Everything we did was classified, and like old soldiers, we didn't' die; we just faded away, if I may use that famous line from Gen. Douglas MacArthur.

The Ghost has already shared much of his approach with you in the book called *All-American*. Now the Darkness invites you to share much of his approach in the book called *The Golden Lions*. The time has come to reveal what we did and how we did it since I believe that my coaching days ended a long time ago. Now that the Darkness has passed away recently, I fear the Ghost just doesn't have it in him anymore. Perhaps that is why the second lion took that final jump at the hunter when he could have run off into the wild; it just wouldn't be the same. However, keeping this knowledge to ourselves wouldn't be right, as all we were ever about was helping people by teaching.

There is a personal reason I have for releasing much of what will follow. You see, for all of those years, I was sworn to secrecy in order to protect my boys from our opponents, and we had many. We had opponents on the field and even more dangerous opponents off the field. Jealousy makes for many enemies; indeed I knew them all.

It wasn't easy for me to hear that the physical education department was not held in high regard. I often wondered why the administration felt secure to send one of us to cover a subject-matter class with five minutes' notice. The reason was because we were talented enough to teach any lesson, and indeed, all we did need was five minutes' notice. It is for all of you out there who are subject to disrespect, who I am now stepping up to the plate. This is an example of what we can accomplish on and off the field.

To my colleagues in biology, math, history, secretarial studies, foreign language, and all other areas of expertise to which I have successfully taught, I have a question. Why is it that in all my years of teaching, anyone of you who covered the class of one of my colleagues could only become a laughing stock in need of rescue by the Ghost? Who among you could write a meaningful and educational book? Who could write two? I am a physical education teacher, and I can write a story!

It was necessary to get that off my chest, or I would not have been able to proceed. If that alienated you, then perhaps you better get off the bus right here, for how will you deal with what to come? What follows is not for goody two-shoes.

Vince Lombardi famously believed that winning isn't everything; it is the only thing! That is the way it was in Ridgewood, and if that offends you, maybe you better do a few extra lesson plans to blow off steam. I am a coach. My dad was a coach. We teach a team how to win; it's what we do! Many a day before or after a game, I would remind the boys that if I had anything of value to teach, it was that! If they would rather learn how to lose, then I advised them to take any number of courses taught in the building!

Branch Rickey, the old Brooklyn Dodger boss, once said that "luck is the residue of design." Leo Durocher once said that "nice guys don't win ballgames." Or some heard it his way by Leo, "Nice guys finish last."

We never subscribed to luck here in Ridgewood. Instead, we were believers in the design that we cleverly took from the world of intelligence and counterintelligence. Yes, the student athletes of Grover Cleveland High School were extremely intelligent, and I must write these pages for them; I owe them at least that much. They were A students. Many couldn't speak English right away, and for that, their intellect was in question. However, when fellow students or teachers found out that one of them was a member of our famous soccer team, the respect meter hit the ceiling. They couldn't cut class. They couldn't be absent from school. For here, they were truly someone to be proud of; here they were big men on campus. You see, it works both ways.

We often would train for a specific opponent and would design a specific coordination more complex than the choreography found in the school dance classes. It would be for a special time in the game. A coordinated plan or design for a special time during the game? Dare I call that a cha-cha? A waltz? The tango? Or shall we now agree to throw political correctness out the window and call it what it is, special ops. Does that sound military? Well, if it does, that's because that is exactly what my boys would soak up like a sponge as we went deep inside enemy lines. Nice guys don't win ballgames, so if this scares you, don't feel too bad. You should have seen the faces on the other team as we rushed in, did the job, and then retreated. Nice guys finish last!

The boys on the team never heard the mention of something called special operations. My colleagues never heard any mention of this, and the sportswriters who covered the games were never informed of this tactic. The only clue that we left behind was innocuous. Everyone playing in or attending the game realized that something just happened, but no one except my boys knew exactly what had occurred. The mission may have succeeded, or it may have failed, but everyone just saw something, and then it was gone. We would withdraw rapidly so as not to leave any information behind. The speed with which we used the special-ops tactic was matched only by the speed of our withdrawal.

If the other team is able to recognize the tactic, then they will doom it to failure. If they memorize the tactic, then you must not use it again on this day. Instead, another tactic must be chosen, but all have the same thing in common—speed. "Speed is the great equalizer," Dad would often declare. For if you operate with speed, it will cover up your vulnerabilities and serve to disguise your intentions.

Speed, however, requires great energy expenditure, and special ops must be chosen wisely and at precise moments. Over reliance on this tactic will drain your team of the energy necessary to see the contest through to a successful conclusion. On the contrary, a successful special operation that results in a goal will lift the adrenaline level of the team to a level here to for unknown.

Caution must be the prerequisite to a special op. There must be no doubt that you have the element of complete surprise; therefore, these events must be chosen wisely. One choice may be an outflanking maneuver, and another option might be an overload done with the attempt to obtain momentary numerical superiority. It only takes the time of a few heartbeats and there the ball rest in the opponent's goal. It happens faster than I can type about the tactic.

The military chooses these same tactics wisely and with precision so as to ensure a high degree of success and the safe return of their men. The mission must be defined so that no doubt exists in the mind of any team member undertaking this perilous action. The attacking force must act quickly, in unison and with conviction. The remainder of the team must be at the ready to cover for a special ops that has gone wrong. You see, a special operation involves only a small group of the team. This group is assembled at a moment's notice by switches so as to capitalize on their individual expertise. The degree of difficulty must be measured and assessed before the special force is signaled to begin rapid deployment. This is how it is done in the military, and this is how it was done here in Ridgewood, New York City.

When reporters asked about spurts in the action that would determine the outcome of the contest the answer would come as forthright as possible. However, it was secrecy I adhered to in order to maintain the integrity of Nosce Hostem. So no one ever heard of the word special op. Not even my boys. It was simply just a play that came to my mind––just a play that came to the mind of a physical education instructor. That's all it was.

However, there were some who knew there was something going on here that just didn't meet the eye. During one of our hotly contested games, a referee ran past our bench with whistle in hand and pulled up short, for he felt compelled to say something to me. In his European accent came the assessment that he had been marveling it, perhaps because we probably sent in one or two special ops too many. The discerning eye of a trained professional saw something only a soccer purist would truly be able to decipher and appreciate. And so he breathlessly blurted out his discovery, and I was happy he was out of earshot from the opponent.

Richard Kihm exclaimed, "I have seen all of the college teams in the area, and I must tell you that your team counters better than any team I ever saw." And off he went in hot pursuit of our counterattack.

Secrecy must be paramount, for what would the league do if it became known that I was teaching my boys to go in hot, do the job, and get the hell out quick! Oh, this is not pedagogically sound. I can just hear them now as they loosen their bowtie to call me in for disciplinary action. Creativity is my province. A letter in your file is their province.

Special operations have merit and find their occasion for usefulness in many stages of a contest. Therefore, these particular events that will occur during certain parts of a game must be prepared for, and training must accompany this preparation so as to leave minimal the chance for failure.

The selection of a special op is undertaken after much thought and information has been assimilated. There is a time during the game referred to as halftime. It is at this juncture that one has the opportunity to meet behind closed doors with his team. These minutes are precious since there are no timeouts in this game except for the one you have right now. Quickly, assemble, rest, sit down, and listen up. I see their strengths and these are them. I see their weaknesses and these are them. This is what we will do about what I have seen. Now, questions. And finally, what have you seen? Hands go up; suggestions run rampant.

This is good stuff! The team is pulsating with thought, and I am loving it for I am their teacher. And this is what we do. Teacher has only one set of eyes, but before me, I have the eyes and ears tantamount to an entire US Army Signal Corps. The information garnered is enormous. We are in an exercise of interpretation and full disclosure of the opponent.

This is not the time or the place for recrimination, or even for jubilation. This is a full-fledged debriefing! From information gained by virtue of this debriefing, we are better able now to select a preplanned array of special-op missions that are to be taken in rapid order so that this opponent will be dispatched in rapid order, immediately and straight out of this locker room! Can you imagine the level of confidence with which this team now takes the field for the remaining half? If we were losing, we now have the plan to win. If we were winning, we now had the plan to secure the victory. This conviction belonged to us now more than ever since we now had their blueprint. We have made our assessment; we have our intelligence. We have our counterintelligence, and now it's a *go*!

The team captain and the two co-captains remain behind as the boys take to the field to resume the battle. There is a chain of command, and consultation must be addressed immediately. We consult briefly about the possibility that all does not go as planned. If that occurs, then these are the contingencies. If time is becoming our enemy, these are the contingencies. If time is in our favor, these are the contingencies. Is this understood? Do we have agreement? Good, then you each know exactly what to do when a contingency may occur, and you have the authority to relay orders to the team depending upon which of these contingencies prevail.

The second half resumes. Which special ops do we use? Well, we trained for each and every one, so this decision will be made by the coach and then relayed to the rest of the team by our field leaders. These leaders have been selected not by popularity—one must be from the last line of defense, one must be from our midfield, and the other must be from the attack line. This so that transitions may be consummated rapidly.

One may begin to realize how it was possible for the boys from Ridgewood to carry on for ten full years of Division A soccer in New York City without allowing a single team to beat them by more than one goal! These boys came to believe in something bigger than themselves. They were smart in many ways. They never heard of Branch Rickey or even the Brooklyn Dodgers, but they knew that luck is the residue of design. These boys were diligent in their approach to representing their beautiful and proud community of Ridgewood. Their work ethic was simply amazing, and when they took to the field, they truly played like the band of brothers that they were.

Their confidence grew with each passing year, along with their fame. All believed that they had a friend out there on the battlefield. That friend was the design of a way to play the game that was stumbled upon by "the Ghost" and "the Darkness."

My soccer teams met with success experienced by many in the first five years. We had our moments in the sun along with our share of rainy days. We became more and more powerful with the passing of the years because of the doctrine that became invincible. This doctrine was woven tightly together from the fine fabric of two distinctly different cloths. This is the doctrine that resulted in the famous streak of an unheard of run spanning ten consecutive years of never losing a regulation game of soccer by more than one goal! How could that be possible? Have the Azzuri ever put together a streak equal to that? Has Juventus, Real Madrid, Manchester United? Has Brazil, Germany, England, or Argentina? Does anyone know of any team of any sport of any time that has done this?

Well, my boys out of Ridgewood, New York City, did just that. And they did it against Division A Public School Athletic League talent. These opponents played club soccer for Inter-Giuliana, Gottschee-Blavweiss, and other numerous sports clubs. Our opponents were trained and accomplished by fine soccer coaches from all over the world. Indeed, the athletes themselves were from all over the world, trained by former coaches, fathers, brothers, uncles in all the best ideas and strategies available worldwide. And we from Ridgewood, New York City, put them all on a streak that will never be matched. We were Italian, German, Yukoslav playing alongside the two components of Serbian and Croatia for our own common cause. We were Romanian, Polish, Spanish, and we came from Haiti, Jamaica, and the Orient. Where in the world except here in New York City, could such an army be assembled?

We loved to win, and for this common cause, we learned American sports, but we learned wisdom from another fabric of a clandestine nature.

This second fabric comes from the world of G2 intelligence sector, US Army's department of counterintelligence. Maj. Charles N. Valenti had crossed the river to the other side. The name of that river is the Adige, and it flows beautifully through the town of Verona, Italy. When he arrived on the other side, there was a dried-up old fountain in a place named Piazza Bra. In the piazza are my friends Sergio, Claudio, Paolo, and they are playing soccer. Watching them intently is Alberto, the ice cream vendor, and another good-looking Italian man. They are sitting above the fountain on the park bench, overlooking the boys. Next to Albert sits a coach with a book in his hands is *Nosce Hostem*.

Beware, all who wish to know. There are many who wish you not to know. Their name is Legion. Be brave all who wish to know, for as a soldier of the Brave Rifle, I have much to teach. Be brave, all who wish to learn, for there are many who wish for you to remain ignorant. Their name is Legion!

I come before you now with knowledge gained from enduring the unendurable. My eyes have seen victory and my ears have heard the sounds of defeat. I have smelled the odor of the battlefield and that of cordite. I have known sheer fright, and I have known jubilation. I have dealt with loneliness while separated from my family, thanks to the camaraderie I was blessed with from the men under my command.

I know what it is like not to know. It is frightening. I knew of this while serving on Attu Island in 1943. Would the enemy come? We did not know. What would we do if they came? That, we did know!

Would they come through the Ardennes? We did not know. Will I ever see my newborn son of which I give my name? I do not know, but if I do, I am holding this book at the ready should he need to learn the knowledge within these pages. Surely, he will need to know what lies beneath these covers, for the knowledge within is what has kept me alive to tell this story.

Within lies the knowledge of my opponent—the knowledge of how he thinks, the knowledge of all his formidable assets. I know where he is strong and where lies his soft underbelly. This knowledge comes my way through the luck of the draw. The luck of the draw simply means that I have survived the war and am alive to tell my tale.

But beware the faint of heart. My son is now in possession of this legacy called Nosce Hostem. With it, he can help you understand the crucial knowledge gained from Knowing Your Opponent. We are the last of the lions––we are the Ghost and the Darkness. And we are here to teach you. It's what we do. Lions do not speak, but they know each other's thoughts, and these we will convey.

––Major Charles N. Valenti

To: John Frost, Editor  Mr. Charles L. Valenti

American Poetry Anthology  150-42 26 Ave.
Flushing
Dept. 31-VNQueens, Long Island, New York
250 Potrero Street  11354
P.O. Box 8403  Tel. 710-359-4802
Santa Cruz, California 95061-8403

"Cleveland, Don't Quit"
    Just three minutes left to play and then it would be done,
    The score was in their favor, they had two goals, we had one.
    So, something had to happen and it had to happen quick,
    Then, a voice came from the sideline shouting, "Cleveland, don't quit!"
    The boys took heart to hear it and dug in a little bit.
    Two minutes are left, and time is passing fast.
    If we keep up this frantic pace, I don't know if I can last.
    With one minute remaining, we're flying at them in a fury.
    "Ten men in now boys," he tells us, "pull the goalie, you have to hurry!"
    "They are never going to do it," snaps a parent, in a fit,
    And then there is that voice again shouting, "Cleveland, don't quit!"
    We get the ball to Vinnie, who is way out on the wing,
    He makes his run, will he cross, or will he bring it in?
    Their defense is in shambles, and the goalie may need a mitt,
    Again, we hear it one more time, "Cleveland, don't Quit!"

> Forty-one seconds on the clock and Vinnie turns to bring it in,
> His shot is true, right on the mark, and bedlam begins.
> Now, the coach has Vinnie firmly in his grip,
> "What's all this fuss about, coach?" asked Vin...
> "Cleveland don't quit!"

A true account by Charles L. Valenti, soccer coach of Grover Cleveland High School (1969–1985) in Ridgewood, Queens, New York City, in a response to an invitation by the American Poetry Association dated March 4, 1987.

*Note: Dad was with me on the sideline that day. It was he who kept shouting to the team, "Cleveland, don't quit!"

They had the great Pele...Franz Beckenbauer, Giorgio Chinaglia, Werner Roth, Shep Messing, and Carlos Alberto. However, lately, things had taken a turn since the departure of many of those premier athletes.

*So what have I got to lose?* I thought. Surely, they would at least lend me an ear and hear what has made my team so consistent. Who knows, maybe they could even learn something.

But there are none so blind as those who will not see! Perhaps they actually read my correspondence and were intimidated by the prospect of having to hear details pertinent to playing an old game in a new way. Perhaps, the reader thought it might even work. Most likely, he or she thought I was crazy. Crazy like a fox!

For, who among you of such high stature learned every American sport proficiently? Who among you would dare to put American concepts out on your foreign field? Scary, it just might work. Oh no, we must stay with the tried and true. That was the statement made to me at a sit down with the Red bull organization in 2007 at their New Jersey offices.

Who among you had the good fortune of a father who became an army professional intelligence officer and passed everything he learned onto his son? Who among you?

Who among you coached a soccer team for ten consecutive years in a first division without losing a single game by more than one goal?

And now, finally, this letter may be viewed by the soccer community, and let us hear what they think about the folly of my ways. It gets real simple. Do you need to win? Or don't you?

And where are you out there? You know where to find me. Put that in your pipe and smoke it! Jimmy Piersall, the baseball player once said, "Fear strikes out."

And I am fearless. Like a fox

---

```
                                        Mr. Charles L. Valenti
                                        150-42 26th Avenue
                                        Whitestone, N.Y. 11357
                                        October 1, 1984


Mr. Peppe Pinton
Managing Director
New York Cosmos
301 Rt 17 North
Rutherford, N.J. 07070


Dear Sir:

This correspondence is in reference to matters that are of an urgent mutual
concern. Although our backgrounds may be diverse, perhaps we have arrived at
a juncture that may serve as a common denominator. You are searching for a
method to sell a product and I may have the method for which you have
searched. You wouldn't have purchased part of the New York Cosmos if you
didn't firmly believe there must be a way of promoting interest and ticket
sales. I wouldn't be contacting you now if I didn't firmly believe that I may
have your answer. As surely as time is running out in search of an illusive
idea, I am certain I have the idea whose time has come.

Would you have the courage to blend your background with mine in order to
enable your product to reach the hearts of the American sports fan? Would you
demonstrate flexibility and deviate somewhat from tradition in order to sell
soccer in America? Will you allow the Cosmos to make an American cultural
commitment to the game? An affirmative response to these questions can set
forth procedures that will put people in the seats.

Being that we are in the media hub, it is apparent what the success of the
Cosmos means to the success of the North American Soccer League. It is toward
that end that I would like to submit material developed to make soccer appeal
in a cultural aspect to the American sports enthusiast. We have seen what
this cultural aspect has done to fill football, baseball and basketball arenas
throughout the country. Soccer can be added to this list by infusing concepts
of certain sports that are rooted deeply in the American psyche and culture.
These concepts would require reinforcement supported by a program to educate
the public in identifying the remarkable similarities between soccer and other
popular spectator sports.

These actions, if undertaken properly, may result in a powerful cultural
commitment to the game on the part of the Cosmos management and team. I have
developed such a program while coaching at Grover Cleveland High School. The
combination of traditional play with the infusion of American concepts has
yielded the reward of a remarkable and visually stimulating game reflecting
the best from both worlds.
```

Mr. Peppe Pinton

The concepts are unique in many ways. I have been fortunate to be proficient in every major American sport and yet six of my early years were spent in Italy as a military dependent of a U.S. Army Major. As a result military tactics and philosophies, combined with proficient knowledge of American sports, tempered by an understanding of the foreign way of thinking, has brought me to the point where I am today.

This approach has enabled me to stimulate foreign and American athletes to achieve a record of 110-39-15 in "A" Division play since 1970. My teams have not lost a single game by over a goal in eight years!

Based on that record and the crucial method from which the record has accumulated, it is hoped that you will not dismiss this correspondence lightly. I sincerely hope that you will match my initiative by arranging for a meeting at your offices so that we can discuss in greater detail what I have to offer your organization.

                                              Yours in soccer,

/se                                         Charles L. Valenti

*The "Golden Lions" 1951 Garmisch, Germany, Dad 34, Me 6*

*1980 Champions and Sons*

*Striped Bass Fishing, Chris-24, Me-42*

# Chapter 16

# Lessons From A Battle

"The 159th entered Germany as 'the Golden Lions.' We began to hear from the men who were there exactly what happened on the morning of December 16, 1944."

"Charlie, there are many lessons to be learned with the information provided by the actual participants," Dad offered.

"What lessons?" I asked.

His reply was, "When I'm done telling you the story, the lessons will reveal themselves, and what you gain from this knowledge is up to you!"

Remember, everything I learned came firsthand and was not watered down by time or propaganda. Nor did enough time elapse for political obscurities to develop and cloud or distort the evidence.

"Charlie, sit down for a while. Would you like some pretzels and a beer?"

This could take awhile!

We were sitting in the den of our home in Whitestone, Queens, New York City, on an afternoon during my senior year at Long Island University, where I was studying to become a teacher and coach. This was beginning to sound like another kind of educational opportunity, an extremely unique one at that, as he would always avoid discussing this particular battle in the past. We had often poured over aps and corresponding field manuals in his studies for career advancement. However, these courses were impersonal, and we could approach them from a distance in a clinical method of detachment. It was strictly business.

This would be personal. This would not come from a detached point of view. This would be very real indeed! I made a halfhearted attempt to lighten the mood since most of the time we behaved something like Abbott and Costello.

"Beer and pretzels?"

"We must be about to learn from the Germans," I said as I eagerly took a seat for this story I had waited years to hear, from the horse's mouth.

And so he began.

"On the morning of December 16, 1944, roaring cannons along an eighty-mile front served notice on surprised American troops that a German attack had begun."

"By 6:00 a.m., first reports had been relayed back to command posts: German infantry could be seen moving forward in the early morning dark. Behind them rumbled tanks, ready to race through gaps cleared by the infantry."

"Dad, is this where the Golden Lions were positioned?" I asked.

"Just let me continue, will you?" he responded.

*I better just eat my pretzels and sip the Budweiser if I know what's good for me*, I thought. It is obvious that this is a story he is telling me not because he wants to, but rather, he has decided that the story's time for telling had finally come.

At this point, I began to realize his affinity with this account as an army intelligence officer when he began this next sentence. "American intelligence officers described the assault as only a local diversion, but by nightfall, the situation was chaotic. Whole regiments had been overwhelmed or cut off."

*I guessed right before*, I thought to myself as I reached for another pretzel. The "Golden Lions" were in deep trouble. How many times had I heard him muttering, "Those poor guys didn't have a chance!" These were "those poor guys," and he would feel even more for them with the passing of time because he had become one of them, and blood is thicker than water.

*Never mind the pretzels, I'm going to need more beer, maybe the whole six-pack to get through this one*, I thought. As they say in the military,

"Loose lips sink ships!" so I better just listen and remain quiet before I sink myself—beer or no beer!

He continued, "Within forty-eight hours, two huge holes had been smashed through the American lines in the Ardennes—and the Panzer columns were sweeping on toward their goal of the port city of Antwerp, Belgium. We were caught napping, Charlie, just like you were the other day when you got picked off first base over at St John's University."

*Did he have to include that analogy?* I thought. *I'm paying attention. What about the triple I hit off their left field wall though?*

*Quiet, Charles*, I reminded myself, but I couldn't resist. "Dad, who was on first and put the tag on me?"

He answered, "I don't know."

"No, I don't know who was on third, but who was on first?"

"What? No, Dad. Who was on second? Vintage Abbott and Costello!" He gave me that same look he gave me years ago when I told him a lizard was under my shirt and resting on my shoulder.

He continued, "The surprise had been complete. Not until weeks later did we learn that the German Army had launched their mightiest offensive on the western front ever, with seventeen divisions and almost two hundred thousand men!"

"How could that many men and their equipment have been concealed?" I asked.

"Exactly, he answered. "And here is where you as a future teacher and coach may benefit from the knowledge given to me by the men who were there. And it is for that reason that I have chosen this time to explain all that had happened in the battle that history refers to as "The Battle of the Bulge"! Do you know why history gave this name to the battle?" he asked rhetorically.

"No," I replied.

"Do you know what a salient is, Charlie?"

"No," I replied once again. If this were a baseball game, I would not be 0 for 2 and at the mercy of the pitcher.

I would never forget what a salient is in the soccer years ahead, for it became our major tactic that enabled my boys of Ridgewood to prevail and dominate the Public Schools Athletic League for ten consecutive years of never losing a soccer game by more than one goal!

"The Bulge" is the salient that the German Army created when it forced a huge wedge to be formed deep into the allied lines. It is like a finger going deep inside enemy territory. The top of the finger is the point of attack, while the sides of the finger protect the flanks from the enemy on both sides. Therefore, the "salient" is a proven battle tactic that can split a strong enemy force at the point of your choosing. When the initial force surges ahead, the reserves patiently await their chance to move in the gap and present themselves as a full-fledged assault on a disorganized and panic-stricken enemy. This was our greatest weapon at Cleveland. With this idea, we would leave the opponent with his knees knocking, his heart pounding, and we would leave him breathless!

Now the reason why my team out of Ridgewood, Queens, would elicit such emotions in our opponents can be traced back to that day we shared in the den of our house. He had saved this lesson for quite some time. It was obvious to me that this was an example of an event that had been meticulously planned well in advance.

"How could seventeen divisions and two hundred thousand men have possibly presented themselves and their massive equipment as a surprise?" I asked him.

That question was met immediately by another as he replied. "How could the Japanese fleet sail halfway across the Pacific Ocean to attack Pearl Harbor by surprise?"

"There were clues, Charlie, to forecasting both events—much like the people on television are able to forecast the weather—and the clues were ignored." This was a matter for the intelligence community of the armed forces to detect, analyze, and interpret, and Dad felt that the intelligence community lacked a keen eye to see information that was available but disguised.

For my development as the soccer coach of Cleveland, this lesson proved priceless. "What do both attacks have in common, Charlie?" he asked.

I answered, "Surprise. A meticulously planned surprise."

"And why did the German army pick the Ardennes sector?" he asked.

I thought back to a question I had asked him years earlier. It had bothered me that a robber had chosen a local bank to ply his craft, and I had asked him, "Why did he pick that bank?" His classic answer was, "Because that's where the money is, Charlie."

"An analysis of deductive reasoning sheds light on why a point of attack is chosen. In this case, the British Army had penetrated in great force to the north under the command of their feisty leader, General Bernard Montgomery. That force was intent on the liberation of Holland, and also had begun to approach an assault on the first big German city of Aachen. Therefore, what could be gained by a surprise attack to the north?"

"To the east, the Russian Bear was waiting for the fierce Russia winter to run its course. What would be the point of an attack in that front with regard to a strategic objective? Men and material are subject to a battle of attrition and are subject to the exhaustion offered by both the enemy and harsh weather conditions. Nothing could be gained."

"To the south appeared the spectra of the American Third Army under the command of a colorful and pugnacious general known as 'Old Blood and Guts,' General George Patton. Although seventeen well-armored divisions numbering two hundred thousand men could wreak havoc even against the highly touted Third Army, what would be the point?"

"To the west appeared an interesting concept that incorporated the possibility of altering the outcome of the war. The German forces moved quickly through the western approach in 1940 and quickly became the masters of the European mainland. Who would expect them to do that again? As the robber chose a bank, because that is where the money is, the Germans chose the Ardennes forest because that was where no one would expect. Surprise, speed, and power through this region would be virtually unopposed."

"Surprise, speed, and power could split the ability of the British to the north and the Americans to the south. With confusion and panic as their only allies, the German Army had its sight set on driving through to take the port of Antwerp, in Belgium, where they hoped to sue for a peaceful settlement to the war. It almost worked until the clouds of war lifted and the combined air force of the British and Americans put an end to the final German attack of the war."

In our favor, as a soccer team, while emulating these historical accounts and concepts, the British and American airpower did not attempt to intervene. Without the help of that combined airpower, the fate of all our opponents was virtually sealed right from the outset. We would go in strong left, then we might try strong right, but we would never go in where they were strong. The decision to switch from right to left depended upon the opponent relocation of force to stop our salient. This was done by a Cleveland High School soccer team out of Ridgewood, NY.

From my father's teachings, my thoughts ran wild with these meticulously planned attacks and counterattacks gained from the applicable knowledge of military intelligence and counterintelligence dogma sharpened by the research of actual historical events studied scrupulously by "The Ghost and the Darkness." The "Golden Lions" bore the brunt of that fateful day of December 16, 1944. But there is one "Golden Lion" remaining, and he had a son.

And that son is me.

And this is what the boys of Ridgewood, New York, learned from me, their teacher from knowledge provided to me from an army intelligence officer I knew as my father. Ten years we spent down on the battlefield in New York City reenacting the tactics and strategies inherent in the famous Battle of the Bulge. Who would ever think to look there for new and mind-stimulating ways to plan such an old game? We did!

But in order for me to identify with these mind boggling concepts found on the hallowed battlefield of the Ardennes, I need to have the answer. "How could the drive through the Ardennes have been a surprise, Dad?"

"Well, Charlie, from accounts taken from my buddies of the "Golden Lions" who were actually there, here is the answer," he said.

"The Germans had for some time amassed, refitted, and reconstituted three separate Panzer Armies. These were attacking armies consisting of various German state of the art tanks known as Panzer and Tiger tanks, supported by artillery units and infantry. There were three separate locations where they had been known to be residing and did not seem to alarm our intelligence people. However, this was achieved by design."

"They were known as the Fourth, Fifth, and Sixth Panzer Armies. From plans to attack, the German war machine rapidly began moving. Sixth Panzer Army, under Dietrich in the lead, began its sudden shift from the Ruhr industrial area where it had been standing guard, and by a series of night moves felt its way toward the weakly held front of r American VIII Corps."

I remained all ears as usual. Meanwhile, to the south, both the Fifth Panzer Army, sparked by their crafty leader Manteuffel, and the Seventh Army under Brandenberger, had successfully completed their secret assembly in the heavily wooded areas of the Ardennes Forests," he continued.

"Manteuffel, like Dietrich, began moving his troops forward, first to the initial assembly areas, and then on the night before the attack, to the final assembly areas from which his troops would move out the next day. Brandenberger carefully shunted his attack divisions into their proper positions, always attempting to prevent detection of unusual movement."

And then came the rub, the part that would always bother him even with the passing of all these years.

"Our forces along the front, I was told, actually heard their movements. As good as they were, even the Germans cannot move seventeen divisions to within a few miles of our frontline completely undetected. Our intelligence interpreted this movement as just a normal relief of frontline divisions, which was often a normal occurrence. One of the intelligence officers whom I became friends with told me, 'Hell, I thought they were moving troops ether to the north or south to meet our attacks from those directions. I knew it couldn't be us they were after as this was the quiet sector where everyone got a rest.'"

"Dad," I asked. "Is it true that the Germans ran out of fuel?"

"Yes, they did, Charlie." That always bothered me throughout my soccer battles in the years to come. I feared that my boys would run out of steam if I pushed too hard in our endless forays into the enemy camp on the soccer fields of New York City. Therefore, at tryouts in September of every year, no soccer ball was to be seen for the first two weeks. There would never be a cut. I never in all my years cut a single soccer player. They would simply cut themselves. We would run and run and run until they would drop out one by one on their own decision. We would be led around and around the field for hours each day for two weeks by an old baseball player out of New York City—me!

The premise was that if a man twice your age can do this, then what is to be your excuse for not doing these arduous tasks of fitness? I do indeed *say arduous*. We had to run up and down the steps of the stadium at Dekalb and Seneca Avenue in our beloved Ridgewood.

After that, you must pick a partner of similar weight and carry him on your back the full length of the field to the goalpost. There you would change, and he would carry you back. And who thought of these tortuous trials? They did! That is how much they demanded to be the best. I could only supply the teaching and drive of a fierce competitor. They supplied the will and determination that I will never forget. Where do you get such men? Where do they come from? I would always wonder. You get them here, in Ridgewood, Queens, and they come here to America from all over the world!

It was the Ridgewood boys who knew that they must not run out of fuel! When the fourth quarter arrived and the issue was in doubt, we always had enough fuel, and never did we never come up short for lack of energy. The boys demanded of themselves that they be superior physically to any team they may encounter from each of the five boroughs—Queens, Brooklyn, Manhattan, the Bronx, and Staten Island. Not one could beat the boys from Ridgewood by more than one goal during that famous ten-year run through the Public Schools Athletic League. Along the way, the boys appealed to me to take them out to Nassau and Suffolk counties of Long Island. "Why?" I asked.

"So we can beat up on those Catholics!" was the answer.

The Catholic schools would begin their season fully two or three weeks to their advantage, and we would assemble our forces and mobilize," as it required a long car ride out to Long Island. You see, the private Catholic school teams were very talented as they offered scholarships to recruit quality players, and we respected those teams. However, we could never convince a single one of them that Ridgewood, New York City, was a wonderful place to come and play ball. They never heard of Ridgewood; however, it was the proposition of coming into big and bad New York City that required us to drive out there and "beat up on them Catholics!"

The German Sixth Panzer Army had tanks and trucks, as did Patton's Third Army. My boys had three broken-down old cars and my 280ZX sports model, and off we went, totally fearless! There were eight soccer players in my 280ZX per trip! Looking back, maybe we should have been afraid after all.

Years later, I was told a story by a man named Kosta Ardeljan. He served my boys well as coach of the team many played for locally on Sunday afternoons. He owned a local garage, and I would pull in off the road every now and then in order to have my old 280ZX serviced since it was not meant to be a troop transport vehicle. We spoke soccer as he replaced my worn brakes, or changed the oil or my high beam bulb.

On one such occasion, he mentioned that several of my players stopped by a few days before with a transmission problem. Kosta was our motor pool mechanic and kept us on the road. He would attend many of our hotly contested league games. I remember one of those visits especially well.

It was a playoff game, and the score was zero to zero, late in the second half. It was apparent that the team who scored and drew first blood would be the winner, and the season would end abruptly for the loser. Kosta began pacing the sidelines, crouching and then standing intermittently as he nervously paced relentlessly back and forth.

Finally, he just couldn't bear the tension and the pressure any longer and blurted out for all to hear. "Valenti, do something!"

I looked over my crossed arms only to tell him that there was nothing I can do. He stared at me in disbelief!

Then he said, "You are Valenti! What do you mean there is nothing you can do?"

"Don't worry, Kosta," I assured him. "Everything will be all right, but right now, that team is better than us! We cannot risk the attempt it will take to score a goal. The boys are well trained and will allow them to penetrate just so far and no farther. We will take them in a shootout!"

Now Kosta had been asking me before the game why I had asked him to check my high beam bulbs. He thought it odd that half my team had asked him to do the same thing this week.

"Valenti, I just have to tell you something," he said in that Romanian accent. "I asked your team what was the most important thing that you have taught them, and you must know the answer. They all agreed that they learned from you not to fear any opponent. From you, they have learned to be fearless, and I think you should know that!"

Kosta and I had become good friends. He was their coach for the First German Sport Club that served the local Ridgewood soccer program. His nephew, Panta Ardeljan, played the midfield position and achieved what few players out of the Big Apple have been able to accomplish. He was selected by Adidas as all-American from our team of fearless athletes from Grover Cleveland High School in Ridgewood, Queens, NYC.

The game went into two scoreless overtime periods while he paced the sidelines, wearing out the carpet in the process, and then the shootout procedure was instructed to begin by the officials. Five of our best shooters went to the eleven-meter line. Each had been trained to perfect a shot from within their own natural talent. These choices included top corner or low corner, left or right, fired sharply or with a chip of finesse. However, as a shooter, you could only select the one you as an individual would be most comfortable taking on behalf of your teammates.

We were a perfect five for five. So were they! Poor Kosta, I thought. I have to take him for beers later at the Eagle's Nest Tavern or maybe McZacks, which Ronnie and I used as our watering hole.

"Five new shooters, step up," demanded the officiating crew.

My five "new" shooters went to the line and calmly and deliberately put five more into the back of the net.

"These are my players," Kosta exclaimed. "I can't believe this! Not even the professional players can do this!"

Our opponent was extremely good and finished their season one goal short. They went four for five! We went on to win the New York City championship with an undefeated record of eighteen victories and no defeats—undefeated! That shootout was the critical moment to separate a champion from the rest of the field. It wasn't as easy as it sounds.

The reason why the high beam bulbs kept burning out on my 280ZX and the four or five other cars is because of an account told to me by Dad while he was gathering information from his "Golden Lions." It was very dark on the early morning of December 16, 1944.

The Sixth Panzer Army, Dad learned, was under the command of Sepp Dietrich, who went by the nickname of "Butcher Boy" for his ruthless attacks in the past. His powerful force had been "hiding in plain sight" while standing guard for all the world to see near the Ruhr industrial area of Germany. Was this by design? We will return to this question later.

"Charlie, it was the Fifth Panzer Army that came in during the darkness with infantry ahead of their tanks. This Fifth Panzer was led by a crafty Field Marshall Manteuffel. Manteuffel's Sixty-Sixth Corps, led by General Lucht, was allotted two infantry divisions to envelop a land known as the Schnee Eifel and the two regiments of the inexperienced 106$^{th}$ Division, who were perched atop the small segment of the West Wall, the German perimeter." An impression was made upon me.

Lights! Use lights in the dark, and you can do as you see fit for as long as you wish. This is how we toiled on into the night at our field in plain sight of the Twin Towers! That is why our high beams were always in need of replacement. We needed an extraordinary amount of time to perfect our shootout procedure after the regular practice and preparation was consummated.

The cars would be rolled out onto the field, and our ten shooters, along with our two goaltenders, were mandated to remain every night during the week prior to the playoffs. Moms and dads were so notified of this order and advised of the utmost importance that every shooter and the two goalies must be present and accounted for or risk being replaced by a more dedicated teammate. Does this sound military? Well, it is! Not one soul could leave after the others departed since the locker room was closed and locked. And now, not one soul could leave until we made ten for ten from the eleven-meter line. And which of you goalies wants to play more than the other? For I am the Ghost with all the tricks, and this idea we undertake in the night I learned from accounts told to me by the Darkness himself—The Ghost and the Darkness—a pair of "Golden Lions."

There is a personal reason I have for releasing much of what will follow. You see, for all of those years, I was sworn to secrecy in order to protect my boys from our opponents, and we had many. We had opponents on the field and even more dangerous opponents off the field. Jealousy makes for many enemies, and since I have been in the business of knowing my enemies, indeed I knew them all.

It wasn't easy for me to hear that the Physical Education Department was not held in high regard. I often wondered why the administration felt secure to send one of us to cover a subject matter class with five minutes' notice. The reason was because we were talented enough to teach any lesson, and indeed, all we did need was five minutes' notice. It is for all of you out there who are subject to disrespect that I am now stepping up to the plate. This is an example of what we can accomplish on and off the field. To my colleagues in biology, math, history, secretarial studies, foreign language and all other areas of expertise to which I have successfully taught, I have a question. Why is it that in all my years of teaching, anyone of you who covered the class of one of my colleagues could only become a laughingstock in need of rescue by the Ghost? Who among you could write a meaningful and educational book? Who could write two? I am a physical education teacher, and I can write a story like Barry Manilow can write a song, only my story is true!

It was necessary to get that off my chest, or I would not have been able to proceed. If that alienated you, then perhaps you better get off the bus right here, for how will you deal with what's to come? What follows is not for Goody-Two shoes.

Vince Lombardi famously believed that winning isn't everything—it is the only thing! That is the way it was in Ridgewood, and if that offends you, maybe you better do a few extra lesson plans to blow off steam. I am a coach. My dad was a coach. We teach a team how to win; it's what we do!

Many a day, before or after a game, I would remind the boys that if I had anything of value to teach, it was that! If they would rather learn how to lose, then I advised them to take any number of courses taught in the building.

# Chapter 17

# The Outlier Chameleons Of Ridgewood

Branch Rickey, the old Brooklyn Dodger boss, once said that "Luck is the residue of design." Leo Durocher once said that "Nice guys don't win ball games," or some heard it this way by Leo: "Nice guys finish last."

The "Golden Lion" I refer to as the Darkness has enabled me to become an "outlier," and with the knowledge, he carefully schooled me to the point where my Ridgewood team also became "outliers." What is an "outlier?" Is this a book about soccer or what? Well, as I have said to the boys on numerous occasions, "If you wish to learn the mundane"—or as I put it to them, how to lose—"there are many teachers in the building who are quite qualified to teach that subject matter. But if you wish to learn what it takes to win, then you must pay very close attention to what I am teaching—because winning is what I do!"

So what is an "outlier?"

Recently, while waiting for an outbound flight at LaGuardia airport in New York City, I began to browse through the books for sale at the gift shop. To tell the truth, my reason was to measure the books available against the two I have written.

*Oh, mine are better than these*, I thought. *Wait a minute. This one could be better than my first one, but my second one is better than this.* You see, I have to win all the time, or I feel terribly disappointed. I know this about myself, but there is nothing I can do about this ailment. I just lose sore, or as some may describe me in a more descriptive verbiage, I am a sore loser. I make that claim hoping it may help e t find a cure. Some say that method is warranted when dealing with alcoholism, so maybe it will work for me. Otherwise, I can pray to St. Jude for help since one refers to St. Jude as the saint of hopeless cases!

However, returning to the point, something St. Matthew refers to in the Holy Bible stands out in my mind. He made the argument, something like this, as close as I can recount. If a young person is given advice, direction, encouragement doled out with great patience and is thus nurtured, he or she has a good chance to succeed in life. He or she may become an "outlier." Even at this late date, I am always seeking an edge. That is why I recently bought a CD of Mozart's most prominent works. Now what does an old coach want with Mozart, you ask? It promised that if one listened endlessly to his creations, the result could be like that leading to becoming an "outlier." I gave it a try, and I am perhaps awaiting the results of how this second book will be received. Lord knows I have no idea yet of how the "all-American" version will be received either. So I am a sore loser who listens to Mozart while hoping to become an "outlier" that has no limits in sight—kind of like the song from *Man of La Mancha*, "The Impossible Dream."

The book I was reviewing discusses how statistics revealed how one's date of birth may affect the ability of an athlete to become an "outlier." That discussion revolved around the premise of a cutoff date after which one may miss out on the opportunity granted to others but denied to him or her. Another statistical point made referred to a village in Italy many years ago as having not one inhabitant experiencing heart failure. They were "outliers."

My point, when taken seriously, and perhaps I have damaged your ability to take me seriously with my attempt at gallows humor...

To continue, as a teacher or a coach, we may have such a chance to attempt fate itself and change the very course or the charges who believe in us and hang on our every word. They will "march into hell for a heavenly cause," and we must be honor bound as educators to give them every opportunity before the chance is missed and it is too late.

An "outlier" isn't someone special. Rather, an "outlier" has had the fortune of being treated like someone special and has responded like the seed blossoms to become the flower. At the beginning of each season back in Ridgewood, the wind of fall would carry the seeds to my friend at Dekalb and Seneca Avenues. By the onset of winter, all the seeds would blossom and become flowers. From there, I wished my "outlier" blossoms, Godspeed, and is sent on his way.

These blossoms had become knowledgeable about what it takes to survive out there in the real world. Their training and learning was not a walk in the park; it was rough. However, in all my years as the drill sergeant, I was never registered with even a single complaint. Was the repetition harsh? Was the dedication harsh? Were the long hours we put in harsh? Of course they were—because we were a team of "outliers."

I realize this appears a bit harsh. I had a wife and two kids waiting for Daddy to come home and tuck them into bed for the night. I had a nice plate of spaghetti waiting for me that would be cold by the time I arrived home. I was tired from my long day at school and exhausted by the conclusion of the "perfect" ten finale. But I needed to win before I needed to eat. I needed to win before I needed to sleep. I wasn't doing this to get paid; I couldn't care less about that. And so, boys, I ask you: Do you just want to win, like everyone else in the world, or do you *need* to win? Make up your mind. They too needed to win.

After these arduous nights I would remind them that someday they would marry their sweetheart. God willing, they would be blessed with children, and someday, "You will sit quietly at home when they became old enough to understand. You will tell them what it felt like to be the very best at what you do. You will tell them how very difficult and almost impossible it will be for them to achieve perfection. You will tell them never to forget this story as you show them your gold medal. You will tell them that once upon a time, there was a team that worked so hard because it needed to own a memory it could take with them for the rest of their lives. And maybe someday, when your children are blessed with children and you are now a grandfather, you can tell them also!"

Thus armed with assistance of an event of a battle past, we had everyone present and accounted for. Not a soul went AWOL (absent without leave). Our only casualty were the high beam bulbs.

Now what about that Sixth Panzer Army "hiding in plain sight" near that position guarding the industrial Rhur Valley? When the night of December 15th fell, they relocated hastily under the cover of darkness in order to present themselves as part of the great attack that would begin the next morning at a very different coordinate. The Sixth Panzer Army behaved with all the natural instincts of a chameleon. Could my army behave in this manner?

## The Chameleon

At this juncture, I must return to an event that occurred back in Verona, Italy, that eventually had a profound impact in building my soccer teams of Ridgewood, New York City, in the years ahead. Many ingredients have been put forth up to this point in producing a division-A team that refused to lose even one single game by more than one goal over a span of ten consecutive years. The Grover Cleveland soccer team benefitted handsomely by this event of mysterious chance. This event taught me the priceless value of transforming an entire soccer team into a chameleon. Now you see us and now you don't!

It happened like this.

As mentioned earlier, the Adige River ran right through the middle of Verona in the shape of the letter *S*. I went down to the riverbank one sunny summer afternoon with a jar in hand to catch bees like we used to do back in the states when I saw lizards scatter. I noticed an Italian fisherman nearby (for there were no American fishermen in Italy).

However, my attention turned to the lizards, and I began to catch them in the jar near the tall green grass that grew alongside the riverbank. They were a beautiful green color and were hard to see as I chased after them with the open jar. I caught a few but fell for an amazing trick they used to escape. When they felt boxed in, they would drop their tail; and as you went for the movement of the tail, they would escape. Wow! What a great idea, I thought. This sure fooled me. This was an exercise in ultimate disinformation, and this tactic was used extensively in the soccer years that were to follow. However, I meant no harm to these creatures and ceased chasing them once I learned of their extreme measure of assuring their freedom.

On the way back home up the bank of the river, I began to release all the lizards one by one from their containment in the jar. As I dropped them out onto the sand, I was amazed to see that these green lizards were no longer green. They were now the color of the sand! How could I ever forget this wonderful talent of disguise? Could a soccer team change in this manner of illusion or optical illusion in order to protect itself from the opponent?

If you wish to backtrack a bit, you will find that there has been no mention of a system or style that may be set in stone. Soccer enthusiasts love to pigeonhole a team in a fixed identification numerically so as that particular team may be identified. All systems and styles have built into them certain identifiable strengths and corresponding weaknesses. So why in the world would I elect to have anyone know me by such an obvious information disclosure? No thanks. I prefer to be the chameleon; none of this 4–3–3, 4–2–4, 5–4–1, 4–4–2 description for the Grover Cleveland team out of Ridgewood, New York City. Nothing obvious about this team from T=Ridgewood except it is a mystery to all who have encountered it on the soccer field. Our style is that of the chameleon. Our identity is unique, as unique as the city we have been so proud to be a part of, for there is New York City, and then there are all the other cities of the world. Frank Sinatra said it best in his song, "New York, New York." If you can make it here, you can make it anywhere, and we not only made it here but we also made it almost impossible for anyone else to make it here. It was all up to us," New York, New York!"

When changing configurations on the field, it is essential that the coach maintain a poker face under extreme pressure so as not to disclose your hand on your emotions. All that can wait for the locker room and press conference after the game. The chameleon story continues to teach me this valuable lesson in self-restraint and composure. You're going to love this part!

Stay with me as we go back to releasing the lizards, and I headed up the riverbank for home as dinnertime was fast approaching. I passed the fisherman and waved as he tipped his cap to me. *He sure looks like he knows what he's doing*, I thought.

Arriving home, I thoroughly washed my hands and took my seat at the table with my family when I suddenly felt something crawl up my left arm and onto my shoulder! I froze. How could I tell my mom and dad that I had a lizard running up my shirt? She had just made a nice baked ziti dinner for us, and I didn't want to ruin everything. Can you imagine this? Could I possibly make this stuff up?

So I sat there for the entire dinner and ate baked ziti with them since the lizard seemed content to sit it all out on my shoulder. At the conclusion of dinner, I signaled Dad to come in the hallway with me, and he followed me into the bedroom.

"Why are you walking so stiff?" he asked. "Did you hurt your arm pitching the other day? What's going on, Charlie?"

"Dad, there is a lizard sitting on my shoulder under my shirt, and I need your help because they are very fast."

He stood in the doorway and just looked at me. Finally, he said, "Are you serious? How the hell did a lizard get on your shoulder?"

"Be quiet, Dad. Don't let Mom hear you, and if you can catch two flies in midair with one hand, then you are faster than this lizard! Are you ready? I'll turn around and lift my shirt up, and you grab him and throw him out the window, okay? They don't have any teeth, so don't worry."

"All right, Charlie, on three," he said, like the quarterback of old. "One, two, three!"

We both shouted and moved like lightning as Mom called, "What's going on in there?"

She disrupted the concentration, and the lizard jumped to the floor and ran alongside the wall. I don't know who was more shook up, me, my dad, or that lizard. There was whooping and hollering, and bedlam broke loose The night table fell over and the lamp hit the floor, and then there was this blur of movement with one hand, and the lizard became airborne as he sailed harmlessly out the window into the yard below.

"What the heck are you two doing?" asked my mom.

Dad walked slowly out the door as I quickly placed the lamp on the night table.

*Wow! Is that guy cool*, I thought as I slowly walked out the door. I guess the apple doesn't fall far from the tree after all.

He made his way out onto the balcony where just a few days before I had ventured while my parakeet rested comfortably on my shoulder. I calmly did a military about face and forward march back inside before that bird even knew he was outside.

"Honey," Mom asked my dad. "What is so funny out there?"

He couldn't even talk, he was laughing so hard. I had kept my cool under pressure, and I felt more pressure than I ever felt in those baseball playoff games. It was a great lesson. Keep your cool always, and everything will be all right.

Anyone can be a cool customer when all is going as prescribed, but as Rudyard Kipling famously wrote, "If you can keep your head about you when all are losing theirs, then you are a man, my son."

Well, that proves the point that measured action in coordination is far superior than spontaneous action taken rashly. The score will not always be in your favor, but with inner calm and perseverance and determination combined with speed of thought and movement, anything is possible. I'm referring not to lizard chasing, to be sure, but to winning soccer games. At any rate, let's chalk this one up for the lizard for a lesson learned.

Soon after that adventure, I ventured back down to the river. I was not looking for a repeat performance with the lizards. It was the fisherman who filled me full of curiosity. My dad and schoolteachers and friends had taught me many things; however, none of these people were fishermen. Maybe I could learn to be a fisherman. It intrigued me that the fisherman is smarter than the fish. As the years passed, I found that my fishing skills landed many lunkers. There were all kinds of fish swimming around in the Public Schools Athletic League in division-A soccer. With the right kind of bait and knowledge of their habits and habitat, we fishermen from Ridgewood reeled them all in hook, line, and sinker. It is the wily knowledge of the fisherman that gave rise to ideas that outfoxed all the unsuspecting opponents who ventured out onto our pond in Ridgewood, Queens, New York City. Our home field was at the juncture of DeKalb and Seneca Avenue. We practiced all these ideas tirelessly by day and often well into the night. Sprawling out there before us was the majestic skyline of Manhattan, which would magically light up as we decided to chase perfection well into the night. What an inspiration to see our wonderful city lit up in all those resplendent colors as the sun went down behind the Twin Towers and the Empire State Building. And so we toiled on into the night perfecting the eleven-meter shootout process, and the corner kicks along with all the directs and indirects, for this was our pond, and we were the fishermen with all the tricks who toiled into the night next to the city that never sleeps. The city where two baseball players named Valenti were born.

We worked harder and longer than any other team because there was so much more for the boys to learn. Saturdays and holidays were part of the routine in our chase of perfection in our throw-in procedures and our mastery of the offside trap and multiple audible free kicks. We were relentless in our drive to win. The boys were schooled in a mental toughness and philosophy that all but eliminated the possibility of being thwarted by chance or by the law of averages.

The following will serve to summarize the dogma to which we all subscribed in our relentless pursuit to accomplish a streak that no other team has even come close to achieving.

> Remember these words...
> First, you must study your opponent.
> Second, you must know how he moves,
> So you will know what he will do,
> Before he does it.
> Third, there will be one moment in the fight,
> Where you can win, and wait for it.
> Fourth is only for the brave,
> And now you will strike
> And not care if you live or die!
> And we had a song to unite us, it went like this:
> Hands in boys. Ready, set, go! And the boys boomed in unison:
> *Uno, due, tre, quarto, cinco, sei*
> *Siki zaka, siki zaka* hey, hey, hey!

After hearing that, everyone in attendance would cheer! Even passersby in the street outside would cheer. It signaled that the Grover Cleveland soccer team was about to take the field; and if you were a spectator at one of our games, you were about to see something you ain't never seen before!

If you were the opponent, it was assured that at the end of this encounter, your knees will be knocking and your heart will be pounding, and we will leave you breathless. For we are Cleveland, and we are coming at you with no fear, and we bring with us an arsenal the likes of which you also have never seen before!

My dad hesitated to relay events of December 16, 1944 through January 8, 1945, because it hurt and troubled him for years. You have to understand that he lost some friends in that battle and learned of the battle particulars from soldiers who survived but lost their friends. I could not fully realize the impact of how he felt until years after I had left Ridgewood. When Tuesday morning arrived on September 11, 2001, we in Ridgewood took casualties, and it is a feeling one must indeed live with forever. Two of my boys come to mind especially.

The Cleveland baseball team needed a coach during the early eighties as my dear friend Ron Mauro had passed away. He would ask me to come down to Glenridge Oval and help cheer the team. He assembled them before a game one day as I stood with him in front of the group.

"I brought Mr. Valenti down today for good luck," he told them. "Maybe some of the success he has had with our soccer team might rub off on us."

That's the way Ronnie was. Over the years, he would often share a bottle of Chianti with me that he had smuggled into the office. We would stay after school and order a pizza, and then he said one day, over that bottle, "I'm real proud of you, Charlie. I'm proud that you have returned the school soccer team to the prominence it had enjoyed under our famous Joe Singer, and that you are Italian makes me even prouder!"

I owed him a season and took over the team. I went around the building knocking on doors to recruit boys I knew and asked for favors if they could give me one season for Coach Mauro. Ronnie, this bud is for you! We finished two games from a city final.

Mike Weinberg had caught for me as a junior varsity player and said to me when I knocked on his teachers' door, "Sure, Vee."

We opened up against Holy Cross High School, the city Catholic school champion from the year before. Each player had been issued a special uniform jersey to wear. This would be a special season, and each eagerly donned the Grover Cleveland High School soccer jersey for good measure.

All my mercenaries were told to report to our home opener at Dekalb and Seneca Avenue where that magnificent view of Manhattan greeted you as you entered the clubhouse; and there they found their name taped to a locker, and on the bench in front of their name was their caps and uniforms folded neatly.

"Did we make the pros?" they asked. And then they played like pros!

What better way to open a season than a direct challenge to the Catholic school champion from the year before. They suited up, took the field, and didn't know it yet, but they would become the "Cinderella" baseball team out of Ridgewood, Queens. Mike Weinerg was the leader.

We were no match for them, but Mike set the stage with a three-run home run to deep center field. The game went down to the wire. Holy Cross was ahead 4 to 3, and we took the bat for our last "licks." We had runners on second and third; however, there were two out, and Mike came up to hit. The outfielders took a few steps deeper. I asked the umpire to call time-out, and Mike stepped out of the box as we met to talk this over.

"Mike, can you do one more thing for me?" I asked.

"Sure, Vee," he would always say.

"On the first pitch after the first strike, I need you to lay one down."

"You mean bunt?" he asked with a look of amazement.

"Mike, they'll never expect it, but you have to go like hell to beat it out, *okay?*"

"What are the runners doing, Vee?" he asked.

"Gaspare is coming in from third on the first pitch after the first strike, and Chris is coming in nonstop right on his ass!"

"I like it, Vee," and he stepped in as I returned to third and flashed Gaspare the steal sign immediately after the first strike came in; the steal sign with my finger pointing to home plate. Now Chris standing on second base got the same exact sign fro me and cannot believe his eyes. He gave me the "repeat" sign back, and I reissue the steal home sign for him as well. Then he acknowledged, Gaspare acknowledged. Mike got the bunt sign so there is no doubt or turning back. It will happen on this pitch no matter where the pitch is. Everyone on the bench came to a speechless standstill.

Here it comes. Mike lay down a beauty to the third base side of the pitcher, and off he went toward first base. The pitcher backhanded the ball as Gaspare crossed the plate unseen. If the pitcher can throw Mike out, the game was over, and Holy Cross would win. Chris was now rounding third and on his way in as the pitcher made his play to first base. The pitcher never even saw him, for his play was to get Mike at first base. The whole team depended upon Mike as the throw went to first base, and Chris crossed the plate. All eyes were on Mike now, and he put on a desperate surge of speed and beat the throw! That was Mike Weinberg, and we lost him on September 11, 2001.

Later that season, Coach Joe Russo of St. John's University called me and offered Mike a baseball scholarship at St. John's. I spoke to Mike's mom, and we were both very proud of him. All of us here in Ridgewood will always remember Mike Weinberg.

Mike knew who Ron Mauro was and what he meant to Grover Cleveland High School. He was our baseball coach and our swim team coach. He was a fine teacher and as good a friend that any teacher or student in the building could ever hope to find. Some members of his swim team had voices like a tenor and would join in unison after a swim meet for their beloved coach. It went like this: "To Mauro, to Mauro, we love you, to Mauro, tomorrow's another day!" Mike and all his hastily recruited friends played that season with a black patch on their shoulder to signify that they were playing this season for the old coach who had passed away from an illness the spring before. We began to win one game after the other, thanks to some old tricks handed down to me by an army baseball player and the inordinate amount of dedication from each and every member of that team.

> **BOARD OF EDUCATION • NEW YORK CITY**
>
> ## Grover Cleveland High School
>
> 2127 HIMROD STREET  •  RIDGEWOOD, N.Y. 11385  •  TELEPHONE: 381-9600
>
> May 15, 1985
>
> Dear Coach:
>
> This letter of recommendation concerns a player of mine here at Grover Cleveland High School. Arturo Santos has proven to be instrumental in our outstanding success this season. Due largely to his pitching and batting efforts, we are currently in 1st. place with an overall 12 & 3 record in Queens Division II.
>
> Art is a lefthanded pitcher and has dominated every team he has taken the mound against. In addition, he hits with power and plays a fine centerfield when not on the mound.
>
> Art is one of our outstanding graduating seniors and he has expressed an interest in attending your institution. Since he is a high quality player, financial assistance is a matter for consideration. We would appreciate it if you could contact Art and send him some information regarding your institution.
>
> You will notice his address and telephone number in addition to my home phone number. Perhaps you would like to see him play in the playoffs which will begin May 23rd.
>
> We look forward to hearing from you some time in the near future.
>
> Yours in Baseball,
>
> Charles L. Valenti
> Coach, Cleveland
>
> ARTURO SANTOS
> 355 WOODWARD AVENUE
> RIDGEWOOD, NEW YORK 10385
> (718) 456-3311
>
> CHARLES L. VALENTI
> (718) 359-4802

We went deep into the playoffs for him as we tried to get to Yankee Stadium for a short at the city championship. However, we ran into a proven "baseball" school in Brooklyn called James Madison, and they took a 13 to 0 lead in the first inning. Dad was at the game, sitting in the stands. Sam Dattolo was our ace, and he had anxiety problems leading to a loss of his usual impeccable control of the baseball. He had to be relieved. So the sign went to our first baseman. I pointed to right field, and that was where Sammy went to pasture. Then the right fielder trotted over to shortstop, and Gaspare, Sam's brother, came in to relieve. I wonder where I learned that from. Dad was leaning forward in his seat. Gaspare retired to the side as Mike shouted to him, "Way to go, Gaspare!" And the boys came in off the field mauled and battered. Their heads were down as they stared at their shoetops.

"Never mind the score, boys," I called out as I went up and down the bench. "Can you give me three runs for Coach Mauro?"

"Sure, Vee, we can give you three." And they gave me four.

"It ain't 13 to 0 anymore, boys!" I shouted. The boys took the field, and I called Sammy back for a private minute.

"What's up, Vee?"

"Sammy, do you want the ball back?" Where have I heard those words before?

"*Okay*, Vee, give me the ball!" Dad looked down from the stands in approval.

He retired the side, three up, three down, and Mike was visibly enthusiastic and shouted, "Way to go, Sammy!" The boys came in running this time.

"Boys, can you give me three runs for Coach Mauro?" I asked. Many heads now bobbing in total agreement now and hollers of "Sure, Vee, we'll get you three more." And that they did! It was 13 to 7. A fan ran down to shout through the screen.

"Coach, I saw Casey Stengel do this one time!" Madison became unnerved and jittery. Their bats had a bit hole in the sweet spot now. Sammy went out and struck out the side.

This place in Brooklyn had now become a zoo!

"Just get me two more for Mauro, boys." Loud shouts of "Yeah, Vee, we'll get you two more" from the dugout. They went out and got me five, and now the score was 13 to 12.

Sammy went out and mowed them down, one, two, three. Mike was calling a superb game and had brought Sammy all the way back.

"How about that?" I thought of the famous quote of the Yankee broadcaster known as Mel Allen.

Last inning now, and we got a runner on first. A sacrifice bunt, and he rested on second base now. A popup, and it was now two outs with a good lefty named Chuck. He got the green from me, and we hoped for the best as he had a homerun stroke in his repertoire. It was a sharp grounder to first base, and our season was over.

We left with our heads held high, and we did it for *Mauro*. The umpire rushed over to our dugout to tell the boys, "It was the damnedest comeback I ever saw!" Ronnie, this Bud's for you!

While working the night center at Grover Cleveland High School during the late seventies, I had an idea. This was around the same time I decided to "mobilize" the soccer team with those "new" ideas. Basketball was taking up the entire gymnasium, and things were boring to many who attended. So I brought in some street hockey equipment that my two sons and I used to start a street hockey game in front of our house. We had enough players, but we had no one willing to play the goalie position. I had a beautiful Irish setter named Shannon, and we chose him as the goalie because no one could get a shot by him. We had so much fun that I just had to bring the sticks and goalie mitt into the night center. Half the gym was devoted to basketball, the other half to hockey. One night, in walked my chairman and fearless leader, Edmund Michael. He stopped to look and then asked, "Can you do this as an elective course structure for the high school curriculum?"

"I guess so, Ed, but we need a lot of equipment in order to pull that off."

"I'll include it in the budget." And so the Public Schools began an experimental hockey elective program.

Enter Irwin Erker. Irwin had a twinkle in his eye that I can remember from the first time I met him as one of the first to sign up for the hockey elective. He had a pageboy haircut that would fly all around when he raced after the puck. He kind of reminded me of Bobby Clarke, the Philadelphia Flyers hockey star with the same haircut and flair for playing all our hockey no holds barred. It was the time of Jean Ratelle, Rod Gilbert, Vic Hatfield, Brad Park and Eddie Giacomin of the New York Rangers; Bobby Hull and Phil Esposito of the Boston Bruins. I had bitten off more than I could chew. The elective drew almost two hundred hockey players. How can I handle this?

Irwin began to notice my frustration and offered to help along with some of his friends from the neighborhood near Fresh Pond Road. They brought in their own whistles and assisted me in the officiating duties as linesmen. The idea caught on, and Irwin helped to organize the class along with some of the more experienced hockey players. We decided that each team will play daily, and one team will rotate as officials on the day they draw the bye. Irwin was full of suggestions and exuberance over the sport, and with the early help of Irwin and his Fresh Pond Road, hockey began to take hold at Cleveland High School in the late seventies. I'll never forget Irwin coming into the office before the class began. I had a particularly bad day at officiating the day before, and Irwin took notice. He peeked in the office door and said, "Hey, Vee. This is for you. The way you called the game yesterday, I think you better read this."

With that, he tossed the *Mylec Street Hockey* rule book onto my desk and then ran out the door with that pageboy hair flying as I made a move to chase him through the hallways. He was too fast for me.

Hockey went on to become a city-wide elective for the city public schools due to our experiment. It caught on, thanks to students like Irwin and his close-knit group of friends. Irwin went on to a prominent role in marsh, and McClennon and was busy at work on the seventy-eighth floor of the World Trade Center on the morning of September 11, 2001. Every time I see a hockey game, I think of Irwin. If Irwin is an example of what the community of Ridgewood can produce, Ridgewood must be awfully proud to have known him. I certainly am!

Perhaps, God willing, someday we will all meet again. Ronnie and I will be coaching baseball together. Mike Weinberg will be our catcher, and Steve Bates, another one of us lost on that fateful day, will be our pitcher once more. I'm sure my dad will be in the stands watching the games with Kosta, and here will be a bunch of hockey players waiting impatiently, looking through the fence, "Come on, Vee. We have a game to play, and we need a ref. So get over here where you belong!"

These were wonderful people. My heart weighs heavy at the loss. I know what it feels like to suffer casualties. It hurts deeply and forever.

No wonder my dad hesitated for many years before telling me what happened between December 16, 1944 and January 8, 1945, for I have just been reduced to tears by the telling to you of my casualties. Now I understand how he felt.

# Chapter 18

# "Charlie, Are You Getting This?"

These words were from my father, when he wanted to ascertain that he had my undivided attention. The reconstituted "Golden Lions" were sent back into Germany. You bet I was getting this, as I hung on his every word. The "Lion was teaching his cub," and now his lesson to me may have relevance to you in this modern day and age. Therefore, it may serve you well to become alert to the perils that may appear innocuous but are a part of the times. I guess these perils were always a part of every time. The say that history repeats itself and that we can learn what the future may hold by looking back into the truths of the past. But beware. As Dad advised earlier in these pages, there are many who wish you not to know. Their name is "Legion." There are many who wish you to remain ignorant, and they go by the same name of "Legion." Well, you wanted to know the other half of the story about my unparalleled soccer team out of Ridgewood, New York City. I promised in my first book called *All-American* that the sequel you are reading now would not be for good-two shoes, and I meant to caution you in that regard. Don't claim I didn't give you a heads up of what is to come.

These are words spoken to me from my father to his son––from one Lion to another. And as promised, Lions cannot speak; however, they know each other's thoughts, and these we will convey. Let not the fog of time hinder your ability to see and hear the message of this lesson once given from a father to a son and from his son to you. Remember, all we were ever about was to help people learn. We are teachers, it's what we do. Listen carefully as he tells you—yes, listen—or you will indeed hear him as I have when he tells you about the turn of the "Golden Lions" to wartime Germany. Take with you what you will, and excuse me for asking, "Are you getting this?"

"Charlie, whether we were to fight our way in or march in to occupy Germany under armistice terms, we would be doing a soldier's job on the soil of the enemy. Our very presence on German soil would serve to convince, as a constant demonstration to the German people, that the master race theory that sent them forth to bathe the world in blood was just so much tragic nonsense. According to its own values, they should have been occupying your hometown instead of us occupying theirs. The 'master race' didn't make their point."

"Charlie, we were in enemy country!" These people were not our allies or our friends. However friendly and repentant, however sick of the Nazi party, the Germans had sinned against the laws of humanity and cannot come back into the civilized fold by merely sticking out their hands and saying, "I'm sorry."

"What do you mean, Dad?" I would often ask in order to be clear about this point.

"Charlie, it would be up to them to prove they deserve a place once more among respectable nations. Don't forget that only eleven years before, a majority of the German people voted the Nazi party into power. Charlie, are you getting this?"

"Yes, Dad," I would reply as I sat on the couch in the TV room of our home in Queens, NYC.

"The German people," he went on, "had all read Hitler's *Mein Kampf*. They knew what Hitler meant to do to the minorities and to the world. That book told them, and a majority of them voted for the National Socialist Party."

"Was that the Nazi party, Dad?"

"Yes, Charlie, and the majority of the people voted for the Nazi party, knowing that this would give them absolute control, with Hitler as chancellor."

"With Hitler firmly entrenched in power, the plan in *Mein Kampf* began to come true—the bullying of races, the destruction of peaceful nations, the march toward conquest. And this gangster racket was enthusiastically supported by the German people as long as it seemed to succeed."

"And it almost worked, didn't it, Dad?"

"Yes, Charlie. God knows what this world would be like if it wasn't for the United States of America. But we were correctly ordered that while in Germany, we were not to carry a chip on our shoulder or disrespect the inhabitants. We were not like the Nazis, but we weren't there on a goodwill errand either."

"It must have been very dangerous, Dad."

"Sure it was, Charlie. We were ordered not to take any chances. We were reminded that we were in unfriendly territory and that our lives may be in more danger than it was during the battles. On the firing line, you kept your eyes open and your wits about you every second. That is why I am still alive to tell you this story of history."

"During the war, Germany kept five hundred thousand black-uniformed SS guards, a branch of Hitler's Gestapo."

"Who were the Gestapo, Dad?"

"They were the German secret police. These soldiers would still be a danger, and we were ordered to remain alert and protect ourselves at all times."

Wow, this was serious stuff for me to imagine, as all my fearful encounters came on the athletic field of battle and not on the firing line, as Dad would often colorfully describe the field of battle. He read my thoughts, as he was so apt to do, and began again.

"You may be realizing that war is not a sport like football or boxing, played under rules and ending with the call of 'time!'"

I had my fair share of fisticuffs around the neighborhood, and Dad had to deal with an irate parent knocking at our door on more than one occasion, so he used boxing as an analogy so I would get the point.

"In boxing, when the bell rings to end the round, only the careless fighter drops his hands. Even then, if his opponent reaches over and clips him once on the jaw and knocks him out, the victim can get justice and relief from the referee. When he wakes up, he will find that his treacherous foe has been disqualified."

"The difference in war and the occupation that follows war is that the person who drops his guard and gets clipped doesn't wake up."

"Didn't we learn that lesson after World War I ended, Dad?" I asked.

"I guess not, Charlie. We were ordered into Germany partly because our fathers forgot so soon what the war was about last time. They took it for granted that the friendly reception the Germans gave them after the armistice in 1918 proved that Germany meant well after all. Our whole country let down its guard too easily last time. So we kept our left out, our eyes open, and trusted only our own."

"But where did they get this attitude toward America from?" I interrupted because I had to know.

"German attitude against America has been concentrated by education, propaganda, and the allied air force bombardment. The German believed that had it not been for the American intervention, this time his old dream of world conquest would have been realized.

"Since 1933, when Hitler came to power, German youth had been carefully and thoroughly educated for world conquest. Charlie, as a teacher, you know that one of the things we take pride in America is the spirit of sportsmanship, decency, and fair play instilled into our boys during their education. You learned that these rules were good ones to take into life with you when school was over, that you belonged to a community of free men with all the rights and privileges inherent in a democracy. That the loyalty you gave to your government was a loyalty to a country governed by representatives of your own choosing."

I was beginning to realize that much is taken for granted here in America, and much can be taken from us if we are not diligent. The nosce hostem doctrine that I applied to the soccer field, in order to know my opponent, is of paramount importance during these tumultuous times. As I have accounted for earlier in these pages, my Cleveland team had enemies on the battlefield and even more powerful foes away from the obvious conflict. Thanks to the major, I knew them, I fooled them, and I schooled them. Is America capable of doing that for her own sake as we come under attack from our opponents? It is toward that end that firsthand accounts experienced by the major must be revealed. So join me on the couch in the TV room of our home and listen to a wise man. Listen to my "Golden Lion of the Nosce Hostem"!

"Charlie, you know that to be born free and equal meant that you were no better and no worse than anyone else but that you would have a decent chance to prove your abilities in fair completion." Yes, I have been free to dance to the beat of my own drum. What a luxury that is, and perhaps it has been the driving force behind my relentless pursuit of winning—a luxury not experienced by everyone and taken for granted by most until it is taken away.

"Well, since the year 1933, the German boy had been taught deliberately the exact opposite. Every man is the product of his early education during the impressionable years."

"The young German, through his most impressionable years, has been taught that the strong are entitled to pick on and destroy the weak. That it is actually noble to squeal on a pal or even inform on a member of one's own family. That a promise or word of honor given is to be kept only as long as it suits its purpose and can be broken at any time."

"Charlie, are you getting this?"

He has been taught to torture and stand torture. He has been told over and again that he is a member of the master race and that all other peoples are his inferiors and designed to be his slaves. He has learned to sacrifice everything, himself, his family, for he has only one loyalty—a fanatical loyalty to a dictator who was only a man, and nothing special at that.

"The German boy was the victim of the greatest educational crime in the history of the world. From childhood, in all his schools, he has heard one teaching. He has been indoctrinated into believing that force, ruthlessness, and blind obedience will carry his people to a position if dominance over all other peoples of the world. By hearing this doctrine constantly repeated throughout his formative years, he has come firmly to believe in it."

"Hitler said that if you tell a lie that's big enough, people will believe you. He made too many believe his propaganda lies about races or faiths or classes. But he failed to put those lies over on the American people, and that's why he lost the war."

"Did we get caught up in the war in order to come to the aid of Britain, France, Poland, and Czechoslovakia?" I interrupted in order to obtain a better feel for this historical disaster called World War II. His answer was unequivocal.

He answered, "We fought that war as Americans for America. We fought against the Germans and the Japanese because our own freedom was threatened. We fought because the interests of our country were tied up with those of the British and French and all other fighters for freedom. Charlie, just as we had defeated them with our weapons and our courage, we had to be ready to defeat lies with knowledge of the truth with clearheaded realization of the issues at stake. Otherwise, we would have to take up arms again. And if not us, then it would be you. And if not you, it would have to be your children. Charlie, are you getting this?"

"Why did our opponents have to finally learn the truth from us?" I wondered out loud. "Why couldn't they find out the truth for themselves and taken steps to avoid the war right from the beginning?"

"So you are paying attention, aren't you?" he asked with a nod of approval. And then he offered reasons why the truth had to come from a free American people.

"To an American, used to the freest press the world has ever known, it seems impossible for a nation to have been almost completely shut off from all external news for four years or more—especially since the perfection of radio—but that is what had happened in wartime Germany."

"Ever since Hitler had come into power with the majority vote of the German people, the entire population had been living in a vacuum as far as the truth and real news was concerned. Into that vacuum, the Nazis have pumped only such news as they wanted the people to have and such lies or misstatements as they thought necessary for their own political agenda. They suppressed all political opposition. Charlie, there was such a grip on the people that they were even forbidden to listen to any foreign or domestic radio broadcasts except those controlled by the Nazis. Can you believe that?" he asked.

I sat in stunned silence and just shook my head from side to side as a thought slowly crept into my mind. If the Nazis were here now and forced me to root for Duke Snider of the Brooklyn Dodgers instead of Mickey Mantle of the New York Yankees. Oh, just might as well shoot me and get it over with. But this was a solemn moment, and as we already know, loose lips sink ships, so I remained quiet and afloat. But I did venture to proclaim, "Boy, we sure take our freedoms for granted, don't we?"

"So the Germans heard only what the Nazis wanted them to hear or read. Charlie, you seem puzzled." He paused to observe, and then he resumed. "If you are still puzzled how such things could happen in the modern age, then maybe you had better pay close attention. It was in Berlin that the Nazis staged a great book burning in which the symbolic knowledge of the centuries was consigned to the flames."

What a terrible repression, I thought, even though I did feel this fate was well deserving of many books assigned to be read by my college professors. I guess I had mixed feelings on that one, although I would be extremely upset to witness the burning of my *Archie and Veronica* comic books or my every issue of *Batman and Robin* or *Superman*. After all, it was how I learned to skim read. I used to imagine that I was Archie and my only problem was that I couldn't decide who I liked better, Betty or Veronica! That was one of my problems, thanks to men like the one sitting across from me in the TV room right now—men of our greatest generation.

"When we entered Germany, Charlie, we were entering a totalitarian state operating under a one-man dictatorship. In this kind of government, the state is supreme. The people have no inherent rights and are slaves and servants of the state as opposed to our way of life in which the government and those who govern are the servants of the people. Previous to the Nazi period and following World War I, Germany was a republic under the Constitution of Weimar issued August 11, 1919. Under the constitution, the Germans voted for and elected a president who was to serve for seven years."

"They had a constitution?" I had to ask. Couldn't their own constitution have served to guide them? Weren't there any voices of reason from the members of the constitution?"

"Charlie, there was one legislative body called the Reichstag. The National Socialist Party contested for seats in the Reichstag, and the people voted them into power because their platform seemed all right, even though the handbook for that party was the book called *Mein Kampf*, which professed Hitler's vision of *My Country*. Who would vote him in after reading his intentions? I had to know. "They were forewarned and had all the intelligence they needed, Charlie, but when an intelligent man fails to heed the clues offered by the intelligence he has available, then he is no longer an intelligent man." Wow! "That cliché is one I will never forget!

"And that was the end of the Republic of Germany. The constitution was suspended. All parties except the Nazis were dissolved. All powers were centered on Hitler. Regimentation under the Nazis was complete. To ensure its rule, the party put its henchmen into every key position in the country. From the central government in Berlin down to every little village, the state and the party became one. All basic policies were made and approved by the party. All legislation was by decree from the top. Finally, the party spread a vast network of police and control organizations over the entire people so as to leave no doubt that its eyes and ears were everywhere in order to keep everyone under control."

"Boy, look what they used their freedom of choice to enable one man to be the drummer for all. And then they danced to his music, like it or not. Dad, it was the herd mentality where the dumb sheep are led by an even dumber human!" We looked at each other and both shook our heads from side to side. The room became quiet for a while. *Did he learn of yet more?* I wondered, and I waited.

And then he looked over at me and asked, "Charlie, are you getting this?"

"We were made familiar with a few names and activities before our occupation of Germany was to begin. We were told by our superiors of the SS (*Schutzstaffelm*) or elite guards, who have become infamous all over the world for representing what is worst and most dangerous in

Nazism. They were in complete control of the police in Germany and occupied Europe and were the strong-arm men of the concentration camps. They had their own military units called the Waffen SS and were responsible for the most brutal acts of terror committed by the Nazi regime. They were assisted in their efforts by the SA (*Sturmabteilungen* or storm troopers.) In addition to these military organizations, the entire German youth of both sexes up to the age of eighteen were forced into HJ (Hitler Jugend or Hitler Youth), where they were prepared for their future military careers and also learned to think the "right way," that is, the Nazi way. All workers had to join the DAF (*Deutsche Arbeitsfront* or German Labor Front), the sole state and party labor union."

"So they actually had a labor union throughout all of this?" Since I thought all freedoms were eliminated.

"Sure, they had a union, and it negotiated all contracts, settled all wage disputes, determined the conditions and hours of work, and even regulated leisure time by a special party-sponsored recreation program called Strength through Joy (*Kraft durch Freude*). Farmers had to join the Nazi Peasants Organization, which told them what to grow, what to sell, where to sell it, and for how much. Practically every German man, woman, or child had fallen into the network of some party organization or was watched by some party agent."

"And these men and women actually voted to live that kind of existence?" I asked. How stupid could they have been to surrender all their freedoms and cast their vote for a fool, whose only verifiable life experience was hanging wallpaper?"

"Be careful what you wish for, Charlie, and be even more careful whom you vote for," he responded.

"It was only recently, owing to modern inventions and the shrinking of distances on the surface of the globe, that the German was able to contemplate realizing his dream of enslaving the world. From that moment on, you and your country were brought within range." Oh, how can history repeat itself!

"The people of Germany and Japan first destroyed their own liberties and then began to use force to destroy the liberty of the neighboring countries. We hoped it was just a series of neighborhood quarrels that were none of our business. But suddenly we began to see that we were part of the world neighborhood. Aviation and radio brought the nations of the world into close touch. Suddenly we began to see things happen that were rotten indeed."

This conversations happened a long time ago, and yet it is as relevant now as it was in the past because history does indeed have a way of repeating itself with the passing of time. If you detect similarities as you gather information and interpret the intelligence, then you are an intelligent man or woman. If you ignore clues from the past recited by the major, then you do so at your own folly and risk. He is trying to help you. He is trying to warn you. Heed his warnings because forewarned is fore learned. Remember, he is a student of the "Nosce Hostem."

"Charlie, in 1938, Germany seized Austria. In the same year, she broke into Czechoslovakia and occupied Sudentenland as Neville Chamberlain, the prime minister of Britain, appeased Hitler and returned from a meeting with a note of promise that Hitler was satisfied with current status and guaranteed "Peace in our Time." Then began the bloody and crazy march of destruction—the remainder of Czechoslovakia in 1939, the blitzkrieg or "lightning war" of Poland in the same year, the invasion of Denmark and Norway followed by the invasion of France and that conquest in 1940. In 1941, invasion of the Balkans and the attack on Russia, despite a nonaggression pact agrees to by both nations. German aggression threatened the entire world." The more things change, the more they remain the same. Follow the clues, they are Legion! Listen to him; he is trying to warn you.

"Charlie, no self-respecting man or nation could live in a neighborhood in which gangsters were having their way without trying to stop them. It was not only a matter of principle, it was a matter of actual personal and national safety."

"The gangsters from all over the world made their alliance against the believers in freedom and burst out of bounds whenever it looked favorable for a successful seizure of a peaceful country."

"The free world couldn't go on taking that forever. Without resistance, the enemy would never quit moving in on and forcing their will and beliefs on other countries. Charlie, the war had been hard on me, your mom, my brothers, Mom and Pop, and millions of others. Let us hope that the honest mistakes of the past made by an older generation may not be repeated. Toward that end, we must be proud to apply Lincoln's words to the fallen men and women of our armed forces in World War II and all future wars we must fight for freedom's sake. We must stay the course for many reasons, not the least of which is to ensure that

These dead have not died in vain.

"Charlie, are you getting this?"

And so, once again, I must repeat the thought. No wonder my dad hesitated for many years before telling me what happened between December 16, 1944 and January 8, 1945. For I have just been reduced to tears by my retelling to you. My casualties. Now I understand how he felt. They didn't have a chance!

And now, my thoughts often return to that day we walked along the bank of the Adige river in Verona, Italy. It was a time long ago in a place far away as I listened to a song sung by a father to his son about me and my shadow, walking down the avenue: "Me and my shadow, no one will ever break this team in two, we'll stick together like glue."

I remember thinking how small my shadow appeared as I hurried to catch up to a much larger shadow. *Someday*, I thought, *I will have a shadow like him*. These days, the shadow cast beside me on the ground seems to move with a smooth and muscular gait because it is a shadow that can only be cast by a Lion! It is him! It is him watching over his cub. It is him forever by my side as we continue to hunt, for we are the ghost and the darkness. It is he who casts the shadow from a Golden Lion of the Nosce Hostem. It is him! It is my father!

We are Lions, and Lions do not speak, but we know each other's thoughts. And what good are words, I say to you? They can't convey to you what's in my heart. If you could hear instead, the thoughts I've left unsaid, Father.

Time after time, I tell myself that I'm so lucky to be loving you. So lucky to be the one you ran to see in the evening when the day was through. I only know what I know. The passing years will show you kept my love so strong, so new. And time after time, you'll hear me say that I'm so lucky to be loving you.

Symbolism:
The blue is for infantry.
The red represents artillery support.
The lion's face represents strength and power.

# The Arsenal: A Review

Our background contains techniques necessary to run pass patterns and overload a zone defense. We know how to fast-break and give-and-go or box out for a rebound. The American athlete knows how to hit the cut-off man or throw a curveball. We even know the principle behind the power play, the power sweep, or the end around, not to mention the flea flicker.

Since the youngsters of today are still playing these games and using these plays, it indicates two positive thoughts. First, it means that the boys we are coaching share our own background. And secondly, since they are still using the same plays, it means they stood the test of time and must be technically correct. And these plays are only a drop in the ocean since there is an endless supply from which to draw. Do you think that the foreign players took the time to learn about all these plays? Well, one day they might out of necessity. However, if they would endeavor to learn these systems, it would take them a lifetime, and they could not persevere even then since we are the best at what we do, and this is reciprocal. Why do we continue to play their game when we could beat them by playing it our way—the American way?

An aggressive nature is part of the American identity, and this nature is obvious when viewing homegrown sports like football, basketball, and baseball. These are sports that are deeply rooted in our culture and national identity, and yet they offer us a bottomless reservoir of knowledge that has gone untapped. If this is true, then one may wonder why none of the international communities has thought to employ some of these ideas into the evolution of soccer. The answer lies with the fact that these ideas do not appear in any sports culture in the world except that of America. Now, it is time for us to carry the ball of soccer evolution and make a contribution to the game. By "us," I am referring to an American approach to soccer. With such an approach, you will find a newfound ability to beat many of your opponents who are shackled with a foreign style.

American coaches have searched afar for what has always been right here in their grasp. We have been competing on terms set down by others and have given little thought to inviting others to compete against us on our terms by using an American approach. It should be remembered that this approach includes the best aspects from both a foreign and domestic athletic educational background. This could offer a distinct advantage since we are not carrying all of our eggs in one basket, as most of our opponents have been accustomed to doing. The advantage of this approach is that we will be challenging our opponent with ideas learned from games that he never played.

Our American players will find that this will lead to a cultural shot in the arm. By integrating skills and ideologies that they confidently possess already with newly learned concepts and skills, we can begin groundwork for a superior soccer program. This will enable American coaches and players to use proven skills handed down from generation to generation. These skills and ideas are drawn from sports at which we dominate the international arena. However, we have learned a great deal from our athletes who were born or raised in a different cultural setting, and these athletes also stand to reap excellent results from learning the best that both worlds have to offer. The American approach is a style acceptable to all nationalities who love to play offensive soccer.

Therefore, it becomes apparent that information provided here will serve to benefit coaches and athletes from all cultural backgrounds in much the same way as we Americans have learned techniques of soccer offered by so many diverse cultures and nationalities. The possibility of an American contribution is at hand, and this occurrence can bring the game closer to the heart of America since these contributions would signify our own cultural statement to the evolution of soccer. In this manner, our own unique style will bring an end to an identity crisis and give rise to a creative and imaginative game that we can call our own. To underscore this message so that the American soccer coach may grasp what this may hold in store for him, I will offer a statistic based upon hard facts.

I have used this American approach while coaching Grover Cleveland High School in New York City since 1970. During this span, we have played against opponents who have used an array of foreign styles too numerous to list. However, Cleveland High School has remained constant throughout these years in the use of our style that is all-American. We have won 186 times as opposed to 33 losses. We haven't lost by more than one goal in any game since 1975. In the process, we have made the city playoffs thirteen times in sixteen years of class A competition, including appearances in four city championships. We have done this with a multiple offense consisting of fast breaks, post patterns, give-and-go, full-court press, strength up the middle, and so much more that are all-American. The paradox here is that half of my athletes were from a foreign background and had to learn these American techniques from the grassroots level. A confident coach can make it happen, especially if he calls upon a background that is All-American.

Throughout this book, I would urge you to search your own background for experiences that will provide you with a new approach. From one American athlete to another, I believe we all share a basic concept of *offense* in American sports. During our years as athletes, we have set a premium on scoring points or bringing runners to home plate from third base. The thrill of a touchdown pass or a basket would be felt among the entire team. The object of our sports philosophy has always been to be the aggressor and bring the game to the opponent. Defense does not have as much prestige with us, and as a result, we have coined an American phrase indicating that the best defense is a good offense.

It should be noted that I am not negating the values of being schooled in the methods of playing defense. Defensive philosophies are valuable and will have a time and a place on the soccer field, but my intentions are that your opponent will spend his time playing defense all over the place. The point here is that we Americans love to see the *home run* and the *touchdown*. We even have a statistic other than the score with which to measure the flow of the game. The statistic is called the time of possession.

As you read on, you will begin to realize how we can remove the shackles and play in the spirited and imaginative manner to which we have become accustomed. In the process of implementing the ensuing American tactics, the time of ball possession will rise dramatically. The premise that offers credence to this philosophy relates to the belief that one cannot get hurt while in possession of that vital object, the ball.

These are many interesting and imaginative ways to sustain a spirited offense while using ideas inherent to your American sports background. Many of the plays and strategies that you have already learned can be adapted to use on the soccer field. Soccer is a unique sport in this regard since it probably is the only sport that lends itself so well to successful application of ideas proven correct in such an array of other sports. Football, basketball, and baseball have some very definite features that can be used effectively by players wearing a soccer uniform. When it becomes apparent that each of the three major American sports can contribute something to the game, then we can realize that collectively the three sports offer something substantial.

In addition, knowledge gained from these American sports enables the coach to offer new and effective concepts in his role as educator. Self-respect and dignity are the partners of confidence.

Given this common-sense approach of your American background, One receiver didn't work then, and it doesn't work to well now, either.

This procedure is unprecedented on soccer fields around the world. The reason being that most of those players have never played the sports we grew up on, bubble gum cards and all.

A case will be made here for play selections on the throw-in.

It will become obvious in the chapters ahead how audibles can prove to be superior to the time-out procedure.

However, you are American, and your ingenuity is legendary. The point will be made that if all you have at your disposal is a key and no tools, then this is not going to be your day.

Which implies that if there is a will, there is a way.

This has been done on the football by using play-action pass plays designed to confuse the defense and influence a defensive flow in the wrong direction.

The double reverse and the end around are technically sound devices that can be used in exercising an outflanking maneuver on the soccer field in an adaptive form. An adaptive version of the power sweep is offered as a means to overwhelm a team when a weakness is detected. Punt-return procedures have merit in the reception of the goal kick and the subsequent stationing of players to ensure delivery of the ball into the area defended by the opponent.

Employing overload procedures usually found in football and basketball will place maximum stress on the opponent, resulting in numerous possibilities by the knowledgeable attacking team using this American approach. Using man-in-motion techniques to disrupt a wall set up by an opponent may gain a screenshot into the goal unseen by the goalie. These American techniques will be outlined in detail as the playbook begins to unfold.

There is a way of simulating the safety blitz techniques to establish your stopper as a potent offensive force within your own defensive backfield. The element of speed and surprise must accompany this bold effort and the methods to achieve this will be explained.

If the opponent has a troublesome individual, your knowledge of the box-on-one will help your team deal with this problem by marking him out of the game in a favorable trade-off situation. There are many give-and-go combinations to be discussed.

There are times when slowing the tempo of the game is desirable, especially for a ball-control team.

The philosophy inherent in the full-court press can be applied to the soccer field in tandem with the offside-trap technique to provide for an overwhelming attack capable of deciding the outcome of the game.

And so I accumulated knowledge of all the varied tactical deployments popular throughout the world. My colleagues, I am certain were also doing their homework, and we were all relegated to the same tedious boredom. No wonder the fans join together to sing songs at international competition. They have to do something to keep the adrenaline going to as not to be put to sleep by what is transpiring before them.

If it appears that I may sound irreverent in these passages, then suffice it to say that I am irreverent and have good cause to make that claim.

Shackles have been put upon the players venturing forth onto the soccer field. FIFA, the governing body of international soccer, has seen to it that all participating must remain within certain parameters or be denied access to the battle. This stifling dogma filters down to the clubs, colleges, schools, and leagues anywhere you would care to witness a soccer game of any level. All the dignitaries and commentators and other authoritarians are comfortable in keeping the status quo. New concepts result in negative behavior on the part of all who do not understand the concepts. Two examples of this come to mind as we were on our record-breaking run through A division soccer in New York City. Flash forward a minute to these samples.

Tony Hlavac, a PSAL referee living in Ridgewood, New York, called at my residence to talk to me about something that troubled him. He had been summoned the night before to an impromptu referee-association meeting. When he arrived, he was astonished to learn the reason for this gathering. The centerpiece of the meeting was a discussion with regard to how Cleveland could be stopped from their continuous domination in the PSAL. He felt he just had to let me know since he lived in the same neighborhood as the boys and did not feel they deserved to be singled out in a negative fashion for their success. As a resident, Tony was proud of what the boys were doing and the record they were relentlessly in the process of achieving. He asked for anonymity, and I assured him he would have that request.

This is what we were up against. All of our opponents needed help for we were just too much for them. We were just too smart for them. We departed way too far away from the norm for them to comprehend exactly what we were doing. We confused every opponent on our relentless trek, and even the referees could not assist in slowing our progress. This went on for ten years!

We were different. We did not play the way the game was drawn up to specifications. We were the opposite of everything any one had seen, and this caused resentment and jealousy. Although, one local college coach and his assistant sought out my services and found me at the library of Cleveland High School as I was entering my marks for the students in my subject area. Bob Montgomery of Adelphi University and his assistant, Paul LeSeur, came with a proposition, and it went like this: "Charlie, we would like for you to consider teaching your methodology to our boys at Adelphi University."

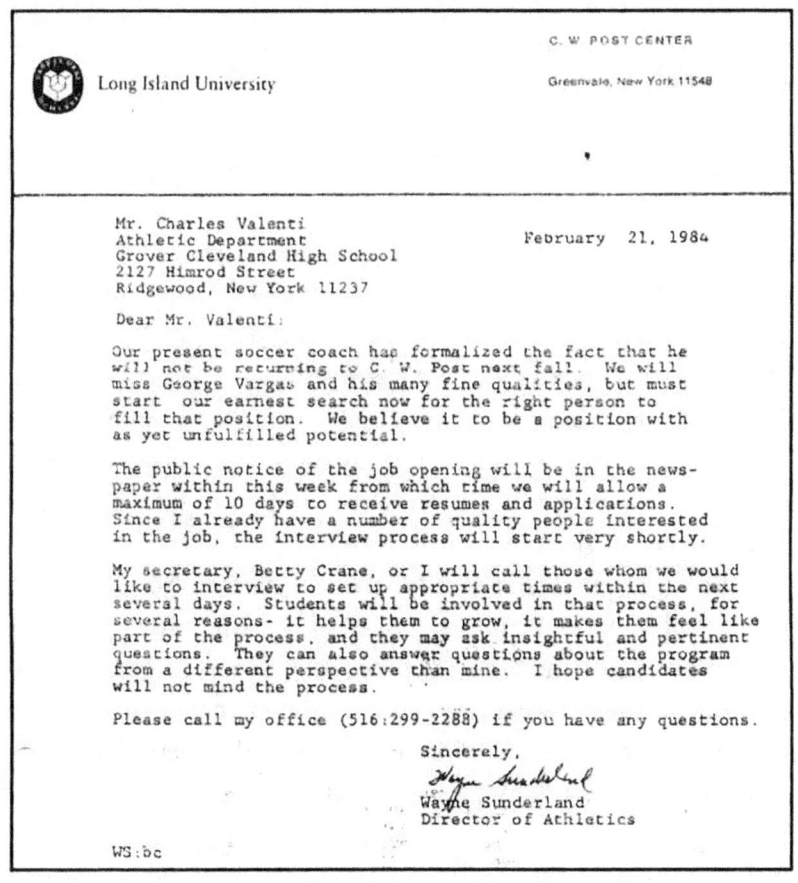

My answer to them was simple. I don't see the challenge in beating up on this PSAL and accepted the offer. Two of my players had been sent to Adelphi and were at the Adelphi team meeting when Montgomery met with his team and expressed his intention in bringing Valenti over here to help us with his myriad ideas. Mike Windishmann, the team captain, voiced opposition to having the prospect of learning a different way. Adelphi went stumbling on, and the PSAL received five more years dosage of Cleveland dominance.

It gets even better than this! Truth is stranger than fiction. CW Post contacted me in their search for a soccer coach, as George Vargas had indicated his retirement. Wayne Sunderland, the athletic director, indicated over ninety applicants had been considered and a final decision was now between two people. He kept me late into the night at the final interview as he discussed in detail the amount of money available for grants, uniforms, meals, travel, and other team expenses. I returned home and happily told my wife that it appears that I have the job and now I have the chance to confound all at a higher pedagogical level where everyone really thinks they know everything. Boy, counterintelligence!

Everyone at the final meeting wanted an answer from me, and the question was, "Why would you want to come here, where we are having a hard time, when you can stay at Cleveland and continue your winning streak? Even here, they knew of the streak.

"Because, if I come here and teach you what I know, then you all will know what it is like to win all the time." This was my final comment to the roomful of players summoned to appear before the athletic director in final judgment.

While waiting the final decision from CW Post, Bob Montgomery of Adelphi called to inform me that the team would rather remain with the tried-and-true method of play rather than depart into the unknown. At the end of our conversation, he mentioned that it was regrettable because he just found out that his assistant, Paul LeSeur, had just been hired as head coach at CW Post University! The handwriting was on the wall.

When I spoke to Wayne Sunderland, in his call, he mentioned the deciding factor was that LeSeur had played for the New York Cosmos.

Mike Windishmann went on to become captain for the US national team. And I went back to the PSAL.

It gets even better! While I was summoned for one interview after another at CW Post, there was someone anxiously waiting outside the door to ask me what I thought my chances were. That supporter was my college baseball coach from Long Island University and current coach at CW Post, Dick Vining.

"Charlie, I hope you get the job so that you can also help coach the baseball team alongside me here at Post," he said.

I thanked the coach for that but had to tell him about something that came up at the final interview. "Sunderland said, 'Coach, you were the shortstop who hit the left-handed grand slam to beat me 5–4 at Pratt when you were playing for Vining at LIU, weren't you?' It sounds like I may have a problem for him to remember that shot, Coach."

My son Ted holding fish.

Son Christian with granddaughter, Christina.

"I'm just working on my boat, and waiting for your call. I'm living the life of a writer, but most days I don't write at all. So, I'm fishing for my living, and waiting for the words. But my muse ain't so amusing, it's a voice I've seldom heard. I've got to get myself together, and if I take the dare. Oh, Jack the Fox, he's coming back, beware!"

# About The Author

My background with regard to the writing of his book can be traced back to the years of growing up in an environment rich in experience gained from participating in the three basic American sports—baseball, basketball, and football. Those years have provided me with far more knowledge than I could learn from reading books on the subject of sports concepts. Growing up with a rich sports background has left indelible memories that have provided me with a unique method of coaching soccer.

Graduating from Flushing High School in New York led to an offer to sign a professional baseball contract with the Boston Red Sox. Instead, a college education was sought by way of a baseball scholarship to Long Island University in Brooklyn, where I continued go develop concepts useful on the baseball field and the basketball court. On the weekends, during the off season, I quarterbacked and played linebacker for the neighborhood football team. In the meantime, I developed a background pertinent to soccer in courses offered at LIU, which had a rich tradition in winning soccer teams.

Accepting the soccer coaching position at Grover Cleveland High School in Ridgewood, New York, provided me with a means to apply my diverse American sports background. In applying that background, I have managed to win at a percentage in excess of .700 while bringing the team into the playoffs fifteen times in eighteen years. During this period, we have appeared in fur city championship games and have posted a combined league record of 185 victories and 33 defeats. From 1975 to 1985, we were never beaten by more than one goal and have made the playoffs every year in succession.

I never played soccer, but I played all the major American sports, and my success in coaching soccer, the beautiful game, is directly attributable to that. This book is my attempt to share with you the rich traditional American sports background that I shared with my players for many years––a background that is all-American.

Currently I reside in Long Island with my wife, Leila, and my dogs, Gizmo and Betsy. I have two sons, Ted and Chris, and two grandchildren, Christina and Teddy.

––Coach Charles L. Valenti

www.ingramcontent.com/pod-product-compliance
Lightning Source LLC
LaVergne TN
LVHW021232080526
838199LV00088B/4318